Popular Movements
c. 1830–1850

Each volume in the 'Problems in Focus' series is designed to make available to students important new work on key historical problems and periods that they encounter in their courses. Each volume is devoted to a central topic or theme, and the most important aspects of this are dealt with by specially commissioned essays from scholars in the relevant field. The editorial Introduction reviews the problem or period as a whole, and each essay provides an assessment of the particular aspect, pointing out the areas of development and controversy, and indicating where conclusions can be drawn or where further work is necessary. An annotated bibliography serves as a guide for further reading.

PROBLEMS IN FOCUS

TITLES IN PRINT

FORTHCOMING TITLES

Popular Movements
c. 1830–1850

EDITED BY
J. T. WARD

MACMILLAN

First published 1970 by
MACMILLAN PRESS LTD
Houndmills, Basingstoke, Hampshire RG21 6XS
and London
Companies and representatives
throughout the world

ISBN 0–333–11137–0

A catalogue record for this book is available
from the British Library.

21 20 19 18 17 16 15 14 13
03 02 01 00 99 98 97 96 95

Printed in Malaysia

Contents

Acknowledgements

The authors are greatly indebted to many librarians and other owners of papers who generously allowed them to use their collections. In particular, they wish to express their gratitude to the following owners for permission to quote from the material under their control: Bradford City Library (Balme Collection); the late Colonel G. W. Ferrand, O.B.E. (Ferrand MSS); the Co-operative Union, Holyoake House, Manchester (Owen Collection); Leeds City Reference Library (Samuel Fenton's diary); London University Library, Goldsmiths' Collection, and Columbia University Library (Richard Oastler's 'White Slavery' collection); Mrs C. M. Lyman of New Haven, Conn. (the late Professor Cecil Driver's collection); the late Professor David Owen of Harvard (Fielden MSS); Sheffield City Library (local pamphlets collection); the National Library of Ireland (Smith O'Brien papers); and University College London Library (Parkes papers).

The editor wishes to thank the following for their kind permission to reproduce extracts from the works listed below:

Messrs George Allen & Unwin Ltd (for Max Beer, *History of British Socialism*); Messrs Edward Arnold (Publishers) Ltd (for Donald Read and Eric Glasgow, *Feargus O'Connor*); the London School of Economics and Political Science (for Sidney and Beatrice Webb, *History of Trade Unionism*); Messrs Macmillan & Co. Ltd (for F. C. Mather, 'The Government and the Chartists', in Asa Briggs (ed.), *Chartist Studies*); and Manchester University Press (for Mark Hovell, *The Chartist Movement*).

Finally, the editor desires to express his gratitude to his colleagues Dr John Butt, who first suggested the theme of the book, and Professor S. G. E. Lythe, who gave invaluable advice on parts of it.

List of Abbreviations

Add. MSS	Additional Manuscripts, British Museum
AHR	*American Historical Review*
CHJ	*Cambridge Historical Journal*
EcHR	*Economic History Review*
EHR	*English Historical Review*
HJ	*Historical Journal*
HO	Home Office
HT	*History Today*
JEH	*Journal of Economic History*
JEccH	*Journal of Ecclesiastical History*
JMH	*Journal of Modern History*
NLI	National Library of Ireland
PP	*Parliamentary Papers*
PRO	Public Record Office
TLCAS	*Transactions of the Lancashire and Cheshire Antiquarian Society*
TRHS	*Transactions of the Royal Historical Society*
UCLL	University College London Library
VS	*Victorian Studies*

Introduction:
Britain c. 1830–1850:
The Background

J. T. WARD

THE second quarter of the nineteenth century had a distinctive character. Sandwiched between the long period of Pittite Toryism and the mid-century liberal dominance, it was an age of change in many aspects of British life. A predominantly rural society was still slowly adjusting to its new role as 'the workshop of the world'. Technological advance and industrial evolution were producing varied results. To some ancient labour aristocracies and the mercantile oligarchies of some towns they had already given a foretaste of a bleak future. For many new 'hands' they had provided a harsh factory discipline – in addition to generally higher earnings. For consumers of all kinds they were starting to provide wider choices and cheaper prices. And for many industrial entrepreneurs they were providing an affluence which permitted major 'social' transformations. Some such 'self-made' men, proud of personal success stories later to be publicised by such industrial hagiographers as Samuel Smiles, now demanded increased participation in national management and decision-making.

This was an era when many seemingly permanent attitudes and institutions – Richard Hooker's Elizabethan equation of Churchman and English citizen; the political and religious settlements of the Restoration and Revolution; the long dominance of the landed interest; the major remnants of mercantilist state interference – were questioned, eroded, amended or ended. The Crown itself was closely involved in the political struggle: George IV at least partly because of his desertion of Opposition causes and his unsavoury divorce; William IV, despite his general constitutional propriety, over 'Reform'; Victoria initially because of her neglect of constitutional propriety. The Church of England was at least equally under attack, as Archbishop Howley discovered when he was stoned at Canterbury. Late Victorians recalled the Primate's 'princely honours' and personal mildness – and the Duke of

Cumberland's report that Howley 'said he would be damned to hell if he didn't throw the [Reform] Bill out'.[1] The peerage, consisting in 1830 of 4 Royal dukes, 18 dukes, 18 marquesses, 92 earls, 22 viscounts and 160 barons, was also under regular attack, above all for its political activities in the House of Lords – where it was joined by 16 Scottish representative peers (elected for each Parliament), 28 Irish representative peers (elected for life) and 26 English and 4 Irish bishops. The Commons, with 658 members – 188 representing 114 county constituencies, 465 representing 262 borough constituencies and 5 representing the universities of Oxford, Cambridge and Dublin[2] – faced another range of assaults. As the House contained two members each for such constituencies as Castle Rising (with scarcely any electors), Gatton, St Germans and St Michael (with 7 each), New Romney (8), Old Sarum and Winchelsea (11), Newport (12), Launceston (17), Orford (22), Lostwithiel (24) and Heytesbury (26) and none for Leeds, Manchester, Birmingham or Sheffield, hostile complaints were widespread and extending.

An older radical tradition was revived in many forms, to provide some 'philosophic' background for many of the attacks on established institutions and entrenched privileges. Most important and influential, because (despite variations of emphasis) most consistent, was the newer utilitarian creed propounded by Jeremy Bentham and his apostles. Benthamite insistence upon the measuring-rod of utility, supplemented to some extent by the hedonistic calculus and notions of 'the greatest good of the greatest number', led to a denunciation of 'the whole class of fallacies built upon authority, precedent, wisdom of ancestors, dread of innovation, immutable laws, and many others, occasioned by ancient ignorance and ancient abuses'.[3] But, despite the wide appeal of radical panaceas, an assortment of more liberal notions attracted the generality of the ever-growing bourgeoisie. The Tory *Quarterly Review*, the Whig *Edinburgh Review*, the Benthamite *Westminster Review* and the ultra-radical metropolitan journals bravely fighting 'the taxes on knowledge' provided no attraction for the northern Liberal manufacturer devoted to his *Leeds Mercury* or *Manchester Guardian*.

On the political Right the conservative defenders of the old order themselves became the organisers of many of the changes in it; indeed, a prolonged rearguard action was transformed into a series of well-planned and competently administered reforms. But controversy inevitably extended to 'new' subjects. Urban life created and extended problems of public health, sanitation, policing, amenity and local government administration (itself involving a myriad of decisions); the changing patterns of industrial labour provoked bitter defensive actions by doomed handworkers and new artisans alike. Religious humanitarians and rationalist Benthamites were equally concerned to discover means of improving the quality and organisation of life. And pioneers in several fields founded a remarkable array of movements to achieve their ends. It is with some of these popular agitations that the present book is concerned.

I

British society in 1830 was highly stratified. The ancient hierarchy of orders still existed more or less explicitly, though it was increasingly complicated by less precise nuances. An age saturated with Gothic enthusiasms and gazetteers of the great families was also the railway age, the age of coal and steam, the age of Manchester. In parts of rural England armorial bearings no doubt exercised a long importance, entitling their owners to social respect and status. At the turn of the century Jane Austen's fictional Coles 'were very good sort of people, friendly, liberal, and unpretending; but, on the other hand, they were of low origin, in trade, and only moderately genteel'. The Coles would have fared little better in Anthony Trollope's Barsetshire half a century later. And in real life, it seems, Lord Braybrooke would have been reluctant to appoint them to the Essex bench in the 1830s.[4] Yet in many counties industrialists had already followed the traditional trek of the successful merchant and banker by converting business profits into landed acres; and most such men (to judge by such criteria as appointment to the magistracy, deputy lieutenancy and yeomanry commissions) appear to have met with a ready acceptance in 'county' circles. This was, after all, an age in which the Conservative party was led by a cotton master's son.

The idea of 'class' – as opposed to 'rank' or 'station' – was only slowly gaining acceptance, however greatly land enclosures and industrial divisions of labour had increased and underlined the fact of class division.[5] The Victorian public school had not yet standardised an upper-class diction, and uncouth *nouveaux riches* from trade and industry were balanced by equally unlettered successors of squire Western among the sporting gentry. Certainly, smooth metropolitan snobs had for long looked down upon socially aspiring (and even socially established) provincials. In 1809 Sydney Smith had found the squire of

Heslington in Yorkshire 'a perfect specimen of the Trullibers of old, [who] smoked, hunted, drank beer at his door with his grooms and dogs, and spelt over the county paper on Sundays' and whose wife 'looked as if she had walked straight out of the Ark, or had been the wife of Enoch'. The 'Railway King' George Hudson was regarded as good for a joke over his accent or for a 'touch' on his purse in the forties. And in the fifties a 'civilised' wife and son hid Sir Tatton Sykes from London Society.[6] But the importance of such matters should not be exaggerated. 'Old Tat' was the greatest landowner in the East Riding and the hero of British sportsmen. 'King' Hudson, who shared his Yorkshire accent and boorish appearance, was a Protectionist M.P. as well as the great railroad manipulator; and his dethronement in 1849, following the unmasking of his dishonest financial arrangements, shocked the growing *rentier* class just as the landed families had been dismayed by the collapse of the rashly spending 2nd duke of Buckingham ('the farmers' friend') in the previous year. Even in adversity, old and new wealth shared experiences; by and large, 'gentility' rested increasingly on wealth, ancient or modern.

Ownership of land still marked the 'arrival' of socially mobile and socially ambitious capitalists as importantly as it buttressed most ancient titles. Landed property, maintained intact by primogeniture and family settlements, and made infinitely more valuable by eighteenth-century agrarian changes (and, in many cases, by industrial, mineral and urban growth), provided the backgrounds, personal interests and family incomes of most prominent politicians. Vast palladian mansions set in classically planned landscapes were still the focal points of county political and social organisation; and their (largely Whig) proprietors often maintained London palaces which were the venues for both glittering high society occasions and complex high political plotting. The greatest landowners, Whig and Tory alike, generally participated to some extent in public life. They provided the Lords-Lieutenant and selected the magistracy. Many of them (most notably the dukes of Buckingham, Devonshire, Newcastle, Norfolk and Northumberland and Lords Carrington, Darlington, Fitzwilliam, Hertford, Lonsdale and Powis) exercised patronal rights over parliamentary elections. Many more were successful businessmen in their own right. Whig and Tory proprietors had both for long supplemented agricultural rents with income arising from mineral rents, royalties and wayleaves, urban leases and rents, port and harbour charges, market dues and canal and turn-pike profits; and now the railway booms added further sums. Landowners might simply receive unearned increments from levies and charges on others' profits; but many (at least initially) played considerable industrial roles, as (for instance) the initial provers and operators of mines and the promoters, provisional committeemen and directors of early railways.

The apparent popularity and permanence of the landed dynasties in the shires both angered and dismayed radical reformers. 'The citadel of privilege in this country is so terribly strong, owing to the concentrated masses of property in the hands of the comparatively few . . .' Richard Cobden complained to John Bright in 1849. 'We are a servile, aristocracy-loving, lord-ridden people, who regard the land with as much reverence as we still do the peerage and baronetage. Not only have not nineteen-twentieths of us any share in the soil, but we have not presumed to think that we are worthy to possess a few acres of mother earth.' Cobden was engaged in a campaign against what urban radicals assailed as 'the land monopoly'; but he scarcely exaggerated his case. The concentration of ownership was to be proved some two decades later. By the nobility and gentry, asserted G. C. Brodrick in 1881, 'Primogeniture was accepted almost as a fundamental law of nature, to which the practice of entail only gave a convenient and effectual expression.' The 'New Domesday' survey of landownership in 1873, despite many omissions and inaccuracies, had by that time shown that about 80 per cent of the Kingdom was owned by about 7000 families.[7] At the apex of the social pyramid was a group of men with property larger than several sovereign German states and rent rolls greater than national treasuries. Such narrowing of ownership undoubtedly benefited British agriculture; but its concomitants of deferential politics and a narrowly based power group provided constant provocation to radicals.

Beyond the 7000 families a population explosion had taken place. 'The most important result which the inquiry establishes is the addition in half a century of *ten millions* of people to the British population', it was asserted in the Census Report of 1851. 'The increase of population in the half of this century nearly equals the increase in all preceding ages. . . . At the same time, too, . . . the populations of the towns and of the country have become so equally balanced in number – *ten millions* against *ten millions*. . . .' This unequalled demographic revolution – occurring despite a huge tonnage of Malthusian tracts warning of the dangers of 'over-population' and despite considerable emigration to the colonies and the United States – was a cardinal feature of the age. It was a major achievement of the new industries to provide work for many of the nation's new citizens; but the achievement was gained at considerable cost.

Backed by (usually bowdlerised) versions of Adam Smith's *Wealth of Nations*, busy industrial entrepreneurs generally had little consideration for anything but production and profit. Their financial responsibilities were to their risk-taking partners; their managerial functions often consisted of enforcing a new industrial discipline, dominated by the clock and the speed of the machine. Those who succeeded often rewarded themselves liberally. The industrial leaders of Manchester, Leeds, Glasgow and Dundee built their villas in Pendleton, Headingley, Pollokshields and Broughty Ferry, leaving Ancoats, Holbeck, the Gorbals and Hilltown to fester. Class divisions were thus accentuated by geography. In 1844 Leon Faucher found 'nothing but masters and operatives' in Manchester, missing those imperceptible gradations of social rank of which British commentators had once been proud. Friedrich Engels 'once went into Manchester with . . . a bourgeois, and spoke to him of the bad, unwholesome method of building, the frightful condition of the working-people's quarters, and asserted that [he] had never seen so ill-built a city. The man listened quietly to the end, and said at the corner where [they] parted: "And yet there is a great deal of money made here; good morning, sir." It was utterly indifferent to the English bourgeois whether his working-man starved or not, if only he made money.' Another foreign commentator drew a similar picture. 'The creation of wealth in England in the last ninety years is a main fact in modern history', wrote Ralph Waldo Emerson in 1856. 'The wealth of London determines prices all over the globe. . . . There is no country in which so absolute a homage is paid to wealth. . . . A coarse logic rules throughout all English souls; if you have merit, can you not show it by your good clothes and coach and horses. . . .'[8]

There remained a very wide range of social groups. Although the techniques of industrial management were evolved only slowly, a new managerial class was growing, partly in industry but most notably among the agricultural agents and mineral viewers of the great estates. A host of variegated categories of workmen – foremen, old and new craftsmen, artisans, mechanics and labourers of all sorts – together with an assortment of self-employed men – ranging from itinerant vendors and struggling shopkeepers to members of developing 'professions' and freeholding farmers – made up a many-patterned social order. Different local traditions, still strong in a Britain only entering the railway age, determined the shape and character of each local hierarchy and the relative status of each group within it. Consequently, broad generalisations about clearly demarcated 'middle' or 'working' classes are not very meaningful. Yet it is certainly possible to sense a growing consciousness of 'class' interests, a growth of 'class' feeling and involvement, an increased willingness to act together for 'class' objectives.[9] Some, at least, of the agitations examined in this book were considerably influenced by 'class' feelings, emotions and consciousness.

II

The time-scale of various movements was inevitably affected – though not necessarily determined – by economic and industrial fluctuations. Some men could be driven almost to militant action by despair over deteriorating conditions. Richard Pilling, for instance, movingly explained his part in the 'Plug Plot' of 1842 during his trial at Lancaster in the following year. The father of nine children, he 'became an opponent to the reduction of wages to the bottom of his soul'. After twenty years as a handloom weaver, ten years in a factory and a year when he was blacklisted by the Stockport masters, he insisted that 'the longer and harder he had worked the poorer and poorer he had become every year, until at last he was nearly exhausted'. If the employers reduced wages by a further 25 per cent, 'he would put an end to his existence sooner than kill himself working twelve hours a day in a cotton factory, and eating potatoes and salt . . .'. Pilling had allegedly become 'the father of this great movement' of noisy strikes at a time of widespread distress, when the legend 'Stockport To Let' was scrawled on one of the borough's 3000 empty houses. But economic fluctuations affected different 'popular movements' in different ways. The prosperity of 1844, said Feargus O'Connor, 'left [the Chartists] scarcely a breath to fill their canvass'. But Cobden considered that 'it was fortunate for the [Anti-Corn Law] League that trade revived', as businessmen were thus enabled to renew their subscriptions. Protest of one sort or another did not require a downward turn in economic activity to attain 'take-off' or preserve momentum. Not all agitations found their strength during cyclical depressions. And for those which did there was a penalty: in Professor Asa Briggs's memorable words, 'the price of dependence on "hunger politics" was the corroding influence of even limited "prosperity".'[10]

After the period of instability and uncertainty which followed the end of the long French wars in 1815, the economy expanded in the early 1820s. Production, trade, investment and real incomes all rose rapidly; indeed, industrial output enjoyed a unique rate of increase. Continued technological advance and agricultural improvement helped to promote a generally sustained fall of prices – which was inevitably beneficial to those employed in 'new' jobs and harmful to such groups as indebted tenant farmers with long leases and handworkers whose skills were becoming increasingly obsolescent. The repeal of the Bubble Act in 1825 at least removed a discouragement to the formation of joint-stock companies, although the subsequent heavy speculation, banking crisis and foreign losses somewhat tarnished the 'new' form of organisation. The success of the new railways spearheaded a further boom between 1832 and 1836. This period of good harvests, expanding trade, high employment and industrial growth yielded to six years of agricultural and industrial depression, with banking crises in 1836 and 1839, high food prices and widespread distress. But the early 'hungry forties' were followed by prosperous years, as another railway mania promoted a boom and a wave of speculation which ebbed after the crop failures of 1846, the commercial crisis of 1847, the fall of Hudson, considerable industrial depression and assorted crises of confidence.[11] By 1850 the forward march had been resumed.

The bald outline of cyclical fluctuations in the economy is not particularly useful as an index of the economic condition of particular groups of people. Men's lives were still greatly affected by regional and local fluctuations or even seasonal changes. For many country-folk existence had been little changed for centuries, and in 1830 'Captain Swing' was organising southern riots against technical changes in the countryside. Standards of living, at least of urban workers, undoubtedly improved as industry expanded; and the process was considerably eased by legislation.[12] While comparative affluence among skilled craftsmen led them to form their craft unions, culminating in the amalgamated societies of the 1850s, lesser rewards led other workers to desert their movements. 'Chartism is dead in these parts', Lord Shaftesbury wrote to Lord John Russell from Manchester in 1851: 'the Ten Hours Act and cheap provisions have slain it outright'. Rural workers, cowed by the repression of their 'revolt' in 1831 and by the prosecution of the Tolpuddle trade unionists in 1834, received little parliamentary attention, despite occasional Radical onslaughts on the authoritarian regime and wretched living conditions of much of agricultural Britain. The bucolic peasantry imagined by sentimentalists on both sides of the political spectrum rarely existed: long hours, low wages and bad housing were widely accepted, and the loss (however legal) of common rights under enclosure arrangements had reduced not only the living standards but also the personal status of many village labourers.[13] Some had stoutly resisted the new ways; but they were defeated, and the rural counties were generally quiet during the 'excitements' in the towns. Only the coming of the railway gave the hinds of remote shires a new opportunity to escape from the natural or institutional disciplines of the countryside. 'I rejoice to see it, and to think that feudality is gone for ever', declared Dr Thomas Arnold, headmaster of Rugby, in a much-quoted comment.

Strictly economic explanations appear to be less valuable than has sometimes been suggested: popular movements in the fourth and fifth decades of the nineteenth century did not wax and wane in accordance with the barometer readings of the Kingdom's economic state. Nevertheless, economic factors necessarily had considerable influence. It was the commissioners' inept decision to apply the bleak new Poor Law in the north during a gathering industrial recession in 1837 that helped to expand a hard core of protesters into a mammoth and militant movement. Pilling's explanation of the 1842 strike wave is more convincing than those of the liberal Bright ('the cause was with Peel and the Aristocracy and in their Corn Laws') and the Tory Croker ('the more we hunt out these Leaguers the viler vermin we shall find them'): hunger and regular wage-reductions, rather than any political theory, drove workers to revolt. And the differing character of Chartism in different localities is at least partly explicable through an examination of local socioeconomic categories and relationships. Cobden himself observed that Birmingham was 'more healthy and natural in a moral and political sense' than Manchester: 'There was a freer intercourse between all classes than in the Lancashire town where a great and impassable gulf separated the workman from his employer'.[14] Behind the differences between the 'moderate' Birmingham Political Union (a collection of 'old women' to the fiery J. R. Stephens) and the militant National Charter Association lay the differences between productive units consisting of masters and handfuls of craftsmen and those with managers and hundreds of 'hands'.

Other local factors also promoted variations. For many a handloom weaver militant action might well appear to be the only alternative to slow starvation; and yet the weavers of literally starving (but sternly religious) Paisley were more celebrated for early literary talents than for later revolutionary zeal. Furthermore, within a single town the same economic facts meant different things to different men. Tory and Liberal, factory reformer and free trader alike complained and protested about northern urban squalor in the early 1840s; and such disparate Jewish observers as Disraeli and Engels could agree on the 'facts' (albeit in very different presentations). The ascription of 'blame' and the provision of panaceas were the divisive issues. An horrific account of proletarian misery in Lancashire towns by the Leaguer and cotton master Cobden would preface a condemnation of a grasping landed class which enforced high food prices. A reply by the Yorkshire Protectionist squire William Busfeild Ferrand would add further detail to the squalid picture and resoundingly blame the greed of merciless capitalists (generally by name and usually including Cobden). Whatever the circumstances of even a purely local 'economy' might be, they alone did not delineate the contours of local agitation. Glasgow (as Edwin Chadwick found in 1842) was already perhaps the dirtiest of urban conurbations; its cotton-spinners (as was revealed in 1838) had an unparalleled record of trade union violence; but its Chartists, under *petit* (rising to *haut*) *bourgeois* leadership, were restrained and mild, and its greatest ground landlord was Sir John Maxwell, the Whig champion of the weavers.

Economists were rather more influential than the economy. The ascendant Ricardian theorists were turning Adam Smith's originally optimistic notions of *laissez-faire* into the 'dismal science' of political economy. To them it was self-evident that 'the natural price of labour was that price which was necessary to enable the labourers, one with another, to subsist and to perpetuate their race, without either increase or diminution'. There was equally little doubt that no 'restriction whatever of the present hours of work could be safely made'. On education,

> . . . all should tell the State
> She has no right to educate.

Commercial free trade was 'the destiny of this age, for free trade principles were recognised and accepted by the intelligence of the age'. And it was essential that the situation of the able-bodied pauper 'on the whole, should not be made really or apparently so eligible as the situation of the independent labourer of the lowest class', for 'every penny bestowed, that tended to render the condition of the pauper more eligible than that of the independent labourer, was a bounty on indolence and vice.' Freedom was the order of the day. 'We ask, then, that we shall be free', declared one nonconformist divine: 'in labour, free; in trade, free; in action, free; in thought, free; in speech, free; in religion, free – perfectly free.' Even public health provisions were suspect interferences with individual freedom. Of Macaulay's famous alternatives of 1846 – 'a paternal government, that is to say a prying meddlesome government . . . or a careless, lounging government' – early Victorian 'intellectuals' generally preferred the latter. 'The only purpose for which power can be rightfully exercised over any member of a civilised community, against his will, is to prevent harm to others', wrote John Stuart Mill in 1859. '. . . Each is the proper guardian of his own health, whether bodily, or mental and spiritual.'[15]

Each agitation had its own background of complaint and tension, its peaks and troughs of strength and its individual appeal to particular groups. While fluctuations in the trade cycle undoubtedly affected the extent and degree of 'militancy', they rarely provided the incentive for a movement's 'take-off'. Traditions of older, eighteenth-century protests – riots over high food prices following a bad harvest (which in turn reduced urban employment by reducing rural demand), Luddite sabotage of new machinery (requiring 12,000 much-needed troops for its suppression at its peak, between 1811 and 1813), 'patriotic' Church and King riots against liberal dissenters in the early war years, earlier metropolitan riots for 'Wilkes and Liberty' and the mob violence manipulated by the crazed Lord George Gordon in 1780 against Popery – still lingered on. Still more men in 1830 could recall Jeremiah Brandreth's Pentrich rising of stockingers in 1817, the Lancashire blanketeers' march of the same year, the charge of the Yeomanry at St Peter's Fields in Manchester in 1819, the Cato Street plot to murder the cabinet and Scottish radicals' 'battle of Bonnymuir' in 1820 and governmental reaction through legislation and the use of secret agents.[16] The ancestry of many agitations lay in the previous century.

III

'The chief grievances of which the people complain', declared Lord John Russell while introducing the Reform Bill on 1 March 1831, 'are these: – First, the nomination of Members by individuals. Second, the Elections by close Corporations; third, the Expense of Elections.' Such complaints linked sections of the Whig aristocracy and of the urban bourgeoisie. But revolutionary action could scarcely be expected from such an alliance between new and ancient wealth, as Whiggish supporters of parliamentary Reform explained in detail. The merit of the Reform Bill to Lord Palmerston was 'that it altered the distribution of political power, and restored the Constitution, by placing the middle classes in that situation to which they were entitled . . .'. Sir James Graham, who helped to plan the measure, 'knew none so safe as the extension of the suffrage to the most intelligent and industrious classes of the community'. Lord Chancellor Brougham (though privately worried by the abolition of nomination boroughs, which had often provided a political entrée for young men without fortunes or connections) differentiated between 'the mob' (or 'the populace') and 'the people' (or 'middle classes'). To him, the latter were 'the most numerous and by far the most wealthy order in the community . . . the genuine depositories of sober, rational, intellingent and honest English feeling'. Reform, maintained the young T. B. Macaulay, should produce 'a complete reconciliation between the aristocracy and the people'. He was alarmed by 'the two extreme parties . . . a narrow oligarchy above; an infuriated multitude below'. The country would be saved by a third party – 'the middle class of England, with the flower of the artistocracy at its head and the flower of the working classes bringing up its rear'. In typically Whiggish form, Macaulay explained

> That government is attacked is a reason for making the foundations of government broader, and deeper, and more solid. That property is attacked is a reason for binding together all proprietors in the firmest union. That the agitation of the question of Reform has enabled worthless demagogues to propagate their notions with some success is a reason for speedily settling the question in the only way in which it can be settled.

As a consequence, the Reform Act of 1832 has fairly been described by one modern historian as seeming to its authors 'essentially conservative, a rescue operation on behalf of rank and property'.[17]

A conservative reform was not particularly surprising from the most aristocratic of nineteenth-century cabinets, consisting of a duke, a marquess, three earls, two viscounts, two barons and four commoners (including an earl's heir, an Irish viscount and a baronet). Subsequent cabinets, as initially constituted, varied considerably: in 1834 Melbourne had a marquess, an earl, a viscount, three barons and ten commoners (including an Irish viscount, two heirs to earldoms, a duke's son and a baronet) and Peel had a duke, three earls, three barons, three baronets and three untitled men; in 1835 Melbourne enrolled a marquess, a viscount, three barons, an Irish viscount, two potential earls, a duke's son, a baronet, and three gentlemen; in 1841 Peel employed two dukes, three earls, three barons, four baronets, an earl's heir and another commoner; and in 1846 Russell (the duke's son) was joined by two marquesses, four earls, two barons, an Irish viscount, an earl's heir, three baronets and two others. For all its parade of past martyrs, its façade of aristocratic sang-froid before tumult, its pose of maintaining the traditions of Athenian democracy or Roman republicanism (let alone the 'Venetian oligarchy') and its innate belief in patrician and rationalist virtues, Whiggism was fundamentally conservative. Sufficiently alarmed by 'the march of progress' to make some strange temporary allies, largely devoted to the politics of pragmatic expediency and always (as Gladstone observed in 1855) exercising 'a more close and marked preference for the claims of consanguinity and affinity than was to be found among other politicians', the Whigs might call on the newer propertied classes to rescue the old. But the alliance between cultured and broad-acred Whig aristocrat and politically determined Liberal parvenu, fighting his way through a fiercely competitive industrial and commercial system, was uneasy long before late Victorian developments made it impossible. For Whigs were inveterate snobs. The reforming Earl Grey had 'regarded the son of an actress as incapacitated *de facto*' (despite an Etonian education) from becoming Prime Minister, when the 'liberal Tory' George Canning was proposed in 1827. And Whigs derived enjoyment from the pastime of pointing out the relatively humble origins of many of their Tory opponents. They would contrast the splendid ducal appurtenances of a Chatsworth or Woburn with the coal-merchanting background of Lord Eldon or the cotton-manufacturing interests of the Peels.

The contrary viewpoint was most strongly expressed by old Eldon, with his advice that 'sacrifice one atom of our glorious constitution and all the rest is gone'. But when the uncompromising leader of the Right spoke, in October 1831, the outworks of the Hanoverian constitution had already fallen. The repeal of the Test and Corporation Acts in 1828, following Protestant demands, finally removed 'a profane prostitution of a sacred ordinance' which legally prohibited non-Churchmen from holding State and municipal offices (but which had long been rendered inoperative by annual Indemnity Acts). This was a comparatively minor measure, though Eldon – who thought it 'as bad, as mischievous, as revolutionary as the most captious Dissenter would wish it to be'[18] – rightly saw it as a portent of further change. The likelihood of such change had been growing since the rise of the 'liberal Tories' from 1822 and had increased with the end of Lord Liverpool's fifteen-year premiership in 1827: the ministries of Canning, Lord Goderich and the 'Iron Duke' himself could not stem a rising tide.

The tide rose dramatically in the summer of 1828, when William Vesey Fitzgerald, a popular Irish squire, stood for re-election in County Clare, on his appointment to the Cabinet. To Tory distress, the demagogy of a middle-aged Roman Catholic barrister, Daniel O'Connell, and the authority of his clerical supporters ('he sent 120 priests into Clare to organise the voters and force them, by threats of excommunication, to vote in opposition to their landlords', asserted Wellington's friend Mrs Charles Arbuthnot) broke Irish voters' deference to even a liberal-minded landowner. The new President of the Board of Trade was resoundingly defeated. 'I care not for anything since I have terminated the contest', he told Peel. 'For the degradation of the county I feel deeply, and the organization exhibited is so complete and so formidable that no man can contemplate without alarm what is to follow in this wretched country.' O'Connell had bluntly challenged the Government in his election address: as a Roman Catholic, he would refuse to take the anti-Catholic oaths required from M.P.s. He 'entertained a confident hope that, if [Clare] elected him, the most bigotted of their enemies would see the necessity of removing from the chosen representative of the people an obstacle which would prevent him from doing his duty to his King and to his country'. And he was right. Faced by a massive new power in Ireland, Wellington and Peel granted 'Emancipation' to Roman Catholics in 1829. 'Little Twitch, *alias* Scroop, *alias* Premier Duke [of Norfolk], Hereditary Earl Marshal' could now take his seat in the Lords, and a handful of his co-religionists eventually entered the Commons. 'The Whigs were as sore as be damned at Wellington distinguishing himself' and 'mad to the last degree that [he and Peel] had taken the Catholick cause out of their own feeble and perfidious hands', observed that delightfully cynical commentator Thomas Creevey.[19] But another result was that the Tory Right was outraged and long remembered and resented the desertion of principle. The arch-Tory Charles Sibthorp felt that 'he had so often been deceived' by Peel 'on important questions of religion as well as agriculture, that he was determined to be deceived no more', when Peel deserted Protection in 1846.

Although Whiggism was still predominant among the 'Revolution Families' and their house-party colleagues in the greatest county and metropolitan mansions, the Tories also had a measure of support among that 'Venetian oligarchy' which Disraeli was to assail. But the principal Tory strength lay in the new nobility created by Pitt, a large number of county families, some traditional mercantile groups and in the Church of England. The Tories' philosophies and attitudes spanned a wide political spectrum: they mobilised Pittite patriots, neo-mercantilists, pioneer free traders, sporting squires from the shires, earnest Evangelicals, latter-day Cavaliers (who reached a mystical apogee in the 'Young England' movement of the forties), merchant-princes, military men and groups of tradesmen and artisans. In general, in 1830 they represented what they took (not always accurately) to be a traditional England and they mainly shared Wellington's belief in the constitution's 'excellence'. But it soon became apparent that they had also enrolled some prominent industrialists; and from 1835 their Operative Conservative Societies were pioneer constituency organisations.[20]

However, the Tories no more than the Whigs constituted a political party in the modern sense. They were banded together not so much by the Tadpoles and Tapers plotting in the Carlton Club (though F. R. Bonham was an astute agent and J. W. Croker an able propagandist)[21] as by personal loyalties, family traditions and connections and (sometimes fleeting) emotions and feelings. The notion of ministers being 'servants of the Crown' in a literal sense led to Wellington's beliefs in the necessity of maintaining government and the comparative unimportance of party.

The events of the early 1830s were seminal in their influence on party development. Whigs might generally agree with Sir Francis Baring's description of them as

a body of men connected with high rank and property, bound together by hereditary feelings, party ties, as well as higher motives, who in bad times keep alive the sacred flame of freedom, and when the people are roused stand between the constitution and revolution and go with the people, but not to extremities.

In 1832 they regarded as Tories simply those who opposed the Reform Bill. But by stages the new Conservatives evolved a wider philosophy. 'If the spirit of the Reform Bill implies merely a careful review of institutions, civil and ecclesiastical, undertaken in a friendly temper, combining, with the firm maintenance of established rights, the correction of proved abuses and the redress of real grievances', Peel told his Tamworth electors in December 1834, ' – in that case, I can for myself and colleagues undertake to act in such a spirit and with such intentions.' In 1838 he told a London rally that

> by Conservative principles we mean the maintenance of our settled institutions in Church and State and also the preservation and defence of that combination of laws, of institutions, of usages, of habits and of manners which has contributed to mould and form the character of Englishmen.

By this time, according to Wellington, Conservatism had attracted[22]

> the great landed, commercial and manufacturing and funded proprietors of the country; the Church almost to a man, the Universities, the great majority of the learned professions in the three kingdoms, and of the professors of Arts and Sciences, of the Corporations of the Empire etc.

From the ashes of Pittite Toryism arose Britain's (and still more England's) predominant political party.

A third political viewpoint – Radicalism, with its many varieties from 'philosophical' to proletarian – was too diffuse and divided ever to offer a single meaningful and consolidated platform. A title used to describe the political views of the traditionalist William Cobbett, the snobbish 1st earl of Durham, the liberal Francis Place, imperialists like Sir William Molesworth and Gibbon Wakefield, capitalists like John Fielden and socialists like William Thompson, Thomas Hodgskin and J. F. Bray has little value. But, despite their numerous sectarian divisions and basic philosophic differences, the assorted Radicals played considerable roles in various political and social agitations.[23] Above all, Benthamite doctrines of the 'greatest happiness of the greater number', the testing of institutions by the standard of strict utility, the involvement of a hedonistic calculus in legislation and the 'scientific' organisation of investigation and inspection exercised vast influence. 'Every law is an evil', Bentham disarmingly explained, 'for every law is an infraction of liberty'; but the logic of his own arguments led from *laissez-faire* to sizeable State intervention. And from an alliance of varied Radicals, Whigs, dissenters and Peelite Conservatives was to emerge the great Victorian Liberal Party.

Party discipline long remained weak. On being offended by transient and normal allies on a particular subject, a group might still follow a prominent personality into entirely different coalitions. Thus in 1829–30 the liberal Tory William Huskisson was prepared to collaborate with the Whig Graham against Wellington; Lord Blandford's Tory platoon allied with Thomas Attwood's Birmingham Political Union;[24] the ultra-Tory duke of Richmond and such Canningites as Palmerston and Melbourne joined Grey's mainly Whig cabinet; the ultra-Tory Richard Oastler collaborated with ultra-Radicals over industrial reform; the Peelites eventually allied with the liberals on free trade. Party commanded a measure of loyalty to generally ill-defined traditions, but major events could upset such allegiances. Lord George Bentinck, successively Whig, Canningite and 'most bigoted and violent of Tories', the arbiter of the Turf, was roused to unexpected political passion by the repeal of the Corn Laws. 'I keep horses in three counties, and they tell me that I shall save fifteen hundred a year by free trade', he wrote in a much-quoted letter. 'I don't care for that. What I cannot bear is being sold.' It was not that maintenance of agricultural Protection was a basic or long-standing Tory principle; certainly it had been defended on many Tory platforms, but the theory of commitment to a 'party policy' was still in its infancy. Neither was Protection, in reality, providing much 'protection' for agriculture.[25] What was important to the Protectionists in 1846 was a combination of their growing aversion to Peel and Graham and their belief that an 'interest' (as distinct from a 'class') was being betrayed.

Nevertheless, in the period between the petering-out of Whiggish reforming zeal in 1835 and the Conservative disintegration of 1845 there was a measure of party order which differentiated the decade from the years of shifting loyalties which preceded and succeeded it. The 'centre party' advocated by Lord Stanley's supporters in 1834–5, when the 'Derby Dilly' hoped to attract an army of moderate supporters to its 'Knowsley Creed', was soon revealed as a sham: conservative and other politicians must continue to choose between Whig and Tory allegiances. And from 1846, despite many false hopes and a greedy grasping of ministries in Lord Aberdeen's government of 1852–5, the Peelites were to learn the same lesson about the polarisation of political loyalties.[26]

IV

Despite the horrors of much early industrial life and labour, the brutality still pervading a wide expanse of society and the uninhibited sexuality of some sections of it (as described in a literary underworld of pornography, assiduously collected by such men as Monckton Milnes), religion played an increasingly important part in forming social and political attitudes during the fourth and fifth decades of the nineteenth century. The religious census of 30 March 1851 may disappoint modern social scientists by its methodological inadequacies; it horrified contemporary readers because it purported to show that of a population of 17,927,609 in England and Wales only 7,261,032 had attended some religious service.[27] Nevertheless, religion permeated every aspect of life and provoked or coloured many of the great national controversies.

The Church of England and its established sister churches in Wales and Ireland provoked the hostility of radical reformer and religious dissenter alike in 1830. The Church's vast total income (estimated at £7,000,000) and the huge personal incomes of some well-connected prelates (the bishop of Winchester reputedly had £50,000 a year and the archbishop of Canterbury and bishop of Ely £30,000)[28] seemed as scandalous to authors of radical *Black Books* as did alleged aristocratic incomes. Sinecures, simony, nepotism and pluralism in the Church could be equated with similar jobbery in the State; a Bishop Sparke of Ely whose way through the Fens was reputedly lighted by the 'sparks' in all the best rectory windows earned equal obloquy with the Cumbrian magnate of whom it was written

> E'en by the elements his pow'r confess'd,
> Of mines and boroughs Lonsdale stands possess'd,
> And one sad servitude alike denotes
> The slave that labours and the slave that votes.

Radicals painted a picture of a wealthy, aristocratic, indolent and corrupt establishment rapaciously insisting on Church rates and its remaining tithes, owning and exploiting huge estates (varying from the dean and chapter of Durham's coal royalties to individual parsons' glebe) and insistently monopolising non-Romanist marriage ceremonies, registration of births and deaths, burials and Oxford and Cambridge degrees. Such a picture was accepted by Churchmen like Bishop Blomfield and the effervescent Sydney Smith, themselves both past absentees. When the Lords rejected the second Reform Bill on 8 October 1831 the majority of 41 included 21 bishops (while 7 abstained and 2 supported the proposal) and hostility to the Church inevitably mounted. At Bristol Bishop Gray's palace was burned down; the

redoubtable Henry Phillpotts's palace at Exeter almost shared the same
fate; episcopal figures replaced the Pope or Guy Fawkes on November
bonfires; and the conversion of Canterbury cathedral to cavalry stables
was proposed amid cheers.

Churchmen were entitled to retort by pointing to their multifarious
good works. The Evangelical movement, originally rooted in the
'Clapham sect' and some Cambridge colleges, had concentrated on
saving souls through personal conversion. An individualist creed based
on individual morality initially sought and found its strength by
recruitment of individuals to the body of the elect – a recruitment
engineered by sermonising about the dangers of eternal punishment in
Huddersfield or Haworth or at tea parties in Magdalene and Queens'.
But concern with individual salvation led to social involvement:
Evangelicals became increasingly concerned to save souls lurking
within whole categories of mankind – Negro slaves, English workers,
aristocrats, businessmen or children. As their individualist theology and
other-worldly acceptance of the temporal *status quo* yielded to a broader
social Christianity, Evangelicals turned increasingly to deal with various
social problems. An early crop of the rich array of nineteenth-century
voluntary societies was one result. William Wilberforce spoke for the
Evangelical–Quaker campaign (a model for several future agitations)
against the horrors of the slave trade (abolished in 1807) and of slavery
(prohibited throughout the empire in 1833). Heathens abroad would be
converted by the Church Missionary Society of 1799, heathens at home
by the Religious Tract Society of the same year, heathens everywhere
by the British and Foreign Bible Society of 1804; prostitutes would be
reformed by the Society for the Suppression of Vice; home missions
would be conducted by the Church Pastoral Aid Society of 1836; a host
of groups would deal with a wide range of social problems from
drunkenness to starvation and child labour to workers' housing.[29] And
from the 1830s Lord Ashley led Evangelical opinion into supporting
many more practical Christian schemes.

While disapproving of Evangelicals' fundamentalist theology and
dissenting contacts, the more sacerdotal High Churchmen had been
equally active. Joshua Watson's 'Hackney Phalanx' had poured its
energies and finances into further extensions of the Church's mission,
backing the Society for Promoting Christian Knowledge (founded in
1698) and the Society for the Propagation of the Gospel (established in
1701) and helping to form the 'National Society for the Education of the
Poor in the Principles of the Established Church' in 1811. 'National'

schools were soon established throughout England and Wales, through the energy of Dr Andrew Bell and large voluntary subscriptions. Protestant and Roman Catholic groups also made some provision for elementary education, and the Quaker Joseph Lancaster's system (from 1814 organised by the British and Foreign School Society) claimed to provide undenominational religious teaching in its schools. Non-conformist 'voluntaryists' were often embarrassed by the Church's much greater generosity in the cause of elementary education. And the Church retained its lead, fending off Whig attempts to extend secular interference in 1839, while accepting modest financial grants from 1833 and proving unable to defeat bitter nonconformist hostility to an alleged extension of its power over industrial schools in 1843.

While the Church admirably maintained its extensive provision of day and Sunday schools, it was inevitably less successful in defending its more moribund sectors. From 1835 the new Ecclesiastical Commissioners energetically inaugurated internal reforms, dealing with such matters as episcopal incomes, Church finance, cathedral chapters and the supplementation of poor livings. In 1836 Parliament enforced the commutation of tithes and considerably changed the ecclesiastical courts. New episcopal supervision of the industrial areas was provided by the creation of the dioceses of Ripon and Manchester in 1836 and 1847. Ecclesiastical charities were overhauled; a great church-building programme (initially aided by public grants in 1818 and 1824) was inaugurated; and the standards of clerical conduct and lay observance were both raised. Increased piety – encouraged by Evangelicals and High Churchmen alike – led to an enhanced sense of the character, history and rights of the Church. The nature of a divinely ordained body must not be made subordinate to the transient fancies of secular society, and seemingly profane state action eventually aroused bitter resentment. 'The Church lays exclusive claim to its own internal regulations', one priest wrote in 1843: 'it jealously protests against Erastian interference; it cannot fulfil its sacred functions if it be crippled and fettered. . . .' Such views were very different from Melbourne's celebrated observation that 'things were coming to a pretty pass when religion was allowed to invade private life'.[30]

The defence of God's institution against profane lay spoliation reached a crescendo in 1833, when Lord Althorp proposed to reduce the sees of the minority Church of Ireland from 22 to 12. On 14 July John Keble, the saintly professor of poetry at Oxford, preached his famous sermon against 'National Apostasy' before the assize judges. Henceforth, Keble and some of his colleagues in the highly intellectual Oriel College – men like Hurrell Froude, J. H. Newman and E. B. Pusey – became the pioneers of a re-examination of the nature, history and theology of the Church. They were attracted by both the medieval concept of an undivided Western Christendom and the Laudian church of the seventeenth century. Their series of *Tracts for the Times* stressed the nature of the priesthood, the importance of the episcopate's apostolic succession, the 'branch theory' of the Catholicism of Anglicanism, Canterbury's *via media* between Rome and Geneva, the virtues of traditional Church practices and the merits of patristic and Caroline writers. Such calls for a restoration of older practices, observances and beliefs attracted a host of followers and repelled a host of Evangelicals and nonconformists by their alleged 'Romanism'. Oxford was bitterly divided between Tractarians and others over such matters as the appointment of the liberal R. D. Hampden to the regius chair of divinity, the Evangelicals' memorial to the Marian martyrs, Pusey's insistence that the Eucharist was a commemorative sacrifice and the creation of a joint Anglican–Lutheran bishopric of Jerusalem.

Beyond the academic community, loyal Protestants were horrified by the 'Oxford Popery', with its interest in reviving the use of all seven Sacraments, religious communities and (rather later) the pageantry, ceremonial and colour of medieval ritualism. 'The Wesleyan Methodists, hitherto friendly to the Church . . .', Ashley told Graham in 1843, 'are actuated by a deep and conscientious fear of Popery in the Church of England.' For long concerned to maintain its special relationship with the Church, Methodism finally passed into the dissenting camp because of its suspicions of Tractarian designs on factory education. A liberal nonconformist divine, Dr Andrew Reed, expressed a widely held view when he told the (predominantly dissenting) British and Foreign School Society that it was impossible to trust the Church 'when so many of her sons were blotting the name of Protestant from their brow as a disgrace, and disturbing the settlement of the very throne, by denominating the Reformation a robbery and the Revolution rebellion!'[31] Anti-Popery for long remained a potent force.

Protestant suspicions – at least in Protestant minds – were increasingly confirmed. Newman's Tract XC, with its provocative reinterpretations of the 39 Articles, raised a storm in 1841; and four years later its disillusioned author entered the Roman Church, to be followed by a trickle of lesser converts. Dr Pusey bravely led the Tractarian majority along a middle but Catholic course between what they considered to be the errors of the Reformation and the Counter-Reformation alike. Sacerdotal, traditionalist, 'mystical' and increasingly ritualistic, the Puseyites shared some characteristics with other reactions to the liberal 'march of progress', such as the Gothic vogue in the arts (ranging from Sir Walter Scott's popular novels to the architecture of Sir Charles Barry and Augustus Pugin and Lord Eglinton's fantastic 'medieval' tournament) and the feudalistic 'Young England' idealism of some romantic Tories. But in the long term the progenitors of modern Anglo-Catholicism were to add a new form of social involvement to the Church's social witness: ritualistic splendour was allied with attempts to implement the Sermon on the Mount. Anglican Catholics were, indeed, to take over the role of socially concerned Evangelicals and F. D. Maurice's mid-century 'Christian Socialists'.[32]

Dissenters – Congregationalists, Baptists, Unitarians, Quakers, Presbyterians and, from about 1843, Wesleyans – periodically continued a noisy campaign against the Church. Edward Miall's *Nonconformist*, with its avowal of 'the dissidence of dissent and the protestantism of the protestant religion', was the most famous of a crop of virulent journals. Its readers would favour disestablishment, voluntaryism on social matters (and especially on education), free trade and largely *laissez-faire* economics; they were among the most important founders of the Liberal party. But in Scotland a sizeable group of Presbyterians, with impeccable Protestant beliefs, reacted as strongly as the Tractarians to State 'interference'. At the general assembly of the Church of Scotland in 1834 the evangelical party carried the 'veto act', giving male heads of families in each congregation the right to veto lay patrons' nominated ministers. A long round of battles ensued between 'evangelicals' and 'moderates', with little charity on either side. The celebrated Auchterarder case led to decisions by the Court of Session and (in 1839) the Lords against the 'act', and passions mounted over theocratic claims (sometimes backed by the harsh disciplining of rivals) against allegedly erastian control. Compromise was tried and failed: to the evangelical leader Dr Thomas Chalmers, the Kirk was 'amenable to no higher power on earth'. Matters reached a head when Peel's government refused, in 1842, to accept the Assembly's 'Claim, Declaration and Protest'. In May 1843 Chalmers led the Disruption, when some 400 ministers established the Free Church of Scotland.[33] Such men made great sacrifices for their principles; and the equally sacrificial devotion of many of their congregations soon covered Scotland with a network of active and socially involved new churches.

Of course, not all early Victorians were involved in the religious, ecclesiastical and theological arguments which divided members of the established Churches of England and Scotland and regularly splintered Methodists and dissenters. But long before the ultramontanes carried their case for papal infallibility in 1870 British Roman Catholics were as bitterly divided over social and political attitudes as were Anglicans over the comprehensiveness of *ecclesia Anglicana*, Presbyterians over their relationship with lay society or Methodists over Jabez Bunting's Toryism and a variety of alternatives. Consequently, a very large number of people were involved in primarily religious arguments. When Roman Catholicism was the subject of the controversy, a huge underswell of opinion would become vocal: Anglicans (liberal-'broad', Evangelical or Tractarian), Protestants of all varieties, Orangemen and secularists; learned readers of Tridentine decrees, earnest readers of John Foxe's martyrology (reprinted in 1843–9) and titillated readers of 'awful confessions' of the Maria Monk (published in 1836) variety might join together. When, in September 1850, Pope Pius IX established a Roman Catholic hierarchy in England, English anger quickly mounted. Already roused by Phillpotts's long High Church opposition to the Evangelical G. C. Gorham and by the trickle of Tractarian conversions to Rome, 'Protestant England' was enraged by Archbishop Wiseman's ineptly phrased letter 'from the Flaminian Gate' in October. Lord John Russell joined what the perceptive diarist Charles Greville called 'the "No Popery" hubbub' with his open letter of protest against 'papal aggression' to the bishop of Durham. Only a handful of M.P.s resisted the panicky Ecclesiastical Titles Bill of 1851.[34]

Religion thus remained a vital cause of controversy, a potent force in society and politics and the constant promoter of many of the voluntary societies which were a glory of the Victorian age. Whether religious influences also prevented some revolutionary outbreak is more doubtful. The distinguished French historian Élie Halévy considered that Evangelical and Methodist pressures had diverted potential revolutionaries among the working and middle classes; and certainly the acolytes of 'Pope' Bunting and the pietist Evangelicals were heavily 'anti-Jacobin', proud of loathing both democracy and sin. On the other hand, some Methodist groups produced several proletarian radical leaders. Furthermore, if such measures as industrial reform helped to pacify discontent, the credit was due to allegedly 'reactionary' Anglicans rather than to 'progressive' nonconformist supporters of *laissez-faire*. It seems likely that 'theology' dampened and restrained possible militancy among members of many churches and sects, with the explanation that

> God made them high and lowly
> And ordered their estate.

But although scores of chapels taught acceptance of present misery in the hope of future redemption, neither religious quietism nor any other easily identified single factor satisfactorily explains Britain's escape from the cycle of continental revolutions. Many people of very different political persuasions talked of 'revolution' in the heat of argument. 'Let the Duke take office as Premier, and we shall have a commotion in the nature of a civil war . . .', wrote Francis Place during the final Reform crisis in May 1832, ' . . . and in less than five days we shall have the soldiers with us.' Richard Oastler, the Tory factory reformer, asked excited audiences whether 'the Law or the Mills [should] be destroyed', threatened sabotage and prophesied social revolution. His Tory friend, the former Wesleyan minister Joseph Rayner Stephens, proclaimed himself 'a revolutionist by fire, by blood, to the knife, to the death'. Some Owenite unionists dreamed of a general strike which would overturn the existing social order. Even bourgeois Anti-Corn Law Leaguers often gave equivocal answers to demands for violence. And, inevitably, Chartists regularly made revolutionary noises and assumed threatening postures, though Feargus O'Connor himself was usually carefully ambiguous and John Frost's 'Newport Rising' of November 1839 – whatever its connections – was a disaster. Much of the oratory of militancy was, as always, bluff and bluster. However greatly reformers in various fields might exaggerate their claims and authorities their fears,[35] it is difficult to believe that Britain really faced the possibility of a continental-style revolution during the second quarter of the nineteenth century.

v

The following essays deal with eight different agitations, in different ways and from different viewpoints. The intention of the authors is to present not only a narrative account but an analysis of different interpretations of eight movements of importance in a vital historical period, together with their personal judgements of these movements.

From 1832 the Reform Act, allegedly and apparently 'final', shaped both the composition of the Commons and the development of political organisations. It is still possible for historians to disagree over the influence of the 'July Revolution' of 1830 in Paris or the 'militant' threats of native radicals in 1831-2 and over the purposes and results of Reform. But the Reform agitation is a useful starting-point for this volume. Its achievement seemed as important to its Whiggish parents as it did to its horrified Tory opponents (when the Second Reading was passed on 22 March 1831, wrote Macaulay, 'many of us shed tears. . . . And the jaw of Peel fell; and the face of Twiss was as the face of a damned soul; and Herries looked like Judas taking his necktie off for the last operation') and to bitterly disappointed ultra-Radicals such as James Bronterre O'Brien (who claimed to have foreseeen that the Act would 'detach from the working classes a large portion of the middle ranks'). But 'finality' was impossible and the demand for suffrage extension continued, until by the 1850s Peter Locke King was proposing annual parliamentary motions.

The pioneer campaign for industrial reform began almost simultaneously with the Reform movement. With its demand for Government intervention, it clearly opposed the 'spirit of the age' and current beliefs in the free play of market forces. As a result it aroused bitter hostility in liberal circles. Shorter industrial hours would destroy competitiveness in overseas markets, slash profits and wages and promote idleness and debauchery; the movement was composed of reactionaries and revolutionaries, both hostile (though for different reasons) to the industrial system, or it was a creature of the great masters designed to ruin smaller competitors; the factory legislation was passed from Tory motives of revenge on the new industrialists. Some of these polemical 'explanations' have had a long life, and can only be assessed by a re-examination of the Factory Movement's history. Much the same political alliance of Left and Right created the agitation against another great shibboleth of the age, the English New Poor Law of 1834. The anti-Poor Law campaigners bravely opposed the plans of Benthamites, economists and the political leaders with appeals to tradition, sentiment and 'morality'. But in addition they raised their agitation to a militant violence which was inherited by some Chartist groups.

An examination of a seminal period of trade union history presents in some ways a microcosmic picture of changing social attitudes. Little convivial clubs and friendly societies had in several cases yielded to larger unions by the late twenties. There followed a period of militancy, syndicalism and socialism largely associated with Owenite trades unionism in the early thirties. And the following decade witnessed the development of the still controversial concept of the Victorian 'labour aristocracy', most notably represented by the Amalgamated Society of Engineers of 1851. An upper crust of time-served craftsmen and 'semi-skilled' workers in such geographically concentrated industries as cotton and coal had established a number of lasting and 'respectable' organisations by the fifties and was in time to exercise some influence on the contours of industrial relations. A much greater working-class movement, and one which was more successful in recruiting so-called 'unskilled' workers, is examined in the chapter on Chartism. The relationship between Chartists and trade unionists remains controversial, as do a host of local and theoretical problems. Many more regional studies are still needed and many more of the 'ifs' of Chartism require consideration. The current state of a developing study is examined in this section.

More immediately successful than most working-class groups was the predominantly middle-class Anti-Corn Law League. Here was an agitation which felt itself fully attuned to the dominant contemporary liberalism, largely financed by the great industrialists and blessed by nonconformist divines. It openly championed a 'class' cause – that of a bourgeois Britian against an *ancien régime* of aristocrats, backwoods squires and 'feudalistic' orders. And it generally condemned industrial reform, Chartism, trade unions and governmental interference with society or the economy. The League was no more monolithic than the Chartists in organisation and philosophy; but its local varieties and groups have received even less attention in the past.

Ireland's manifold and manifest problems have for long periodically influenced the course of British politics. In 1829 an Irish election led to the 'emancipation' of Roman Catholics and in 1846 an Irish famine provoked the repeal of the Corn Laws. Irish agitators – Bronterre O'Brien, Smith O'Brien, Daniel O'Connell and Feargus O'Connor – and their followers; Irish religious differences between equally intractable factions – a Roman Catholic majority rigorously controlled by its episcopate and priesthood, an established Anglican group of landowners and tenants and a rabidly Protestant Presbyterian class of farmers, industrialists and workers; a tradition of protest against 'alien' land-ownership and rule and an apparent denial of local nationality – such were some of the ingredients of Irish politics. Fact and myth about the distant past constantly exercised some influence on Ireland's uniquely complicated political and social life. And the most 'religious' section of the United Kingdom became the most 'revolutionary', violent, murderous and bigoted. The principal Irish views are examined in the seventh chapter. The final essay in this volume is concerned with the campaign for public health reform, itself not a particularly 'popular' movement but of major importance to the populace of a dirty and often diseased nation. As John Heysham of Carlisle had pointed out in 1782, disease was largely 'the offspring of filth, nastiness and confined air, in rooms crowded with many inhabitants', but insanitary conditions persisted – and not only in dreary urban conurbations. At Cambridge the river acted as the main sewer for the town and colleges, and such palaces as Wentworth Woodhouse had bad drainage systems. Attempts to improve public health faced every kind of hostility and apathy, and the Public Health Act of 1848 was a major achievement in the circumstances, however short-lived some of its provisions were. Furthermore, the subject leads to further consideration of those wider Benthamite and humanitarian influences which were to influence the mid-Victorian administrative revolution.[36] The essays as a whole are offered as a contribution to the understanding of the continuing debate on a seminal period of British history.

NOTES TO INTRODUCTION

1. G. W. E. Russell, *Collections and Recollections* (1903 ed.) pp. 68, 81.

2. A. S. Turberville, *The House of Lords in the Age of Reform, 1784–1837* (1958), p. 478; J. H. Philbin, *Parliamentary Representation, 1832: England and Wales* (New Haven, Conn., 1965), p. xxi.

3. *The Book of Fallacies: from Unfinished Papers of Jeremy Bentham, by a Friend* (1824), p. 390.

4. Jane Austen, *Emma* (1816; 1909 ed.), p. 175; William Addison, *Audley End* (1953), pp. 212–15.

5. See Asa Briggs, 'The Language of "Class" in Early Nineteenth-Century England', in A. Briggs and J. Saville (eds.) *Essays in Labour History* (1967 ed.), pp. 43–73.

6. Hesketh Pearson, *The Smith of Smiths* (1948 ed.), p. 160; R. S. Lambert, *The Railway King, 1800–1871* (1964 ed.), pp. 174–83; Christopher Sykes, *Four Studies in Loyalty* (1947 impr.), p. 18.

7. Cobden to Bright, 1 Oct, 4 Nov 1849 (Lord Morley, *The Life of Richard Cobden* (1910 ed.), pp. 517–18); G. C. Brodrick, *English Land and English Landlords* (1881), p. 99; *PP* (1874), lxxii; cf. John Bateman, *The Great Landowners of Great Britain and Ireland* (1883 ed.). For very different interpretations, see Turberville, op. cit., pp. 407 ff. and O. R. McGregor, 'Introduction Part Two' to Lord Ernle, *English Farming, Past and Present* (1961 ed.), *passim*.

8. Léon Faucher, *Manchester in 1844* (1844), p. 41; Friedrich Engels, *The*

Condition of the Working-Class in England in 1844, trans. Mrs F. K. Wischnew-etzky (1892), reprinted in *Marx and Engels on Britain* (Moscow, 1954), p. 311; R. W. Emerson, *Works* (1884 ed.), v, 145.

9. See Sidney Pollard, *The Genesis of Modern Management* (1965), David Spring, *The English Landed Estate in the Nineteenth Century: Its Administration* (Baltimore, 1963); E. P. Thompson, *The Making of the English Working Class* (1968 ed.), *passim*. See also R. S. Neale, 'Class and Class-Consciousness in Early Nineteenth-Century England: Three Classes or Five?', *VS* xii (1968), suggesting a five-class model – upper, middle, middling and working class A and B (roughly industrial and other workers).

10. *The Lancaster Trials* (1843), quoted in Max Morris, *From Cobbett to the Chartists* (1951 ed.), pp. 180–3; *Northern Star*, 1 Mar 1845; Cobden to Konig, 1 Oct 1844 (Norman McCord, *The Anti-Corn Law League, 1838–1846* (1958), p. 162); Asa Briggs, 'National Bearings', in A. Briggs (ed.), *Chartist Studies* (1965 impr.), p. 291.

11. W. G. Hoffman, *British Industry, 1700–1950*, (trans. W. O. Henderson, W. H. Chaloner) (Oxford, 1955), B. R. Mitchell and Phyllis Deane, *Abstract of British Historical Statistics* (Cambridge, 1954), *passim*; C. N. Ward-Perkins, 'The Commercial Crisis of 1847', *Oxford Economic Papers*, NS, ii (1950).

12. See G. Rudé, 'English Rural and Urban Disturbances on the Eve of the First Reform Bill, 1830–1831', *Past and Present*, 37 (1967). On the continuing 'standard of living' controversy, see T. S. Ashton, 'The Standard of Life of the Workers in England 1790–1830', *JEH Supp.* (1949); R. M. Hartwell, 'The Rising Standard of Living in England, 1800–1850', *EcHR* 2nd ser., xiv (1961); R. M. Hartwell and E. J. Hobsbawm, 'The Standard of Living during the Industrial Revolution: a Discussion', ibid., xvi (1963); A. J. Taylor, 'Progress and Poverty in Britain, 1780–1850: a Reappraisal', *History*, xlv (1960).

13. Shaftesbury to Russell, 26 Nov 1851 (G. P. Gooch (ed.), *The Later Correspondence of Lord John Russell* (1925), i, 214); W. E. Tate, *The English Village Community and the Enclosure Movements* (1967).

14. Bright to Mrs Priestman, 14 Aug 1842 (G. M. Trevelyan, *The Life of John Bright* (1913), p. 81); Croker to Graham, 28 Jan 1843 (J. T. Ward, *Sir James Graham* (1967), p. 193); cf. G. S. R. Kitson Clark, 'Hunger and Politics in 1842', *JMH* xxv (1953); A. G. Rose, 'The Plug Plots of 1842 in Lancashire and Cheshire', *TLCAS* lxvii (1957). Cobden quoted in Asa Briggs, *Victorian Cities* (1968 ed.), p. 189.

15. David Ricardo, *Principles of Political Economy and Taxation* (1819 ed.), p. 83; N. W. Senior, *Letters on the Factory Act* (1837), p. 16; Spencer Murch, *Ten Objections against the Factories Education Bill* (1843), p. 10; Philip Harwood, *Six Lectures on the Corn-Law Monopoly and Free Trade* (1843), p. 119; *PP* (1834), xxvii, 228; Andrew Reed, *Factories Education Bill. A Speech . . .* (1843), p. 12; Herbert Spencer, *Social Statics* (1851), *passim*; *Speeches of the Rt Hon. T. B. Macaulay, M.P.* (1854), p. 436; J. S. Mill, *On Liberty* (1859), *passim*.

16. F. O. Darvall, *Popular Disturbance and Public Order in Regency England* (1934), p. 1; G. Rudé, *Wilkes and Liberty* (Oxford, 1962), *passim*; R. J. White, *Waterloo to Peterloo* (1957); D. Read, *Peterloo* (Manchester, 1958); J. Stanhope, *The Cato Street Conspiracy* (1962), *passim*. Cf. the interesting argument in E. J. Hobsbawm, *Labouring Men* (1964), pp. 126–57 and the 'social tension chart' in W. W. Rostow, *British Economy of the Nineteenth Century* (Oxford, 1948), p. 124.

17. D. G. Southgate, *The Passing of the Whigs, 1832–1886* (1962), p. 21.

18. *Christian Observer*, xxvii (1828); H. Twiss, *The Public and Private Life of Lord Chancellor Eldon* (1844), iii, 45.

19. Francis Bamford and the Duke of Wellington (eds.), *The Journal of Mrs*

Arbuthnot, 1820–1832 (1950), ii, 196–9; W. Vesey Fitzgerald to Peel, 5 July 1828 (Lord Mahon and E. Cardwell (eds), *Memoirs of Sir Robert Peel* (1856), i, 115); R. Huish, *Memoirs of Daniel O'Connell* (1836), p. 438; J. Gore, *Creevey* (1949), pp. 306–7.

20. See G. S. R. Kitson Clark, *Peel and the Conservative Party* (1929); W. J. Wilkinson, *Tory Democracy* (New York, 1925); W. Paul, *History of the Origin and Progress of the Operative Conservative Societies* (Doncaster, 1842 ed.), *passim*. For some curious statistics of party allegiances, see J. R. Vincent, *Pollbooks: How Victorians Voted* (Cambridge, 1967).

21. See Norman Gash, 'F. R. Bonham: Conservative "Political Secretary" 1832–47', *EHR* lxiii (1949), *Politics in the Age of Peel* (1953), *passim*; M. F. Brightfield, *John Wilson Croker* (1940).

22. Bernard Mallet, *Thomas George, Earl of Northbrook: A Memoir* (1908), pp. 32–3; Norman Gash, *The Age of Peel* (1968), p. 77, *Reaction and Reconstruction in English Politics, 1832–1852* (Oxford, 1965), p. 132; L. J. Jennings (ed.), *The Croker Papers* (1884), ii, 217.

23. See S. MacCoby, *English Radicalism, 1832–52* (1935), *The English Radical Tradition, 1763–1914* (1952); Max Beer, *History of Socialism in England* (1919–20); Élie Halévy, *Growth of Philosophical Radicalism* (1928).

24. See Asa Briggs, 'Thomas Attwood and the Economic Background of the Birmingham Political Union', *CHJ* ix (1948).

25. Chester Kirby, *The English Country Gentleman* (n.d.), ch. 2; cf. Derek Walker-Smith, *The Protectionist Case in the 1840s* (Oxford, 1933).

26. D. W. J. Johnson, 'Sir James Graham and the "Derby Dilly"', *University of Birmingham Hist. Jour.*, iv (1953); Ward, op. cit., chs. 10–12; Asa Briggs, *The Age of Improvement* (1959), *passim* – the best modern textbook.

27. See Brian Harrison, 'Underneath the Victorians', *VS* x (1967), 'Philanthropy and the Victorians', ibid., ix (1966); K. S. Inglis, 'Patterns of Religious Worship in 1851', *JEccH* xi (1960). For an excellent introduction to this and many other themes, see G. S. R. Kitson Clark, *The Making of Victorian England* (1962), *passim*.

28. J. R. H. Moorman, *A History of the Church in England* (1954), pp. 332 ff.

29. See R. Coupland, *Wilberforce* (1945 ed.), G. R. Balleine, *A History of the Evangelical Party in the Church of England* (1933 ed.), Ford K. Brown, *Fathers of the Victorians: The Age of Willberforce* (Cambridge, 1961); Lord Annan, *Leslie Stephen* (1951).

30. G. W. Sandys, *A Letter to the Rt Hon. Sir James R. G. Graham . . .* (1843), p. 9; Lord David Cecil, *Melbourne* (1955), p. 151; cf. J. T. Ward and J. H. Treble, 'Religion and Education in 1843: Reaction to the "Factory Education Bill"', *JEccH* xx (1969).

31. Ashley to Graham, 26 Apr 1843 (J. T. Ward, *The Factory Movement, 1830–1855* (1962), p. 266); Reed, op. cit., p. 11.

32. R. W. Church, *The Oxford Movement* (1891); Y. Brilioth, *The Anglican Revival* (1925); S. C. Carpenter, *Church and People: 1789–1889* (1933), C. E. Raven, *Christian Socialism, 1848–54* (1920).

33. Arthur Miall, *The Life of Edward Miall* (1884); Robert Buchanan, *The Ten Years' Conflict* (Glasgow, 1852); William Hanna, *Memoirs of the Life and Writings of Thomas Chalmers* (Edinburgh, 1852), vi; Thomas Brown, *Annals of the Disruption* (Edinburgh, 1877).

34. C. C. F. Greville, *A Journal of the Reign of Queen Victoria from 1837 to 1852* (1885), iii, 366 ff.; T. C. Edwards, 'Papal Aggression: 1851', *HT* i (1951).

35. Élie Halévy, *History of the English People in the Nineteenth Century*, trans. E. I. Watkin and D. A. Barker (1949), i, 423–8; E. J. Hobsbawm, 'Methodism

and the Threat of Revolution', *HT* vii (1957); R. F. Wearmouth, *Methodism and the Working-Class Movements of England, 1800–1850* (1947), *passim*; Place to Sir John Hobhouse, 18 May 1832 (Graham Wallas, *Life of Francis Place* (1918), p. 316); *A Report . . . of Public Meeting . . .* (Oldham, 1836); *Northern Star*, 6 Jan 1838; D. Read and E. Glasgow, *Feargus O'Connor* (1961); D. Williams, *John Frost* (1939); F. C. Mather, *Public Order in the Age of the Chartists* (Manchester, 1959).

36. Gwen Raverat, *Period Piece* (1954), p. 18. See J. B. Brebner, 'Laissez-Faire and State Intervention in Nineteenth Century Britain', *JEH Supp.* (1948); W. H. Coates, 'Benthamism, Laissez-Faire and Collectivism', *Journal of the History of Ideas*, x (1950); David Roberts, 'Jeremy Bentham and the Victorian Administrative State', *VS* ii (1959); O. MacDonagh, 'The Nineteenth-Century Revolution in Government: A Reappraisal', *HJ* i (1958), *A Pattern of Government Growth, 1800–60* (1961); H. Parris, 'The Nineteenth-Century Revolution in Government: A Reappraisal Reappraised', *HJ* iii (1960).

1. The Agitation for Parliamentary Reform

DEREK FRASER

THE essential success of the parliamentary Reform movement in the years 1830–2 lay in the effective mobilisation of public opinion in a situation of political excitement and flux. This success can be analysed in the narrow chronological confines of the Reform Bill crises but it is important to realise that in both ideology and tactics the Reform movement had a history stretching back at least sixty years. As one observer put it, 'The feeling in favour of Reform is no meteor flash, no transient burst of passion – but a deep seated, fervent unquenchable fire – a fire that has been long smothered but never extinguished.'[1]

The ethos of the Reform movement in terms of its ideology had three component parts, overlapping and interdependent yet at the same time distinct and identifiable. The first component originated with the Reform movement of Wilkes in 1769–70 and the County Association movement of Wyvill in 1780–5. Wilkes was able to arouse the lower classes, particularly in London, in favour of changes in Parliament, and Wyvill's political programme included shorter Parliaments, an extension of the suffrage and increased county representation. Yet they were not really anticipating a mass democracy: their main motive was to limit the power of the executive. In trying to create that public opinion of which Burke had spoken they were looking back to 1688 and Locke, to the idea that the people had a duty to oppose a misguided executive, and they sought to strengthen Parliament as a means of controlling the executive, to bring to reality that separation of powers which Montesquieu thought he detected in the eighteenth-century constitution. Hence the important corollary of Wyvill's movement was the economical reform movement of the Rockingham Whigs by which the patronage of the Crown was limited. Thus the Whigs became associated with parliamentary reform.

The second component was the Radical working-class attitude to reform which originated in the Corresponding Societies of the 1790s. Formerly the continuity between the Corresponding Societies and earlier reform movements was stressed, but now historians feel that in the 1790s a new dimension was added by the emergence of political activity in the lower parts of the social scale. Prompted by the political ideas of the French Revolution and Tom Paine's *Rights of Man* and by economic hardship, working men formed a political tradition appropriate to their 'class' before a distinct working-class consciousness had fully emerged.

Many working men believed that their interests could be effectively protected only by their own representatives in Parliament. They sought to solve their social problems by first gaining political power, and so their programme was an attempt to create the opportunity for 'poor men to turn the wheels of history'. Universal suffrage, annual Parliaments and the ballot were the shibboleths of this working-class tradition, which survived the war years and which revived in the post-war depression to produce the Reform movement of the Hampden Clubs, the Blanketeers and Peterloo.

The third component of the reform ideology may be termed a middle-class or commercial philosophy of reform which in the context of 1830–2 became the decisive factor in the build-up of public pressure. The essential difference between 1819 and 1831 was, according to a provincial journalist, that 'from the principle of radical reform being confined almost exclusively to the operative classes, the employers have now joined in the same ranks'.[2] What had prompted this movement had been a growing concept of the representation of interests within the political framework, not seen as in the working-class tradition in personal terms, but in economic, almost geographic terms.

In 1760 many Englishmen were content with the political system because it was a fairly accurate reflection of the social structure in a society dominated by landed wealth. The political system was based on consent, not of the whole nation but of the political nation, which was largely speaking connected with the landed interest. It was the mercantile groups of London and other ports who first began to view their own economic activity as an interest quite distinct from that of the landed oligarchy and an interest deserving of special representation in Parliament.

Only slowly did this view gain ground in the newer industrial centres of growing population, and in 1785 Pitt's abortive proposals for a reform of Parliament were received very coolly. Under Pitt's plan a self-acting mechanism would have been created whereby social changes could have been echoed in the political system by a redistribution of seats. At that time and later many manufacturers believed that elections were unnecessary interruptions in the more serious business of economic activity, but even so, gradually the idea developed that economic changes were creating new and separate interests which required special attention. This idea may be traced from the General Chamber of Manufacturers of 1785 through to the urban commercial opposition to the Orders in Council in 1812 and to the urban versus rural controversy of 1814–15 over the Corn Law which in some towns united Whigs and Tories in opposition to the landed interest.

Manufacturing groups in towns like Birmingham began to find their local county representatives inadequate in representing their interests, and 1812 was the first occasion on which Birmingham manufacturers tried to sway a Warwickshire county election. By 1819 George Edmonds, a man who could straddle both the working-class Radical and the more moderate middle-class movement, was announcing that 'the people of Birmingham have a *right* to choose a member or members to sit in the Commons House of Parliament. . . . If the people are refused their *right* fie upon the laws.'[3] In fact in 1819 Birmingham did elect its own 'legislatorial attorney' to sit in Parliament, and Peterloo may well have been an example to prevent this sort of thing spreading.

There had always been middle-class sympathisers with the working-class demands regarding the suffrage which had been expressed in public meetings and in the Press. Thus one editor believed that [4]

When members shall be made annually responsible to their constituents and when the elective franchise shall be made more general, we may expect to have a Parliament watchful over the rights, the privileges and the property of the nation.

However it was not until the 1820s that a more general demand, based not on the suffrage but on the redistribution of seats, became familiar in middle-class pronouncements. Redistribution was necessary to give adequate representation to unrepresented interests glaringly ignored in a situation where Leeds, Manchester, Birmingham and Sheffield had no M.P.s. In 1820 Birmingham tried to get Richard Spooner elected for Warwickshire, and in 1826 Leeds was successful in nominating John Marshall as one of the members for Yorkshire (mainly because of his great wealth). The idea of redistribution was further aired by the discussions in the 1820s about the possibility, not acted upon, of transferring the seats of disfranchised boroughs to industrial cities. In 1821 Grampound's seats were suggested for Leeds, and in 1828 those of

Penryn and East Retford for Manchester and Birmingham. Nothing came of these ideas, but by the end of the 1820s redistribution was firmly embedded in middle-class ideas. By then, too, a reform ideology comprising a Whig tradition of reform, a working-class Radical programme and a middle-class demand for the representation of industrial interests was emerging as a powerful force in politics.

The translation of that ideology, or at least parts of it, into political reality involved the mechanics of political change and the tactical consideration of how best to organise extra-Parliamentary activity. The tactical origins of the 1830–2 Reform movement may be identified in the County Association movement of the 1780s, with its attempt to inspire petitions from all parts of the country. Yet there are far clearer tactical antecedents to be found in the nineteenth century, and two can be identified as being of precise ancestry to the Political Unions. These were the agitation against the Orders in Council in 1812 and the success of the Catholic Association in 1829.

The 1812 campaign was the prototype of several later urban industrial agitations. In personal terms it saw the emergence of two great Reform Bill figures, Thomas Attwood and Henry Brougham, the former at the head of a national extra-Parliamentary agitation based on Birmingham (a dress-rehearsal for 1830) and the latter enhancing his reputation with the manufacturers by his handling of the movement inside Parliament. It was a successful and peaceful mobilisation of manufacturing opinion in the face of older mercantile interests, many of which were not at all hostile to the Orders in Council. Many saw a dangerous precedent in the public meetings held in the spring of 1812, which appeared to be exercising 'a sort of supplementary jurisprudence by holding a kind of self-created Parliament in every town'.[5] An even more significant precedent than the movement itself was its success, which meant, in the words of one enthusiast, that 'the voice of the people triumphed over the strange infatuation of the men who preside at the head of affairs'.[6] Attwood learnt a valuable lesson at his political baptism: even the unreformed political system was susceptible to public pressure if properly organised.

The same lesson was the legacy of 1829, which registered the success of O'Connell's Catholic Association. Peel and Wellington were persuaded to 'rat' on their former beliefs because of the practical needs of the Government to maintain order in Ireland. Yet what threatened public order was the effective control of the Catholic Association over the Irish populace. Like some latter-day influential American campaign manager, O'Connell could deliver the block vote of the Irish Catholics and they would jump when and where he commanded. Attwood quite consciously modelled his Political Union on the Catholic Association, whose success legitimised the lobbying of this sort of pressure group. Many realised this point:[7]

> We never were the advocates of self-constituted political clubs until our present ministers confessed they had succumbed to the Catholic Association and by the enactment of the Relief Bill, sanctioned the means by which it was obtained.

The tactics of 1830–2 thus evolved from the successes of 1812 and 1829. The combination of a reform ideology and the tactical methods to bring it to fruition produced the sustained public pressure which was needed to get a reform bill passed. On both sides of the political fence it was agreed that the strength of public opinion would be the decisive factor. As early as 1820 Peel, the product of the new society himself, detected this growing public opinion:[8]

> Do not you think that there is a feeling becoming daily more general and more confirmed – that is, independent of the pressure of taxation or any immediate cause, in favour of some undefined change in the mode of governing the country? It seems to me a curious crisis – when public opinion never had such influence on public measure and yet never was so dissatisfied with the share which it possessed. . . . Can we resist – I mean not for the next session or the session after that – but can we resist for seven years Reform in Parliament?

Grey, who had introduced his first reform measure in 1797, had announced in 1810 that he would not propose reform again until the people had 'seriously and affectionately' taken up the issue. In 1820 he told his son-in-law that public opinion was not strong enough to carry reform 'during my life or even yours' and seven years later he told the House of Lords that reform had not enough public support to justify making it 'a *sine qua non* in forming an administration'.[9] The theme of Grey's beliefs was that a massive expression of public interest was not only necessary for reform to have any chance of success but a prerequisite to his own readoption of the question. In 1830 he believed the pressure was such that reform demands could no longer be delayed and this was also the view of Melbourne, among the least enthusiastic of the

Whigs, who had always said he would support Reform when public opinion justified it.

When the Whigs in the crises over the Reform Bill talked of the great public pressure and interest which had to be placated they were referring to a reform movement which was an amalgam of discontents, policies, motivations, activities and personalities of fluctuating chronological and regional intensity. It is possible to identify six strands in that reform movement whose opinions had become so decisive during 1830.

The first element in this movement was in many ways the most surprising, for it comprised the reform demands of the ultra-Tories, a direct legacy of 1829. Their view was that if Parliament could pass a Roman Catholic Emancipation Act in direct contravention of what they believed to be public opinion, then it really did need reforming since it was not truly reflecting the nation's wishes. Thus from 1829 to 1831, both inside and outside Parliament, there was the strange combination of ultra-Tories and Radicals united in demands for reform, and while the former soon learned the error of their ways, even as late as April 1831 it was still possible to find Tories saying that Catholic Emancipation was the main reason for the necessity of a reform of Parliament.

In an ironic reversal of roles these ultra-Tories had adopted the Whig theory of opposition to the executive, since their main complaint concerned the rotten and pocket boroughs, often referred to as nomination boroughs. Radicals believed that nomination boroughs should go because they were corrupt excrescences of a bygone age, but ultra-Tories believed that they should go since they enabled the executive to dominate Parliament. This was an important point. Nomination boroughs were certainly useful to a Government in an age when constitutional convention demanded that a Minister should stand for re-election on his appointment to an office. Peel was very thankful to be able to buy the seat for Westbury from its Jewish patron Sir Menassah Lopez when he was rejected by the University of Oxford in 1829.*

---

* This episode produced the following typical example of Ultra-Tory opposition to Peel and to nomination boroughs, a verse entitled 'The Jew of Westbury and Mr Peel'.

> Once Peel, the Rat, for Oxford sat
> Of *Christian* men the choice;
> But now he's sent to Parliament
> Without one *Christian* voice.

Even in the Whig Cabinet there were doubts on this score. Brougham, supposedly the champion of reform, was complaining in the Cabinet meetings of spring 1831 that after the wholesale abolition of these boroughs there would be no way of getting seats for Ministers, and a year later Melbourne was reported as saying that the Government could not be carried on without rotten boroughs. Peel summed it up: 'How are thirty offices vacated to be filled with efficient holders and the return of those holders secured?'[10] It is clear that the ultra-Tories had accurately gauged the usefulness of nomination boroughs to the executive. The attachment to the cause of reform of such ultra-Tories as the Marquis of Blandford, who for a while was allied with Attwood,[11] was of great significance in making the cry for reform more general, while inside Parliament their desire for revenge was decisive in bringing down the Wellington government.

The second element in the public pressure for reform was the political excitement, particularly in the larger cities, consequent upon the 1830 general election and the July Revolution in France. It is now clear that news of the July Revolution came too late to affect many of the contested elections, and it has been estimated that only about forty or so constituencies were contested late enough to have been influenced by the events in France. There was already excitement enough, and though the results were confused there were some spectacular successes against aristocratic influence, the most notable of which was the election of Brougham for Yorkshire at the suggestion of Edward Baines of the *Leeds Mercury*. Though the anti-slavery groups in Leeds were responsible for his success, parliamentary reform dominated Brougham's campaign, which ended with his boast 'I will leave in no man's hand now that I am member for Yorkshire, the great cause of Parliamentary reform.'[12]

It may have been a Tory myth that the election itself was influenced by the July Revolution, but it was certainly true that after the election events in France helped to maintain the political excitement already created. For several months meetings were held celebrating the July Revolution, and these meetings naturally discussed the domestic

---

By Christians spurned where e'er he turned
He brib'd an old *Hebrew*
A borough bought for many a groat
And represents a *Jew*.

It appeared in *Leicester Journal*, 13 March 1829 and *Birmingham Monthly Argus and Public Censor*, April 1829.

situation. In some areas it was the decisive last straw which brought out into the open hitherto silent groups. In Manchester the middle-class coterie that eventually led to the Anti-Corn Law League was stimulated to action by the July Revolution and as Mark Philips, Manchester's first M.P., said, 'France is making rapid strides, England is standing still.'[13] In the political excitement which grew as the autumn wore on, one issue stood out above all others. The people had by the end of 1830 many demands, and among these the principal was a reform of Parliament.

The third component of the Reform movement, and one which helps to explain the existence of discontent even before the election of 1830, was the economic distress which affected both rural and urban areas from 1829 to 1832 and which compounded with the cholera epidemic of 1831–2 to maintain the intensity of discontent. It had long been acknowledged that in the political movements before 1830 there was a close connection between political and economic discontent, in the years 1815–20 for instance. As early as 1812 one observer had perceptively asked:[14]

> Are the people discontented in prosperous times? Are the labouring classes ripe for mischief when their hands are full? Of what avail are the arts of the incendiary when a flourishing trade diffuses riches and plenty?

It was the depression in Birmingham's trade which in 1829 prompted Attwood to launch the Political Union, with its special 'Brummagem remedy' of currency reform. In February 1830 Grey spoke of 'a state of general distress such as never before pressed on any country', and in the first three months of 1830 twenty-two county meetings were held on distress or taxation. The poor harvests of 1829 and 1830 ushered in this depression, and throughout the Reform Bill crises there were frequent reports from both rural and urban areas of high poor rates, high unemployment, slack trade and low wages. It was because it was so general that the depression acted as a widespread and continuing motivation to political action.

Out of this third element of distress sprang a fourth and most menacing aspect, attacks on property. Both opponents and supporters of the Reform Bill were agreed that England was standing on the edge of a precipice of disorder throughout the years of agitation. The knife-edge balance was particularly difficult for the Reform movement to maintain, for it had to make real the threat of attacks upon property which underlay the reform demands yet at the same time prevent disorder, the reaction to which might drown the chances of reform in a welter of repression.

It was attacks upon property which both Whig and Tory feared, and there was plenty of evidence to justify such fears. In the south of England in 1830 there had been widespread disorder and arson stretching from Kent to Dorset and known as the 'Swing Riots'. These had been repressed by Melbourne with a harshness reminiscent of Peterloo days, and many of the Whigs' own supporters were shocked when nine people were hanged and nearly a thousand transported or imprisoned. Similar repressive action followed the Merthyr riots of June 1831, in which over twenty civilians were killed and during which the red flag was first used in Britain as a symbol of rebellion. Melbourne, looking for a scapegoat to shock the whole nation into submission, gave birth to the legend of the probably innocent martyr Dic Penderyn.

In October 1831 the politically motivated rioting spread even further when the Lords' rejection of the Bill led to outrages at Worcester, Bath, Derby and Nottingham, which culminated in the seizure of Bristol by rioters. There was usually a specific local personality involved, like the most notorious of the borough-mongers, the Duke of Newcastle, who admitted that he dare not even visit manufacturing districts where he owned property as 'I should either be murdered or raise a riot by appearing'. Peel was most uneasy at leaving his children at Drayton 'with Birmingham political unions on one side and Derby and Nottingham on the other', and he was anxious to form 'a select cohort of persons on whom I can thoroughly depend who may constitute an armed garrison for my protection and that of my family in case of actual attack'.[15]

Nobody in authority was happy about civil disorder – but neither were the leaders of the Reform movement, who judged aright that the threat of potential disorder was a powerful lever, while actual disorder might become political suicide. Attwood was quick to point out that it was in areas where there was no strong political union that trouble had occurred, and that the very purpose of his organisation was to canalise discontent through legal channels. In Nottingham, where there had been an early but inactive political union, one of the reform leaders, Thomas Bailey, pleaded with his followers after the burning of the castle:[16]

What evil spirit my dear countrymen has possessed you . . . to ruin the best cause in the world by the adoption of the worst possible means for its alleged support. . . . The cause of *Reform* my country-men needs not such an auxiliary as persecution! It utterly disallows the aid of violence in its support . . . and must prevail unless joined in unholy alliance with outrage. Britain peaceable must be enfranchised.

Thus threats to property, feared by the oligarchy and embarrassing to the reformers, were an integral aspect of the Reform movement.

The fifth element in the Reform movement was the enormous influence wielded on behalf of reform by the 'fourth estate', the Press. In March 1830 Grey was already blaming the Press for 'destroying all respect for rank and station and for the institutions of the Government',[17] while a year later William IV was bitterly complaining to his Prime Minister of the 'poisonous influence of a licentious and unobstructed Press'.[18] Peel, too, believed that the Press together with the Government had created the excitement. By 1830 the Press was indeed well equipped to fulfil its function. From the time of Wilkes Parliamentary reporting was allowed and the development of shorthand meant that both inside and outside Parliament speeches could be fully covered. From the 1790s onwards the provincial Press began using editorials extensively in order deliberately to influence opinion, and the Press with its copious reports and lengthy editorials was admirably placed both to guide and reflect local opinion.

By 1830, too, many of the leading London papers were supporting Reform. *The Times* and the *Examiner* both cited parliamentary reform as one of the great issues of the moment, while the *Globe* and the *Westminster Review* fully discussed the English electoral system. Of great significance was the support given by the leading Whig paper, the *Morning Chronicle*, which did much to reaffirm that the Whigs really were the party of reform.

But it was in the provinces that the real strength of the reform press lay, for the fulcrum of the agitation rested not in London but in Birmingham and the provinces. By the time of the Reform Bill there were provincial newspapers and journalistic families who had been supporting reform of Parliament for a generation, like Edward Baines, senior and junior, of the *Leeds Mercury*, Thomas and James Thompson of the *Leicester Chronicle*, or Charles and Richard Sutton of the *Nottingham Review*. These papers had supported Reform long before it was fashionable and their editors had sometimes, like Charles Sutton, paid for their opinions with a term of imprisonment. Add to these and many like them papers of more recent origins, such as the *Manchester*

Guardian of John Edward Taylor, or the more Radical *Manchester Times* of Archibald Prentice, and its Leeds counterpart, John Foster's *Leeds Patriot*, together with recent converts to the cause of Reform, like the *Birmingham Journal* edited by Jonathon Crowther, and one finds an enormously varied and powerful phalanx of local reform newspapers which kept the agitation alive. All regions and interests were represented, Merseyside by the *Liverpool Mercury*, Tyneside by the *Newcastle Chronicle* and Sheffield cutlers by the *Sheffield Independent*. In addition to these reform journals were to be found, temporarily at least, supporters from the Tory side – and not only scurrilous ultra-Tory papers like Allday's *Argus* in Birmingham, or the *Leicestershire Herald* representing the corrupt arm of the Leicester Corporation – but also the moderate Tory papers like George Stretton's *Nottingham Journal*.

There was an important link between the political unions and the Press, for the seventh duty of a member of the Council of the Birmingham Political Union was 'to consider the means of organising a system of operations whereby the Public Press may be influenced to act generally in support of the public interests'. The political unions sought to make the Press their advanced guard, rounding up troops to join the armies of reform which the political unions commanded.

It is to the political unions themselves that we must now turn, for they were both the sixth element in the Reform movement and at once the means by which the other five were mobilised. In the reform agitation the typical local lobbying unit was a political union which organised local opinion into the dual channels of petitions and public meetings. They were nearly all modelled in structure and ideas on Attwood's Birmingham Political Union, which he had contemplated as early as 1819 and which he finally founded ten years later. The B.P.U. was intended as a permanent body to lead local reform movements and to replace that temporary and vacillating enthusiasm which had produced in every city a cycle of political excitement and apathy. At the first public meeting of the B.P.U. in January 1830 there were 15,000 people present; by May 1832 the union attracted over 100,000 of whom about a quarter were actual members.

Attwood's son believed that the B.P.U. had achieved three things during the Reform Bill crises: first in creating a public opinion; second in showing this opinion without law-breaking; and third in keeping enthusiasm at boiling-point.[19] This was no mean achievement and contemporaries believed, and historians confirmed, that Birmingham led the nation in these years, which in effect meant that Attwood led the nation. Attwood and Birmingham bequeathed to the Reform movement two characteristics. The first was legality, for the motto of this and other political unions was Attwood's 'Peace, Law and Order'. The second was class co-operation, which reflected the social structure of a city where an artisan could achieve through social mobility a middle-class respectability. Attwood's aim was to unite cordially together masters and men in political action, and this the B.P.U. did. In some other areas like the North East and Sheffield political unions did combine working- and middle-class elements; in others they did not.

The Birmingham artisan identified himself with the middle-class philosophy because he could recognise his own interests therein, but the Manchester weaver, the Leeds cropper or the Leicester framework-knitter could not, so in places like these the Birmingham model could not be precisely imitated. In Manchester, Prentice's Political Union did not attract the extensive support of either the operatives or the wealthy manufacturers, while in Leeds there was the fragmentation of three organisations, Baines's middle-class Leeds Association, the middle- and working-class Leeds Political Union, led by the Radical glass manufacturer Joshua Bower, and the working-class Leeds Radical Political Union of the Radical printers Mann and Foster. There was also a competing but related agitation led by Richard Oastler for factory legislation.

London, too, exhibited its own hybrid brand of Radical agitation, and Francis Place was the centre of a hive of political activity. London had become far too big to unite its disparate elements into a movement whose strength could be commensurate with the size of its vast population, but it was a great centre of ideas and two associations of significance originated there in 1831. In October Place began his National Political Union to unite the Radical middle classes with those working men who sympathised with the Bill. Earlier in the year William Lovett (later to be the author of the People's Charter) and Henry Hetherington of the *Poor Man's Guardian* had launched the National Union of the Working Classes, inspired by Owenite ideas, which rejected the Whig Bill entirely. In many ways these two bodies personified the working-class dilemma in 1831–2. Place's N.P.U. represented the view put out by Attwood that working men could benefit from the Bill since it gave representation to the middle-class industrial interest, and what was good for the masters was good for the men, while Lovett was the inheritor of that 'working-class' tradition already discussed which held out for universal suffrage, annual Parliaments and the ballot to give real and actual working-class representation in Parliament. This then was the Reform movement, comprising the ultra-Tory discontent consequent upon Catholic Emancipation, the excitement of 1830, the economic distress, the violence and threats to property, the outpourings of sections of the Press and the activities of the political unions; and it was the success of this movement rather than the details of the Bill which made 1830–2 revolutionary years in British history. It was the passage of the Bill which was of greater significance than the Bill itself, and in John Bright's famous phrase, 'It was not a good bill, though it was a great bill when it passed.' It is a truism, often unstated and unnoticed, that it was the unreformed Parliament which passed the Reform Bill. The Whigs hated to admit it, but the Reform movement was the essential battering-ram which finally broke the back of reaction and resistance, and it is possible to analyse within the chronology of the passing of the Bill the precise occasions when public pressure was of greatest significance.

It is as well to have that chronology in mind. The general election of July 1830 was followed by Wellington's declaration against Reform and his subsequent fall in November. Grey's first Bill was introduced by Russell in March 1831 and it passed its second reading by only one vote (302–301), to be defeated in the Commons committee stage on the Gascoyne amendment in April. There followed a dissolution and in the election the Whigs gained a majority; hence the scene shifted from the Commons to the Lords. The second version of the Bill passed the Commons in September and was rejected by the Lords in the following month. Parliament was recalled in December and Russell's third bill went to the Lords, raising the issue of the creation of Peers needed to pass it. In April 1832 the Bill passed its second reading but in May it was delayed in the committee stage, and Grey resigned when the necessary peers were not created. Wellington tried and failed to form a government in May, and the return of Grey signalled the passage of the Bill without the new peers in June.

It would not be untrue to say that in the two years from the summer of 1830 England was in a state of seething political excitement; and within that time there were four periods of decisive and crucial public pressure, November 1830, April–May 1831, November 1831 and May 1832. It is often argued that Wellington's speech against Reform in November 1830 made a reform bill inevitable, because he completely failed to recognise the intense enthusiasm for it. It was the timing as much as the content which made Wellington's statement ill-judged.

After all, utterances about the perfection of the Constitution had been made before and people could not really be surprised to hear a Tory defending it. The most shattering part of Wellington's statement was in fact his belief 'that the legislature and the system of representation possess the full and entire confidence of the country'.[20] What made him an embarrassment as Prime Minister was his complete failure to recognise the state of public feeling and so he fell from power, defeated by a House of Commons which in August 1830 had not looked particularly hostile. Public pressure, which, as both Peel and Attwood later explained, existed prior to the Duke's statement, dictated that an anti-Reformer could no longer be Prime Minister.

When the first Bill was lost on 19 April 1831 by 299 votes to 291 the Whig government stepped up its demand for a dissolution which would in effect be a sort of referendum on Reform. There had been no precedent for a one-issue election. On occasion, as with the Catholic question in Leicester in 1826, a locality concentrated on one issue, but in April and May 1831 the whole country would be asked to decide on Reform. Given the state of political excitement this would be a most dangerous precedent for the delegation of Parliament's authority to the nation, and in March William IV had warned Grey that the state of the country imposed on him 'a sacred duty, the obligation of resisting any proposal for the dissolution of Parliament at this period'. Yet the selfsame reason was cited by the Cabinet as the overwhelming need for a dissolution:[21]

> The bill had been generally approved, public expectation had been raised high, and the effect of a disappointment seemed greatly to be feared as likely to disturb the peace of the country. To prevent, therefore an agitation of so formidable a nature, your Majesty's servants felt themselves called upon humbly to advise your Majesty to dissolve the present Parliament.

Grey got his dissolution because of the public pressure, and in the subsequent election the same political enthusiasm ensured that the House of Commons would be safe for the passage of the Bill.

Once the election was over the big question for the next year was 'What will the Lords do?' and the riots following the rejection of the Bill in October 1831 have already been mentioned. So too have the shocked reactions of the Reform leaders. The violence was not only dangerous to authority: it was also dangerous to the Bill itself, and it is no coincidence that the October riots were followed by a period of doubt and rumour of betrayal. It was then that serious talk took place between Ministers and the 'waverers' led by Lords Wharncliffe and Harrowby, then that there was a real possibility of a severe dilution of the Bill's provisions, or even its abandonment, then that there was widespread talk of a falling away of public interest. Here was the crucial challenge for Attwood and the Political Union: the Whigs' morale must be underpinned so that their nerve held.

What the B.P.U. did in November 1831 was perhaps of greater importance than any of its other actions, although at first sight it seemed the height of folly. A plan was drawn up to put the union on an armed, pseudo-military footing, with a ladder of ranks and authority to maintain public order. This was clearly illegal, but it was intended to goad the Whigs into activity at a time when their intentions were under justifiable suspicion, and it was accompanied by widespread accusations that the Whigs intended to arrange a long delay before the recall of Parliament and then to introduce a watered-down Bill. The Tories, many Whigs and the King wanted the suppression of the Unions but Grey, though he would not tolerate illegality, knew that suppression would merely create greater dangers. The plan had its effect, for it convinced Grey even more that only by destroying the discontent on which the unions were built could they themselves be put down. Hence he persuaded the King that the passing of the Bill as speedily as possible was the necessary answer, not the prosecution of Attwood. Secretly, Joseph Parkes was approached by Ministers[22] and he persuaded the B.P.U. to drop its plan prior to the Royal Proclamation against such arrangements. By then what Attwood had wanted had been achieved. The Cabinet was revitalised in its determination to get the Bill through and, significantly, Parliament was recalled early in December and the Bill was reintroduced.

The decisive nature of the B.P.U.'s action in November 1831 was probably hidden from most contemporaries, in sharp contrast to the 'days of May' in 1832 of which everyone knew. The Duke of Wellington, so people believed, had been prevented from forming a government by the massive expression of public opinion hostile to him and the Lords had been finally cowed into submission. In fact the truth was otherwise. The famous run on the banks, urged on by Place's motto 'To stop the Duke go for gold', never really materialised and Place's great plan of a national uprising led by the Political Unions was still-born. What was crucial in Wellington's failure to form a government was his failure to win over Peel, for whom the memories of 1829 were too painful to contemplate a repeat performance of eating his own words. This was a ministerial crisis in which public pressure played little part, as was true of the final assent of the Lords.

It should not be forgotten that the most famous of all the Reform Bill meetings, the great 'Gathering of the Unions' in Birmingham on 7 May 1832, described recently as 'one of the high points in the political history of provincial England, a striking physical expression of the strength of nineteenth-century provincial public opinion',[23] was specifically called to persuade the Lords to pass the Bill. Yet the Lords, perhaps motivated by courage, perhaps by blindness, still held their course. What persuaded the Lords was not the public commotion of eighteen months' duration but the threat of the creation of peers. Only when they were given the 'alternative of the Reform Bill with an addition to the Peerage, or the Reform Bill without it'[24] did the Bill pass.

Yet to argue that 'the days of May' failed to influence Wellington or the Lords is not to deny their great significance. In May 1832 what people thought was happening was of more importance than what was actually happening, for in these 'ten days of the English Revolution' a popular myth was born which was to dominate extra-Parliamentary politics for a generation. There was unprecedented activity including many meetings, like the county meeting at Wakefield called by the Leeds reformers, of over 100,000 people, and probably well over 500 meetings in just over a week produced nearly a thousand petitions. A number of supporters thanked the Lords for giving England this opportunity to discover its own strength, for even in cities previously divided on the Bill there were huge meetings. It was generally believed that England was without a government and that the peace of the Kingdom rested with Thomas Attwood. It was understandable in view of the intense activity and its apparent result that men should have believed that the Whigs had been brought back on the shoulders of the people. The days of May provided the logic and inspiration for all subsequent agitations; only the strength of the pressure need be repeated to achieve similar results.

Had Grey known in November 1830 that the passing of the Bill would involve a 'democratic' election, coercion of the peers and dependence on continual extra-Parliamentary excitement he might well not have embarked on his reforming path. At a time when the Whigs shared the King's view of the period – 'the times are awful' – two motives kept the Whigs on their course, the needs of conservatism and finality. The basic Whig argument, frequently reiterated, was that in order to preserve both society and constitution it was necessary to make those potential rebels who supported Reform allies in defence of the existing order. The Whig view was, in the words of Macaulay, that 'the danger is terrible and the time is short' and that, as Grey pointed out, it was necessary for 'a great influence to be yielded to the middle classes', for inaction would 'lead rapidly to republicanism and the destruction of established institutions'.[25]

The Tories feared exactly the same thing, but they viewed concession as a harbinger of that disorder which the Whigs sought to avoid. In the view of such Tory alarmists as Croker, 'the Reform Bill is . . . a stepping stone in England to a Republic' and 'the Bill once passed, good night to the Monarchy and the Lords and the Church'.[26] Thus both Whigs and Tories feared revolution, which Whigs believed could be avoided and Tories believed would be invited by the Reform Bill. By abolishing illegitimate influence the Whigs thought they could strengthen the legitimate influence and authority of rank and station on which society, as they conceived it, rested. The deferential social ladder would be reinforced by allowing the industrial interest to exercise in the urban areas that necessary influence which the landed interest already wielded elsewhere.

This conservation was closely allied to the Whig belief in finality, that the Bill had to be of such a nature as permanently to satisfy the demands of the reformers. Looking back now, we may well construct a lineage from 1832 through the Chartists to 1867, 1885 and beyond; but this was never Whig intention. In the words of the 'Committee of Four' who drafted the Reform Bill, it was ministers' desire 'to effect such a permanent settlement . . . of such a scope and description as to satisfy all reasonable demands, and remove at once, and for ever, all rational ground of complaint'.[27] Even the most ardent of the reforming Whigs did not intend this as an instalment and so, for instance, when Earl Fitzwilliam was asked to support further reform a few years later he refused:[28]

> We have gone through one revolution, for now that we can speak of those events historically, it is idle to call by any other name the transactions of 1830, 31 and 32. By God's mercy we went through it peaceably but are we to repeat such experiments every eighth or tenth year?

Much of the Reform Act becomes explicable when seen in terms of these Whig intentions, and the provisions of the Act were concerned with two main points, redistribution of seats and the franchise. The redistribution was made possible by the disfranchisement in Schedules A and B, whereby 56 boroughs lost both seats, 30 boroughs lost one and Weymouth dropped from 4 to 2. In the first two Bills the size of the House of Commons was to be reduced. However, in the event all the seats available were redistributed by awarding 22 large cities two seats each and 20 smaller cities one each, while 7 counties got 3 instead of 2, 26 counties got 4 instead of 2 and Yorkshire rose from 4 to 6. The remaining seats went to Wales (5), Scotland (8), Ireland (5) and the Isle of Wight (1).

Every schoolboy knows of the anomalies of the old system like Old Sarum, yet the new system was not without anomalies of its own, as the Tories were quick to point out. There were, for instance, five boroughs with fewer than 200 electors and twelve with over 3000 so that in one constituency 50 votes might swing an election while in another 5000 were needed. In England the counties had 56 per cent of the electorate and only 31 per cent of the seats while Scotland's population was three times as great as Wales yet it got fewer than twice as many seats. However an exact ratio of seats to population was never intended, for no Parliament in 1832 would have passed a plan for equal constituencies which would have given to population that weight of political power which then rested with property. The worst anomalies were removed and the newer cities given some representation so that a fairer distribution of seats was possible.

In terms of voters there were separate qualifications for the borough and county franchise. In the boroughs a property test was applied and the £10 household was the minimum qualification for a vote, so that in place of the old multifarious borough franchise a new uniform franchise was created. It has been justly pointed out that varying property prices throughout the country gave the £10 householder a varying economic and social identity; yet despite this, minor variations did not detract from the conclusion that this was a middle-class franchise. The £10 test was an attempt to define sociologically the groups who were considered safe for the vote; and, as Grey had said, there was an overwhelming need to enfranchise the middle classes, defined by Brougham as 'those hundreds of thousands of respectable persons the most numerous and by far the most wealthy orders in the community'. Some Tories pointed out that in the old system potwalloper seats like Preston and Coventry enabled the working-class interest to be represented, whereas the new franchise would sever 'altogether the communication between this house and all that class of society which is above pauperism and below the arbitrary and impassable line of £10 rental'.[29] This was the intention, and although the old franchise continued in the lifetime of the voter classes who had the vote before 1832, their successors were to be deprived of it. The extent of working-class representation can be assessed by the example of Leeds, where out of a population of 123,000 there were only about 5000 voters.

In the counties the old 40-shilling freeholder retained his vote and there was added a mixed group of tenants, such as £10 copyholders and £50 tenants at will. The enfranchisement of the latter was easily the most important of the changes in the Bill made by the Commons when they passed the famous Chandos clause in August 1831. The enfranchisement of these tenants was supported by Radicals, who believed that any extension of the suffrage was a good thing, but opposed by the Cabinet and by many of the Reform leaders on the ground that no matter how wealthy these tenants were they were still dependent upon their landlord. Many Whigs and Tories supported Chandos simply because his clause would mean in the absence of secret ballot a strengthening of landed influence. As one observer remarked:[30]

> What the great borough holders have lost by the disfranchisement of boroughs they will much more than compensate by the enfranchisement of the yearly agricultural tenantry. If so we have come round to the same point, after all the stir about reform which has been exerted and have indeed shifted the influence which was so loudly and extravagantly complained of but have neither destroyed or lessened, it, may perhaps increased it.

In order to counteract the effects of the Chandos clause ministers decided to allow borough residents qualified for county votes to vote in county elections.

The overall effect of the franchise changes were to add something like half a million votes to an electorate of about 400,000 in a population of 24 millions. This meant that in the whole country one in seven adult males had the vote (the figures were one in five for England and Wales, one in eight for Scotland and one in twenty in Ireland). There were other changes too. Polling districts were devised within large constituencies, which reduced the cost of election, and the duration of the poll was lessened, which reduced the excitement. A boundary commission was appointed, which ensured that the larger boroughs had a chance to spread without overspilling into county constituencies and that very small boroughs had a sizeable slice of the neighbouring countryside attached to them to strengthen landed influence further.

The most important and far-reaching of these minor clauses were those dealing with registration of voters, which acted as a great stimulus to local party organisation. Voters had to be registered on electoral lists and partisans soon saw that by successfully objecting to the opposition's voters in the annual revision court elections might be won. Well before Peel's famous 'Register, register, register' plea to the Tory party, many spectacular successes were recorded to show that elections could be won not in the polling booth but in the revision court. Leeds, for instance, was the first of the new industrial cities to return a Tory in 1835, and this was largely the result of a mass objection in the revision court to all Whig compounded ratepayers. Not only did the annual revision stimulate party organisation, it also necessitated continual and careful attention and elevated to some political importance quite humble men:[31]

> Regular persevering systematic effort is the thing wanted under the Reform Act. A plodding shopkeeper on a Committee who sees that the Registration is attended to does more good than a dozen wealthy squires who reserve all their energy for the Election itself.

Elections after 1832 were put on a much more organised footing and professional party agents began to emerge.

This survey of the characteristics of the new system enables a judgement to be made of how successful the Whigs were in their twin motives of conservation and finality. On the former they were relatively successful. The Whigs intended that the Reform Act should preserve and not destroy landed influence, and that is why Grey called it 'the most aristocratic measure that ever was proposed in Parliament'. There was continuity, despite the great changes, between the pre- and post-1832 systems, for the landed gentry continued to dominate both society and politics. The middle classes were being hitched to the constitution but not being allowed to dominate it. They were given the semblance, not the reality, of power and the rule of the middle classes was not yet being ushered in. Cobden believed that 1846 made 1832 a reality and that then the middle classes inherited the political kingdom, for, as he told Peel, 'The Reform Bill decreed it; the passing of the Corn Bill has realised it.' Yet 1846 and even 1867 may also be regarded as timely concessions by the landed classes to preserve their power. Middle-class men did not dominate the new Parliament (Cobden said he was regarded as 'a Gothic invader') and in the words of the diarist Greville in 1833, 'a reformed Parliament turns out to be just like any other Parliament'.

Their success in preserving the old system contrasts sharply with the Whigs' complete failure to achieve finality. Such failure was inevitable in view of the method which had been used to pass the Bill. Popular pressure both in 1829 and 1832 had produced results and so the precedent had been established. Peel had recognised that the Whig tactics would be imitated:[32]

> These are vulgar arts of government; others will outbid you, not now but at no remote period – they will offer votes and power to a million of men, will quote your precedent for the concession and will carry your principles to their legitimate and natural consequences.

Two sorts of extra-Parliamentary agitations would inevitably follow 1832. First there was bound to be pressure for a further extension of the suffrage, for not only had many working-class Radicals rejected the Bill as too moderate but even those who supported it believed, in the words of Bronterre O'Brien, that it was no more than 'an instalment or part payment of the debt of right due to us . . . capable of expanding and purifying itself into a perfect representation system'.[33] Secondly, inherent in the reformers' demands was a whole series of improvements expected to flow from the new system. The Whigs saw the Reform Act as an end in itself, the reformers saw it only as a means to an end. In Cobbett's often quoted words, 'What did we want the Reform Bill FOR? that it might do us some good . . . not for the gratification of any abstract or metaphysical whims.'[34] In Birmingham men expected the first action of a reformed Parliament would be currency reform, in Manchester repeal of the Corn Laws, in Leicester municipal reform; but, as Melbourne had anticipated, the Bill was not 'attended with any of the benefits expected from it' – and so further popular movements were necessary.

BIBLIOGRAPHICAL NOTE

Two outstanding works are essential reading, J. R. M. Butler, *The Passing of the Great Reform Bill* (Longmans, 1914) and N. Gash, *Politics in the Age of Peel* (Longmans, 1953). Butler illuminates the manoeuvres involved in the passage of the Bill and Gash masterfully analyses the workings of the new system. The Whig policies are explained in G. M. Trevelyan, *Lord Grey of the Reform Bill* (Longmans, 1920), which may be supplemented by dipping into Earl Grey (ed.), *Correspondence of King William IV and Earl Grey*, 2 vols (1867). The Tory point of view may be gleaned from the correspondence in C. S. Parker (ed.), *Sir Robert Peel from his Private Papers*, 3 vols (1891–9), ii and L. J. Jennings (ed.), *Correspondence and Diaries of J. W. Croker*, 3 vols (1884), ii. The working-class attitude to reform may be traced through the comprehensive study by E. P. Thompson, *The Making of the English Working Class* (Gollancz, 1964) and a selection of relevant documents may be consulted in G. D. H. Cole and A. W. Filson, *The British Working Class Movement, Select Documents* (Macmillan, 1955).

G. S. Veitch, *The Genesis of Parliamentary Reform* (Constable, 1913) gives the eighteenth-century origins of the reform movement, and the nineteenth-century context is discussed in D. Read, *The English Provinces* (Arnold, 1964). The Birmingham Political Union is discussed from different standpoints by Asa Briggs, 'Thomas Attwood and the Economic Background of the Birmingham Political Union', *CHJ* ix (1948) and H. Ferguson, 'The Birmingham Political Union and the Government', *VS* iii (1960). An indication of the varying regional approaches to reform is given in Asa Briggs, 'The Parliamentary Reform Movement in Three English Cities', *CHJ* x (1952), which successfully relates economic and social structure to political action. Far less successful is the attempt to give a sociological analysis in D. C. Moore, 'Concession or Cure: the sociological premises of the first Reform Act', *HJ* ix (1966), which fails in discussing the borough freeholder and the boundary commission to justify a new interpretation. Economic rather than political motivation was largely discerned by G. Rudé, 'English Rural and Urban Disturbances, 1830–31', *Past and Present*, 37 (1967). This is further illustrated in the comprehensive study of the rural disorders of 1830, E. J. Hobsbawm and G. Rudé, *Captain Swing* (Lawrence & Wishart, 1969).

NOTES

1. *Birmingham Journal*, 27 Aug 1831.
2. *Nottingham Review*, 7 Jan 1831.
3. *Edmonds Weekly Recorder and Saturday Advertiser*, 10 July 1819.
4. *Leicester Chronicle*, 6 Apr 1816.
5. *Birmingham Commercial Herald*, 30 Mar 1812.
6. *Midland Chronicle*, 20 June 1812.
7. *Birmingham Journal*, 23 Jan 1830.
8. L. J. Jennings (ed.), *Correspondence and Diaries of J. W. Croker* (1884), i, 170.
9. G. M. Trevelyan, *Lord Grey of the Reform Bill* (1920), p. 215; J. R. M. Butler, *The Passing of the Great Reform Bill* (1914), p. 25; D. G. Southgate, *The Passing of the Whigs* (1962), p. 4.
10. C. S. Parker, *Sir Robert Peel* (1891), ii, 187.
11. See Asa Briggs, 'Thomas Attwood and the Economic Background of the Birmingham Political Union', *CHJ* ix (1948).
12. Quoted in Norman Gash, 'English Reform and French Revolution in the General Election of 1830', in R. Pares and A. J. P. Taylor (eds), *Essays Presented to Sir Lewis Namier* (1956), p. 285.
13. Archibald Prentice, *Historical Sketches and Personal Recollections of Manchester* (1851).
14. *Midland Chronicle*, 25 Apr 1812.
15. Parker, op. cit., ii, 190–1.
16. *Nottingham Review*, 14 Oct 1831.
17. Grey to Ellice, 2 Mar 1830, quoted in M. G. Brock, 'The Reform Act of 1832', in J. S. Bromley and E. H. Kossman (eds), *Britain and the Netherlands* (1960), p. 180.

18. William IV to Grey, 24 Apr 1831 (*Correspondence of King William IV and Earl Grey* (1867), i, 246).

19. C. M. Wakefield, *Life of Thomas Attwood* (1885), p. 193.

20. Quoted in W. N. Molesworth, *The History of the Reform Bill of 1832* (1865), p. 59.

21. William IV to Grey, 20 Mar 1831; Cabinet minute, 21 Apr 1831 (*Correspondence*, i, 159, 238).

22. Parkes was sworn to secrecy because, as Althorp told him, 'it would not be fitting for a member of the Government to be known to have taken any indirect measures to prevent proceedings which approach so near to levying war against the King'. (UCLL, Parkes Papers, Althorp to Parkes, 18 Nov 1831).

23. Donald Read, *The English Provinces* (1964), p. 92.

24. Sir Herbert Taylor (the King's secretary) to Grey, 20 May 1832 (*Correspondence*, ii, 444).

25. Quoted in Trevelyan, op. cit., p. 237.

26. Jennings, op. cit., ii, 140, 148.

27. *Correspondence*, i, 461.

28. *Leeds Intelligencer*, 6 Feb 1841, Earl Fitzwilliam to J. G. Marshall, 21 Dec 1840.

29. Peel in the House of Commons, 3 May 1831, *Hansard*, 3rd ser., ii, 1346.

30. *Nottingham Journal*, 27 Aug 1831.

31. *Leeds Mercury*, 26 Nov 1836.

32. *Hansard*, 3rd ser., ii, 1350.

33. *Midland Representative*, 18 Feb 1832.

34. *Political Register*, 22 June 1833.

2. The Factory Movement

J. T. WARD

FACTORY legislation, affirmed William Newmarch in his opening address to the economics section of the British Association's Manchester meeting in September 1861, 'had consolidated society in this part of the island, swept away a great mass of festering and growing discontent [and] placed the prosperity of the district on a broad, solid and safe basis: on the orderly, educated, contented labour of Lancashire . . .'. Such were the results of 'the sagacious, persevering, and moral exertions of the advocates of the Ten Hours Bill'.[1] The greatest of those advocates, the 'Factory King' Richard Oastler, died a fortnight before this tribute was paid; and already most of his colleagues in an agitation which had once inflamed the factory districts were dead or almost forgotten.

The movement to reform factory conditions was inevitably rooted in the industrial counties, although its demands were ultimately achieved through parliamentary action. Since historians have sometimes seen the controversy solely in terms of the struggle at Westminster, they have been inclined to exaggerate the (undoubtedly important) contribution of Lord Ashley, the reformers' principal champion in the Commons. Yet, as Samuel Kydd, the first historian of factory reform, wrote in 1857, the movement 'occupied many years of the lives of some self-sacrificing, strong-minded, persevering, and benevolent men, ultimately commanded an over-ruling share of public attention, and left the mark of its existence on the legislation of the country . . .'. Furthermore, its 'efforts in the factories, on the platform, through the press, the pulpit, and the parliament, called into existence almost every shade of controversy, religious, moral, social, economical, political, philosophical and parliamentary . . .'.

The reformers had to fight against the whole liberal ethos, as enunciated by pedagogues, maintained by political devotees of *laissez-faire* and exploited by industrial employers. Ashley (by then 7th earl of Shaftesbury) recalled in 1866 that he 'had to break every political connection, to encounter a most formidable array of capitalists, mill-owners, doctrinaires, and men, who, by natural impulse, hated all "humanity-mongers" . . .'. And there were other problems: 'To "practical" prophecies of overthrow of trade, of ruin to the operatives themselves, I could only oppose "humanity" and general principles . . .', recorded Shaftesbury. 'Out of parliament, there was in society every form of "good-natured" and compassionate contempt. In the provinces, the anger and irritation of the opponents were almost fearful . . .'. Oastler and his friends had faced much greater hazards in the woollen and cotton towns.

By 1861 many old opponents had changed their attitudes. As 'Parson Bull' declared in an Oastler memorial sermon, 'there is now scarcely a manufacturer to be found, who does not thank God for the factory regulation laws, which were forced from an unwilling government by the energy of Oastler and his friends . . . chiefly of humble rank.' And Bull could fairly ask 'where now is the "Ruin" that the chief organs of our opponents predicted as the result of legislative restriction and control?' Even Nassau Senior, that pillar of the dismal science who had lectured on an 'iron law of wages', advocated a harshly 'Malthusian' Poor Law, condemned 'a ten hours bill . . . [as] utterly ruinous' and insisted that profit was created by the last hour's labour, reversed his stand. He now hoped 'that the wise and courageous men who carried the Factory Acts against such opposition as no law ever surmounted – an opposition in which men of the most dissimilar habits of thought, statesmen, manufacturers, and philosophers, all joined – were not disposed to leave their work imperfect . . .'.[2]

Hostile politicians, who had confidently repeated the economists' theoretic 'laws', had also moved with the times. T. B. Macaulay, who insisted in 1832 that 'however unpleasant it might be to work, it was still more unpleasant to starve', warned the Commons in 1846 that 'over-worked boys would become a feeble and ignoble race of men, the parents of a more feeble and more ignoble progeny'.[3] Other 'con-versions' required a longer period. In 1844 Sir James Graham, as Home Secretary, preferred resignation to following Ashley's 'dangerous course' and 'Jack Cade system of legislation' – to which he 'had an insuperable objection'. Sixteen years later he 'endeavoured to make some amends' by supporting the Bleaching and Dye-Works Bill. Another bitter opponent announced himself 'Ashley's convert' at the same time. In 1844 J. A. Roebuck had asked Parliament to condemn any 'inter-ference with the power of adult labourers in factories to make contracts respecting the hours for which they should be employed'. At this time 'it would not do to come down to [Parliament] with exaggerated descriptions of misery, of want and of suffering', for Roebuck 'denied them all'. By 1860 he was telling Shaftesbury that 'we ought never to trust to the justices and humanity of masses of men whose interests are furthered by injustice and cruelty. The slave-owner in America, the manufacturer in England, though they may be individually good men, will, nevertheless, as slave-owners and masters, be guilty of atrocities at which humanity shudders; and will, before the world, with unblushing faces, defend cruelties from which they would recoil with horror if their moral judgements were not perverted by their self-interest.'[4] By the sixties, it would seem, few public men any longer cared to be associated with the 'classical' economic doctrines which had tolerated and even justified the overworking of women and children.

After a century of varied experience, some historians have reacted against often politically motivated distortions of working-class conditions under Industrial Revolution capitalism. Occasionally, indeed, they have reacted so strongly that historical retinting has degenerated into wholesale 'whitewashing'. However, the general consensus of opinion would probably be that while the general hues of the 'dark satanic mills' were over-blackened in the past, early factory life was often dark indeed.

Despite the subsequent wide approbation of industrial legislation, the battle for the Factory Acts was both bitter and long.

I

The Factory Movement underwent a long period of gestation. Long hours of labour were traditional in the British textile industries, and eighteenth-century observers generally found the fact commendable. 'No hands being unemply'd, all can gain their bread, even from the youngest to the antient', Daniel Defoe approvingly noted of Halifax parish, in a much-quoted passage in 1726: 'Hardly any thing above four years old, but its hands are sufficient to it self.' In 1768 an anonymous Norwich clergyman typically considered that a particular virtue of the weaving trade was 'the little time that it giveth either servant or master (but servants especially) for idleness. Idleness (especially in youth) is the source and fountain of almost all the debauchery that polluteth the world, and all the beggary with which we abound.' Certainly excessive labour should be avoided, but in general 'the lesser time for idleness any trade allows, the better it is'.[5] It was in line with this attitude, which usefully combined approbation of industrial development with 'moral' condemnation of juvenile relaxation, that John Wesley praised a silk mill which maintained '250 children in perpetual employment' in 1787.

In 1844 Friedrich Engels imagined a 'Merrie England' before the coming of the factories. It was an idealised rural society in which 'the workers vegetated through a passably comfortable existence, leading a righteous and peaceful life . . . did not need to over-work . . . did no more than they chose to do, and yet earned what they needed. . . .' The children 'grew up in the fresh country air, and, if they could help their parents at work, it was only occasionally; while of eight or twelve hours work for them there was no question'. This type of sentimental dream was periodically shared by ultra-traditionalists and anti-capitalists of both the Left and Right in politics. The reality of the domestic system was more prosaic and bleak. George Crompton, the eldest son of the weaver–inventor, 'recollected that soon after he was able to walk he was employed in the cotton manufacture', treading cotton in a tub of soapy water. And Samuel Bamford, the Lancashire Radical, remembered a childhood largely spent at the family bobbin-wheel and loom. The normalcy and presumed virtues of child labour inhibited early protest. Custom, necessity and what passed for theology alike justified the practice; and the transition from the home (where, according to an informant of William Cooke Taylor in 1842, children worked 'as soon as they could crawl' for parents who 'were the hardest of taskmasters') to the early mill involved no apparent change of principle.

Early opposition to the conditions of child-workers developed in the late eighteenth century. The water-power requirements of the spinning mills led the textile entrepreneurs (notably the cotton masters) to site their ventures in often remote riverside areas, where it was difficult to recruit labour. The hostility of many agricultural communities and the demographic revolution together encouraged the adoption of a recruitment policy fraught with hazards. Much mill work could be performed by children; a sham 'apprenticeship' system could be resurrected; and hard-pressed Poor Law authorities would welcome opportunities of reducing both parochial rates and personal responsibilities by sending cartloads of pauper and orphan children to the North. Undoubtedly the lives of such children varied enormously, ultimately depending upon the whim of individual masters – who ranged in contemporary reminiscences from allegedly rapacious sadists like Ellice Needham of Tideswell to comparatively benevolent despots such as David Dale of New Lanark. At the best mills, the 'apprentices' might attend school, visit a library or even play after 12 or 13 hours' labour: at the worst, harshly treated, overworked and underfed children might be treated as virtual slaves. As the stories of starved, tired young workers mutilated by beatings or injuries seeped out to the 'civilised' sections of the public, the first protests were raised.

At least four distinguishable groups participated in the varying strands of the initial, unorganised demand for legislative reform. Old labour aristocracies, such as the East Midland framework-knitters, the Yorkshire woollen croppers and worsted-combers and the ubiquitous handloom weavers, originally despised the new developments. But as technological innovations ruined both their prestige and their incomes, such men fought desperate rearguard actions against factory industry as a whole. Some indulged in Luddite machine-wrecking; some battled through early trade unions; some participated in groups opposing child employment.

Secondly, some courageous pioneers of social medicine drew attention to the pernicious effects of factory labour on health. For instance, the celebrated John Aikin of Warrington wrote of 'children of very tender age . . . transported in crowds, as apprentices to masters resident many hundred miles distant, where they served unknown, unprotected, and forgotten' and were 'usually too long confined to work in close rooms, often during the whole night'. After periodic investigations of child-workers' health following a fever epidemic at Radcliffe Bridge in 1784, Thomas Perceval of Manchester organised a pioneer board of health in 1795. The board published a report on the large cotton establishments on 25 January 1796, asserting that[6]

> 1 – It appears that the children and others who worked in the large cotton factories are peculiarly disposed to be affected by the contagion of fever. . . . 2 – The large factories are generally injurious to the constitution of those employed in them. . . . 3 – The untimely labour of the night, and the protracted labour of the day, with respect to children, not only tends to diminish future expectations as to the general sum of life and industry . . . but it too often gives encouragement to idleness, extravagance and profligacy in the parents. . . . 4 – It appears that the children employed in factories are debarred from all opportunities of education, and from moral or religious instruction. 5 – From the excellent regulations which subsist in several cotton factories, it appears, that many of these evils may, in a considerable degree, be obviated; we are therefore warranted

by experience, and are assured we shall have the support of the liberal proprietors of these factories, in proposing an application for Parliamentary aid (if other methods appear not likely to effect the purpose) to establish a general system of laws for the wise, humane, and equal government of all such works.

A long succession of surgeons and physicians followed this lead – which in fact announced the bulk of later reformers' policy and propaganda points. Perceval's fourth assertion inevitably interested a third group. Northern clergymen were to play important roles in the successive factory campaigns. Priests of the old High Church tradition and men tinged with new Evangelical enthusiasm both participated; but the reformers were predominantly Anglicans, with a sprinkling of Primitive Methodists and in Scotland a considerable number of supporters of the 1843 secession. Roman Catholics, Wesleyans and the range of English Protestant dissenters were, with a few honourable exceptions, conspicuously absent from the roll. Oastler, the ever-active 'Church and King Tory', was 'not a Latitudinarian . . . Puseyite . . . of the Low Church [or] High Church, [but] a sincere member of the established reformed, Protestant, national episcopal Church'. He insisted in 1836 that throughout his campaign 'his only object had been to establish the principles of Christianity, the principles of the Church of England in these densely peopled districts', for 'the Factory-question was indeed . . . a Soul-question – it was Souls against pounds, shillings and pence' and 'the Clergy of the Church of England must either resist the Power of Mammon, or renounce their God.' Looking back in 1860, he could still write that 'his aim was . . . especially to show the working classes that their best interests were bound up in the well-working of the Church.'[7]

The close connections between prominent nonconformist divines and leading capitalist opponents of reform led reformers to indulge in considerable 'religious' polemic. Oastler never hid his contempt for dissenting opponents, ascribing their hostility to the influence of wealthy chapel-goers. 'Wesley would not have been silent on this question . . .', he declared in a Primitive Methodist chapel in 1833, when Bradford Methodists had refused accommodation for the Movement's first conference. 'I do know that John Wesley, had he been on earth, would have been our mighty champion, and would have let us have his chapels, no matter who had rented the front seats in the gallery.' On occasion he lashed out angrily. 'Now, my little Bradford Factory

Children, my poor little degraded pets, degraded by those wicked men, let me ask you, who are the greatest tyrants?' he wrote in a highly contentious paper of 1834. 'You know I answer truly when I say the "liberal" Whig proprietors of the "Bradford Observer" – and the pious, praying, canting, "Deaconized" Dissenters.' If self-styled Christians thought only of financial gain, Hell must be full of Christians, he told the Congregationalist Edward Baines in 1835 – 'and your filthiest Brothels will be the fit receptacles for all your spotless Dissenting Virgins. . . . These men, these 'Deacons', are as like the pure sample of Christianity *embodied* in Jesus Christ, as the Arch Fiend himself! and, depend upon it, Baines, they are just as Holy, as Pious, as Devout, *as* is the filthiest strumpet who walks the streets of Leeds – and not one whit more so.' And in 1843 he insisted that dissenters 'as a body, cared not one rush what became of the poor factory children'. He recalled that 'for many years . . . the Dissenters have been my most inveterate enemies. . . . Their ministers and deacons and members were, with few exceptions, the flatterers or apologists of the monster tyrants. They were my stoutest opponents – my bitterest revilers – my most malignant persecutors.'[8] Any analysis of Oastler's Northern opponents proves the truth of his more factual remarks.

A fourth group of reformers might be characterised as 'traditionalists'. Some were literary men. 'In what sense, not utterly sophistical, can the labour of children, extorted from the want of their parents, "their poverty but not their will consenting" be called *free*?' Samuel Taylor Coleridge pertinently asked in 1818. His colleague Robert Southey believed that the new liberal capitalists 'would care nothing for the honour and independence of England, provided their manufactories went on . . .'; he protested at 'a new sort of slave-trade' in workhouse children. And William Wordsworth loathed the 'outrage done to nature' by night-work:[9]

> Then, in full many a region, once like this
> The assured domain of calm simplicity
> And pensive quiet, an unnatural light
> Prepared for never-resting Labour's eyes
> Breaks from a many-windowed fabric huge;
> And at the appointed hour a bell is heard,
> Of harsher import than the curfew-knoll
> That spake the Norman Conqueror's stern behest –
> A local summons to unceasing toil!

Michael Thomas Sadler, a Leeds and Belfast linen merchant, was no Lakeland Poet, and had spent his youth in Evangelical good works and Tory mercantile endeavour rather than in Cambridge undergraduate radicalism. But he was moved and enraged by the new industrialism. 'I was talking with a man at the London Coffee House on the manufactory system', he told his friend Samuel Fenton in January 1829:[10]

> I said count your gains, Sir, place your golden image on the *plain of your purse*. . . . Infants are not made to leap through fire to your Moloch – that would be merciful – but through the fetid corrupted atmosphere of your manufactories, to which any of your prisons are palaces. You disturb the peace of nature making your towns like to cities in a siege blazing with illuminations and calling infant existences into perpetual labour. . . . And you do not [consider] the health and morality of a whole population, and after all what do you gain? Nothing. Look at the statistics of crime in the manufacturing districts. Let it increase as it has done for 50 years and every man in them will be a felon. Marriage too, instead of being entered into to gratify the affections, is made a matter of mercenary calculation and a man counts from their birth the gain he shall make of his children by their infant slavery in these accursed manufactories.

A host of 'sentimental' paternalists, squires and businessmen, and equally 'reactionary' Radical demagogues and workmen followed this line.

Undoubtedly, some landowners were at least partially influenced by 'class' hostility to the *nouveaux riches*. Colonel Charles Sibthorp, the ultra-Tory Member for Lincoln, became famous as the archetype and prototype rural hater of industrialism as a regular *Punch* cartoon character in the 1840s. And the 'Young Englander' Alexander Baillie-Cochrane long recalled the country gentlemen's delight at the Yorkshire squire William Busfeild Ferrand's appearance at Westminster in 1842, as 'the great denunciator of all manufacturing wrongs, of tyranny and fraud . . . a Danton, a Mirabeau, addressing the Convention . . .'.[11] Some later writers perpetuated the view that the factory reform campaign was simply – or largely – an aristocratic and squirearchic counter-attack on the presumptuous capitalists who dared to assail the entire concept of the politics of deference.

Such explanations dominated the older textbooks and were sanctified by a curious alliance of liberal and Marxist writers. 'The factory question from [1844] down to the passing of the Ten Hour Act', wrote John

Morley, 'was part of the wider struggle between the country gentlemen and the manufacturers. The Tories were taunted with the condition of the labourers in the fields, and they retorted by tales of the condition of the operatives in factories.' This assertion was given a 'social' twist by G. M. Trevelyan's claim that 'it was owing to this fortunate antagonism between the country gentlemen and the manufacturers that the working people began to get their heads above water, and obtained Free Trade and the Factory Acts.' Decades previously, Karl Marx had told American readers that 'the landed aristocracy', beaten by the bourgeoisie over the Reform Act and challenged over the Corn Laws, 'resolved to resist the middle-class by espousing the cause and claims of the working-men against their masters, and especially by rallying around their demands for the limitation of factory labor'. Later, 'having received a deadly blow by the actual abolition of the Corn Laws in 1846, [they] took their vengeance by forcing the Ten-Hours Bill of 1847 upon Parliament'. Such was Marx's 'secret history' of the controversy.[12]

There was, perhaps, just enough truth in this analysis to enable it to enter historical folklore and to be repeated, more or less faithfully, by authors who were unable, unwilling or for some reason reluctant to examine the question in its chronological, political and social context. Certainly the explanation satisfied generations of socialists hostile to both landed and bourgeois wealth and liberals embarrassed by the alleged illiberalism of their forebears. But the facts were rather more complicated than is suggested by a picture of serried ranks of Protectionist squires engaged in rearguard actions against an advancing phalanx of liberal manufacturers. The 'Agricultural' and 'Industrial' interests were far from being monolithic bodies; and Tories, Whigs and Radicals were divided over both industrial reform and free trade. Great Whig landowners like Earl Fitzwilliam or the earl of Radnor sympathised with the free trade case most loudly proclaimed from Manchester; and such Tory manufacturers as John Wood and William Walker of Bradford, Henry Edwards of Halifax and Montague Feilden, John Hornby and William Kenworthy of Blackburn provided invaluable support for factory legislation, together with the Radical manufacturer M.P.s John Fielden of Todmorden, Charles Hindley of Ashton and Joseph Brotherton of Salford.

The 'tidy' theory of a sudden Protectionist switch to industrial reform in 1847 for motives of revenge on the free traders cannot be substantiated. It would be more realistic to argue that, freed of the restraining influence of Peel and Graham (strongly exercised over Conservative backbenchers in 1844), the Protectionists returned to a natural and congenial course. Oastler had consistently expounded Protection to Northern workers: 'Whenever I hear a British artizan shout "cheap foreign corn", I always fancy I see his wife pulling his coat, and hear her crying out "low wages", "long labour", "bad profits" . . .', he declared in December 1832. 'My principle of legislation is this – to encourage home growth, home labour, home trade, and home consumption.' His disciple Ferrand, Tory M.P. for Knaresborough from 1841, 'Young Englander' and 'Working Man's Friend', shared his views. His rescue of a freezing child-worker from a snowdrift on a winter's morning in 1833 had a traumatic effect: 'From that day [Ferrand] became a "Ten Hours Bill man" and the unflinching advocate of "Protection to Native Industry".' And it is possible to see some consistent principle in Ferrand's demand of 1846 for 'Protection for our Protestant Religion . . . for the Monarchy . . . for the Peerage . . . for the Aristocracy . . . for the Landowners . . . for Agriculture . . . for the farmer . . . for the farm labourer . . . for the home trade . . . for the manufacturing operative's labour. . . . Protection for all, destruction to none'[13] – whatever one makes of the hierarchy of preferences. In 1852 C. N. Newdegate not unfairly pictured his colleagues as 'Protectionists of the interests of the poor . . . of the labour of young people employed in factories . . . of the Christian character of the State . . . of the Protestant character of the Constitution and of the national independence . . .'.[14]

Notions of squirearchic paternalism and semi-feudal benevolence stumblingly propounded by tongue-tied Members from the shires and most notoriously expressed in Lord John Manners's lines

> Let wealth and commerce, laws and learning die,
> But leave us still our old Nobility

inevitably aroused contemporary and later parody. But in an age when decrepit mercantilism was lingering through its death-throes, State intervention held a variegated appeal. Proletarian militants, socialist theorists, Evangelical Northern Tories; the sentimentalised medievalism of a Southey, the idealised 'Merrie Englandism' of a Cobbett, the pseudo-Jacobitism of the smart but sympathetic young men of Disraeli's 'Young England'; the social Christianity of a host of Anglican priests and the amorphous 'humanitarianism' of an increasing section of the public – such were the disparate elements involved in the demand for what to many contemporary observers appeared to be a

retrogressive denial of the 'March of Progress'. Strange allies were
to appear in the future: pioneer social scientists disciplined in cold
Benthamite doctrine and academic economists amending their 'laws' to
suit changed circumstances would have some influence, but only after
initial appearances as opponents.

Across the great divide, politically, economically and socially, liberals
of all party persuasions recognised the consistencies of the conflicting
groups in a way often blurred by later writers. When answering the
Radical manufacturer Fielden, the Liberal manufacturer R. H. Greg
thought it a telling point that 'the soundness of [Fielden's] judgment
might still further be impeached, as the advocate for a *legislative interference with wages, and the establishment of a board for the regulation of
them* . . . [he] could scarcely have heard of the name of Adam Smith'.[15]
Richard Cobden talked of the Tories' 'socialist doctrines', though
parliamentary experience led him to amend generalised condemnation
of the sincerity of all Protectionist factory reformers and to think (in
1842) that 'the Tory aristocracy were liberals in *feeling*, compared with
your genuine political bigot, a cotton-spinning Tory'. The Whig Lord
Melbourne professed to consider Ashley 'the greatest Jacobin in [Queen
Victoria's] dominions'. And middle-class Radicals certainly disapproved
of that 'unholy alliance' which ensured that in 1841 Northern 'Chartists,
such as were voters, had almost to a man supported the Tories'. For men
who publicised their 'progressive' liberalism as a modern antidote to
'feudal', 'reactionary' Tory *étatisme* it was inevitably disturbing to see
Ferrand addressing (in Manchester, of all places, in December 1843) a
rally of 'Eldonites, Cobbettites, O'Connorites, Stephensites, Oastlerites
. . . '. They sought to explain the phenomenon. 'The itinerant lecturers
of Chartism want money, the Monopolists want support from the
masses', asserted the Anti-Corn Law League in 1844: the Protectionists
had been deceived by agitators, dismissed workmen and socialists into
establishing 'the principle of interference between the employers and
the employed . . .'. Such Protectionists as George Bankes, J. C. Col-
quhoun, Ferrand and Lord George Bentinck were 'the most ardent
champions of the Ten Hours Bill' in 1846, and 'among the manufacturing capitalists [the League], did not know one advocate of [it] who had
not been a supporter of the Corn Law' – apart from Fielden, a luke-
warm free trader. Liberals might be infuriated, but they understood the
rival attitudes. 'The Protectionists were at least consistent in their vote
in favour of the Factory Bill', commented the Dundee Liberal organ,
protesting at the support of some Liberals.[16]

II

The early industrial reformers had little or no organisation. Despite some notable precedents, 'agitation' was widely regarded as somewhat improper; and the 'genteel' inhibitions of the gentry and professional men were matched by workers' fears of victimisation. Consequently, early legislative efforts largely depended upon benevolent individuals. The 'Health and Morals of Apprentices Act' of 1802, restricting cotton apprentices to 12 hours daily labour, was the work of the first Sir Robert Peel, cotton magnate, squire and Tory M.P. When steam-powered mills employing 'free' children developed in urban areas, the 'socialist' millowner Robert Owen of New Lanark set off a campaign in 1815 to limit child labour to $10\frac{1}{2}$ hours. Investigations by a Commons Committee and two Lords Committees (under the sympathetic Tory Lord Kenyon) led only to Peel's Act of 1819, restricting cotton-mill children generally to 12 hours. But there were the first signs of a supporting organisation in the cotton districts. A few brave spirits formed a Manchester operatives' committee in 1814; Anglican priests and medical men collected and published information; and the Manchester merchant Nathaniel Gould reportedly spent £20,000 on the campaign.

In 1825 three Bradford Tory masters, John Wood, John Rand and Matthew Thompson, unsuccessfully appealed for a voluntary 10-hour day in the worsted industry. And a group of Lancashire workers under John Doherty and James Turner resumed the 'cotton' campaign. But again any hope of success rested primarily with the parliamentary leader, the radical Whig beau John Cam Hobhouse – who gained two minor improvements in 1825 and 1829. It was at this stage that Oastler burst upon the scene. Wood's horrifying revelations about child-labour in September 1830 set his course. Believing that an exposure of industrial conditions and an emotional appeal to Yorkshire morality would secure reform, he sent his famous letter on 'Yorkshire Slavery' to the *Leeds Mercury*, describing children's 13 hours of toil in 'those magazines of British infantile slavery – *the worsted mills in the town and neighbourhood of Bradford*'.[17] Instead, he provoked a furious con-troversy in the Yorkshire Press. During the winter of 1830-1 the rival views were polarised. Edward Baines's *Mercury* became the voice of opposition, supporting dissenting liberal masters like John Marshall of Leeds, Jonathan Akroyd of Halifax and William Ackroyd of Otley. And behind the Tory *Intelligencer* and Radical *Patriot* were gathered Wood's group (still ineffectually appealing for voluntary reform), old-style Tories, increasing numbers of workers – and Oastler.

Employers' emasculation of Hobhouse's last proposals (which eventually resulted in another weak Act) enraged Oastler and his friends, who from 1831 demanded a 10-hour day. When Hobhouse asserted that 'nothing could be more idle', Oastler predicted that future legislators 'would hardly believe it was ever possible for a Christian Parliament to refuse such an Act'. In the spring workers' groups in Huddersfield, Leeds, Bradford and Keighley had formed 'Short-Time Committees' and in June a delegation of Huddersfield men prevailed upon Oastler to link his Tory paternalism with their Radical reformism. By the autumn Oastler was urging operatives to '*manage this cause themselves* . . . [and] establish, instantly establish, committees in every manufacturing town and village, to collect information and *publish facts* . . .'.[18]

Thus began a new type of organisation. For over two decades a variable number of committees – generally composed of Radical and Tory operatives and tradesmen, patronised and largely financed by Anglican clergymen, Tory squires, and Radical and Tory industrialists – spread across the textile districts of England and Scotland. The Lancashire reformers soon rallied again, under Doherty, Turner and Thomas Daniel. Apart from mobilising local support and arranging Oastler's tumultuous winter campaign, the committees – almost invariably operating from taverns – organised a concerted campaign in support of the Ten Hours Bill movingly proposed by Sadler on 16 March 1832. Subsequently they selected witnesses for Sadler's controversial Select Committee and supported his unsuccessful candidature at Leeds in December.

Throughout the early years of the Factory Movement Oastler acted as the pivot and central organiser. His speaking tours revealed a wide histrionic ability; he controlled the central funds, mainly his own savings and Wood's contributions; he unceasingly planned and argued and wrote; and he imparted the crusading tone to the Movement. 'God prosper your righteous cause!' he wrote to Daniel in 1832:

> Operatives, – This Cause is your own. Never desert it. Bend your thoughts always to it – publish the Horrors of the System – subscribe what you can, by what you can – and be assured God will prosper the right. Oppression has reigned long enough. Let the Nation see you have resolved your Sons and Daughters shall be free. . . . Be united.

Be firm. Be courteous and obedient to your Masters – but resolutely bent on using every means the Law provides, to remove Slavery from your helpless little ones. God bless you and the Holy cause.

But a basically 'moral' approach never precluded heated rhetorical outbursts. Oastler was enraged by magisterial connivance at factory-owners' offences under the Factory Acts. 'You cannot keep Labour down, if you try, much longer', he warned George Goodman of Leeds in 1836. ' . . . If it is still allowed to sleep, expect the Giant to awake, – and that right suddenly.' In a notorious speech at Blackburn he mused over the relative values 'in the eye of the law of England' of children's lives and masters' spindles, threatening to sabotage the machinery of law-breaking proprietors. Such men he lashed as 'lawbreakers, tyrants and murderers'.[19] Oastler's home at Fixby Hall long remained the Movement's planning centre; but the organisation was gradually formalised.

As the number of local committees grew, central committees were established to co-ordinate Yorkshire and Lancashire activities and to arrange periodic assemblies of delegates. Modelled to some extent on Methodist precedent, conference was to assume an executive role; at least ostensibly it made the major policy decisions. After Sadler's heartbreaking defeat, twenty delegates (with mandates from two Scottish, ten Lancashire, one Nottingham and eleven Yorkshire committees) assembled at Bradford in January 1833. This first conference authorised Bull to select a new parliamentary leader. Bull's choice, the Evangelical Tory Ashley, took over Sadler's Bill, but was compelled in April to accept investigation by a Royal Commission. Edwin Chadwick's Benthamite-tinged Commissioners inevitably aroused anger and apprehension in the North, and a Manchester conference planned a boycott campaign. Bitterly complaining of hostile demonstrations, Chadwick's colleagues nevertheless worked quickly to report in June. They found that children worked adults' hours, consequently suffered from sicknesses and lack of education and were not 'free agents'; they therefore considered 'that a case was made out for the interference of the Legislature . . .'. In a curious and long-term way some utilitarians were thus converted to some measure of reform.

A tumultuous Northern campaign failed to deter Government: Ashley was defeated and the seminal Factory Act of 1833 was passed. Children aged 9–14 were restricted (by stages) to 8 hours actual labour in most textile mills, with 2 hours at school; young persons under 18 were limited to 12 hours; and four Factory Inspectors would enforce the Act. It was hoped that by employing children in relays it would be possible to maintain long adult hours. But for the moment it seemed that the Oastlerites had been 'outbidden in humanity'. They formed a 'Factory Reformation Society' at Birstall in October, to continue their campaign. But in November, at Manchester, Owen and Fielden announced a 'Society for Promoting National Regeneration', with an impractical though inevitably popular demand for an 8-hour day with 12 hours' pay. The loyalists rejected 'Regenerationist' invitations. 'You must alter your name or you will never get on, "12 hours wages for 8 hours work" is *Unjust*', Oastler told Owen. 'You might as well say "12*d* for 8*d*". The poor creatures have only had 8 hours Wages for 12 hours work.' Furthermore,

> We have no delegated Power. Our Delegates' Meeting sanctioned the 10 Hour Bill and our Local Comees have done the same, and the only power to alter . . . rests with the Public Meetings. . . . I shall never argue against an 8 hour Bill. . . . But the people must drive me by the Majorities at Public Meetings, from the 10 to the 8 hours Bill.

And Bull berated Bradford Regenerationists as 'a rope of sand':[20]

> There are too many of you that would not give up one hour's occupation, one hour's comfort, or the price of one glass of ale, to save *your own class* from distress and ruin. . . . Now, therefore, do exercise a little forbearance and keep your little political playthings still and quiet, when great practical questions are under discussion.

'Regeneration' failed with the general Owenite collapse of 1834, carrying with it much of the 'Short Time' agitation.

From 1834 the Factory Movement had a chequered history. Oastler and his friends became increasingly involved in anti-Poor Law campaigns – in which they were spectacularly joined by the violent Tory ex-Methodist minister Joseph Rayner Stephens of Ashton. In 1836 Poulett Thomson's attempt to prevent the full implementation of the 8 hours provision provoked an angry (and successful) campaign. But thereafter many Northern reformers devoted themselves to the Poor Law and Chartist agitations. And there were always local differences. Lancashire reformers, for instance, experienced in evasions of previous legislation, for long demanded that the mill engines should be stopped at set times to make enforcement certain – a policy at which Oastler would 'greatly rejoice' but 'dare not ask for', in 1832. Furthermore, some of their parliamentary spokesmen, such as Hindley and Brotherton, were often prepared to compromise on the Ten Hours demand. They had supporters among Lancashire workers: Thomas Pitt of Ashton, for example, always thought it was 'a great error' to reject Hindley's gradualist approach and Brotherton's '11-hour' proposal. But other men hotly opposed any weakening of policy: in 1835 Doherty bluntly told Hindley of 'a strong and rather growing feeling of distrust of [his] sincerity', while Stephens constantly assailed his 'unsteadiness, time-serving and tergiversation',[21] In Liberal Scotland the committees tended to rely upon the support of professional men and Presbyterian ministers: the Dundee committee was founded in 1831 on the proposal of a mill manager and appointed a newspaper editor as its secretary; and the Aberdeen, Arbroath, Edinburgh and Paisley agitations were largely organised by middle-class men. While the Glasgow movement was undoubtedly proletarian in origin, at some time after the cotton-spinners' troubles of 1837 it also passed under largely 'bourgeois' control. And the Quaker-dominated London committee was, as Oastler recalled, 'sterile and unfruitful'.[22]

Yorkshire, with its popular Tory–Radicalism, was less prone to division and controversy within the organisation. Even here, however, there were differences. In Leeds, asserted Baines, Sadler was supported in 1832 by 'operatives of that nondescript and mongrel class betwixt ultra-Radicals and ultra-Tories'. But the varieties of local Radicalism led to sectional struggles. In June 1833 Oastler rejoiced that 'in Bradford they are red hot and even in Leeds united and firm – nay, even enthusiastic.' In July he had 'no fears from the enemy. My fear alone arises from the spirit of concession, which Satan has put into the hearts of your leaders', he told the Keighley leader, Abraham Wildman. 'We are all right at Huddersfield, Holmfirth, Manchester, &c. &c. Leeds is divided, I believe, as indeed it always is.'[23] Leeds reformers' instability led to the Yorkshire headquarters being transferred from Leeds (where the county secretary was William Osburn, a Tory wine merchant and Egyptologist) to Bradford (where the most notable organisers were the Tory workmen Matthew Balme and Squire Auty). The Huddersfield committee was dominated by Radical workers, of whom the most famous was Joshua Hobson, weaver, printer, journalist, Chartist and eventual Conservative, while Keighley was led by the Radicals Wildman and David Weatherhead, a pioneer spiritualist.[24] Lancashire committees also varied: Manchester had a unique trade union backing; Blackburn was Tory-dominated; Ashton was ever divided; Bolton was the most generous to visiting speakers.

The activities of the central committees were subsidised by Oastler, Wood and Fielden. Sometimes they published journals – *The British Labourer's Protector and Factory Child's Friend* in 1832–3 and the *Ten Hours Advocate* in 1846–7 – in addition to a continuous outpouring of pamphlets, petitions and tracts. Sometimes they could afford to employ staff, such as the 'missionaries' Cavie Richardson of Leeds, Mark Crabtree of Dewsbury, Philip Grant of Manchester and Joseph Mullineaux, the Lancashire secretary from 1845. The principal benefactors were also expected to help in emergencies: Lord Feversham's committee made up the difference between the 'Oastler Liberation Fund' and Oastler's debts in 1844; Wood, Walker and Fielden met the deficit on Oastler's *Fleet Papers*; the Fieldens paid for the *Advocate*; and Wood, Ashley and Fielden helped Grant's business ventures.[25] In its early days the Movement organised such spectacular mass demonstrations as the 'Pilgrimage to York' at Easter 1832 and the mammoth Wibsey Moor rally of July 1833, but later it concentrated on a wide series of public meetings. Stephens's imprisonment for sedition in 1839 and Oastler's for debt in 1840 perhaps marked the change: the chastened Stephens and weakened Oastler did not subsequently favour wild rallies, although Ferrand's tumultuous campaign in the winter of 1843 to raise funds for Oastler's release revived much of the old excitement.

Propaganda campaigns were sustained and varied. Sadler himself produced two typical but very different publications in his 'sentimental' verses on 'The Factory Girl's Last Day' in 1832, and his posthumous *Factory Statistics* of 1836. Medical men contributed such volumes as Charles Turner Thackrah's pioneer investigation of *The Effects of the Principal Arts, Trades and Professions . . . on Health and Longevity* of 1831 and 1832 and Charles Wing's anthology of 'reformist' evidence in *The Evils of the Factory System* (1837). Oastler provided a host of pamphlets exhibiting every mood of his extrovert character; Fielden published his classic on *The Curse of the Factory System* in 1836; alleged autobiographies of child labourers were provided by Robert Blinco, William Dodd and James Myles. And in 1840 Frances Trollope devoted a novel to the *Life and Adventures of Michael Armstrong, The Factory Boy*.

The pace of the campaign of the 1840s varied considerably. Ashley had failed to inject 'ten hours' provisions into Fox Maule's unsuccessful Bills of 1838, 1839 and 1841. But now the Inspectors themselves favoured further legislation: in 1840 the celebrated Leonard Horner considered that 'it would be a matter of great regret if another session should be

allowed to terminate without an amending Act having passed. . . .'
Hopes also rose with the return of the Conservatives, under the second
Sir Robert Peel, in 1841. But despite the 'reform' activities of many of
their Northern supporters, Peel and his Home Secretary, Graham (who
seemed to Yorkshire delegates 'to have drunk too deeply at the fount of
the Malthusian policy') shared liberal economic attitudes. By February
1842 Ashley felt obliged sadly to inform the committees that Peel had
'signified his opposition'. The riotous 'Plug Plots' in the summer
speeded Government action, however, and in March 1843 Graham
introduced a new Bill, which would restrict children aged 8–13 to $6\frac{1}{2}$
hours' work with 3 hours' daily education in improved schools largely
controlled by the Church. A massive campaign by dissenting groups,
stressing the virtues of 'voluntaryism' and professing fears about the
'Romanising' effects of the Oxford Movement, led to the withdrawal
of the measure in the summer. Reinforced by the newly liberated
Oastler and by numerous Anglican clergymen, the Ten Hours men
mounted a major campaign in the spring of 1844. Ashley had some early
success in his efforts to engraft a '10 hours' clause on Graham's new
Bill; but 'Ministerial influence' and Peel's threatened resignation
deterred Tory back-benchers. In May Ashley was 'utterly, singularly,
prodigiously defeated by a majority of 138!!' and could only console
himself with the knowledge that 'the majority was one to save the
Government', irrespective of the merits of the case.

Graham's Act of 1844 actually effected considerable improvements.
Children became 'half-timers', working $6\frac{1}{2}$ hours; dangerous machinery
was to be fenced; women shared the teenagers' 12 hours restriction. But
the disappointment in the textile towns provoked compromises and local
negotiations. A series of conferences sought to maintain unity by
reviving the Ten Hours Bill at Westminster, and after a wide winter
campaign Ashley moved for leave to introduce it in January 1846. The
debate over industrial conditions was now overshadowed by the nation-
wide controversy over the Corn Laws, with their emotional undertones
of landed 'privilege'. Ashley was one of the few 'Peelite' Conservatives
who felt morally obliged to resign their seats on changing their views,
and Fielden (M.P. for Oldham) took his place as parliamentary leader,
only to be defeated by 203 votes to 193 in May. As another mammoth
campaign was mounted in the autumn a gathering industrial recession
weakened the case for opposition; even the *Manchester Guardian*
confessed that 'there certainly never was a time, in the history of the
cotton manufacture, when a limitation to ten hours would interfere less

with the engagements of the masters, or the earnings of the workpeople, than the period now before us. . . .'[26] Final Whig attempts to compromise on 11 hours were defeated, and Fielden triumphed by 151 votes to 88 in May 1847. Lords Ellesmere and Feversham (as Lord Francis Egerton and William Duncombe old friends of the Bill) piloted the measure through the Lords, and the Ten Hours Act received the royal assent on 8 June.

Northern rejoicings were still premature, however. From 1848 there were reports of evasions in Lancashire and of masters' campaigns to repeal the Act. Above all, a small group resorted to a relay system, 'giving meal-times at various periods of the day, and . . . changing the hours of work and meals of every hand employed, arbitrarily from day to day', so that (reported Horner) 'no restriction of the hours of work could be enforced in the factories of artful men'. Gradually, a new agitation grew to protect the Act, but it became increasingly obvious that the Movement was sadly divided, with Ashley, Hindley and a 'liberal' group prepared to tolerate some compromise and Oastler, Stephens, Ferrand, Manners and Fielden's Conservative sons intransigent. The bitter internal struggle, inflamed by Oastler's oratory and Stephens's angry papers in the *Ashton Chronicle* and *The Champion*, mounted after the failure of the test case of Ryder *v*. Mills before Baron Parke in the Court of Exchequer in February 1850. Stormy conferences exacerbated the situation, by appointing Manners and Bankes as Ashley's associates in the parliamentary leadership. And Ashley provoked charges of 'treason' when he accepted Sir George Grey's so-called '10½ hours Bill', which would increase weekly hours from 58 to 60 in return for banning relays by establishing a working day between 6 a.m. and 6 p.m. Ashley had been tricked: his attempt to include children in the standard day was as unsuccessful as Manners's struggle to retain the ten hours. Consequently, men might work 15 hours, aided by relays of children beyond the hours allowed for women and young persons. The Act received the royal assent on 5 August 1850. 'Free Trade in everything, especially in flesh and blood, is henceforth to be the order of the day', asserted Stephens, as 'the meanness of the Manchester school . . . triumphed over the honour of the English gentlemen.' He thought that 'the name of Lord Ashley would for ever stink in the nostrils of honest men'.[27] The children only received their fixed day by Lord Palmerston's Act of 1853; and the '10 hours' was only restored by Disraeli in 1874. In the meantime, however, similar legislation had been extended to a wide range of workers.

III

The Factory Movement was in many ways a strange agitation. Most of its founders, most of its parliamentary champions and most of its foremost regional leaders were Tories and Churchmen. 'If you chuse, I will take Yorkshire round, Town by Town; and in each Town, at PUBLIC Meetings, we will enquire the names of 12 of the best masters and 12 of the worst', Oastler told Baines in 1835, 'and I will engage that, on the average, 9, at least, of the BEST, will be Church-goers or Tories, and 9 of the WORST will be Dissenting Whigs.'[28] If 'best' and 'worst' can be taken as meaning 'supporting' or 'opposing' factory reform, Oastler was undoubtedly right. Tory industrialists have been curiously neglected by historians, presumably because of the attraction of a simple Liberal–industrial–nonconformist and Tory–agricultural–Anglican dichotomy. But even more curious were the alliances, often very firmly made, between old enemies from the Tory and Radical ranks in the Northern industrial towns. Certainly, the Factory Movement can only be described as a Tory–Radical agitation, with the different components of the alliance varying in influence in different areas at different times. Later partisan writers often oversimplified the demarcations: to the end, not all Protectionists were supporters, while Peelite Conservatives were generally bitter opponents; 'Radicals', as ever, were divided; Whigs and 'Liberals' included such old supporters as Sir George Strickland and new sympathisers like Macaulay, as well as a host of opponents. As Oastler told London ultra-Radicals in 1835, he hoped 'to persuade a few labouring men . . . to look at *principles*, not *names*'; he pointed out that 'Poulett Thomson is a Whig, so is John Maxwell; Sir Robert Peel is a Tory, so was poor Michael Thomas Sadler; Joseph Hume is a Radical, so is John Fielden.'[29] Furthermore, the hated 'centralising' Benthamites were eventually to have an important influence on the factory legislation campaigned for by the humanitarians.

The Movement left its own considerable literature. Oastler's first biography (by Stephens) was published in 1838 and Sadler's only 'Life' appeared in 1842. Oastler's secretary, Samuel Kydd, published the first history of the agitation in 1857; Philip Grant (latterly a supporter of Ashley) issued a shorter, self-justifying account in 1866; W. R. Croft of Huddersfield produced an even less accurate narrative in 1888; and in 1903 B. L. Hutchins and Amy Harrison published the first edition of their general history of British factory legislation. Biographies of Shaftesbury have appeared regularly since Sir Edwin Hodder's work of

1886, but have added little or nothing to knowledge of the factory agitation. The readable exaggerations of J. L. and Barbara Hammond have long influenced twentieth-century textbooks. When confounded by Sir John Clapham, 'socially concerned' writers fought back in a variety of ways against equally involved liberals, and the Factory Movement fell to the status of an occasional footnote in the continuing war between 'pessimists' and 'optimists' over the social effects of the Industrial Revolution. More recently some writers attempted to reopen the investigation, mainly by examining relevant subjects more carefully. Such investigators provoke some extraordinary 'remarks' and 'reviews' – but, unfortunately, very few rationally argued publications of substance – from the embattled warriors in the dialogue between those who imagine themselves as Adam Smith's new interpreters and those who claim to have reinterpreted Karl Marx. Historians who find such rival disquisitions occasionally informative but increasingly uniformed, repetitious and unproductive, may be grateful for the increasing availability of some of the classic accounts of a strange but productive agitation.

Certainly there were exaggerations in reformers' propaganda and excesses in their threatening oratory. Certainly their sentimental hyperbole infuriated lazy politicians like Melbourne and overworked ministers like Graham. But, starting with low chances, they were among the most successful of contemporary agitators.

BIBLIOGRAPHICAL NOTE

Contemporary material on factory reform is widely dispersed. The most important collections are those of Richard Oastler (in the Goldsmiths' Library at London University and Columbia University Library) and Matthew Balme (in Bradford City Library). Samuel Kydd's (pseud. 'Alfred') pioneer *History of the Factory Movement* (2 vols, 1857), based on Oastler's papers, is still useful (1 vol impr., Cass, 1966).

Several publications which influenced the course of the agitation have been reissued. The 1832 edition of *The Effects of the Principal Arts, Trades and Professions . . . on Health and Longevity* by C. T. Thackrah, a Leeds Tory surgeon, factory reformer and pioneer of social medicine, is reprinted in A. Meiklejohn, *The Life, Work and Times of C. T. Thackrah* (Livingstone, Edinburgh, 1957). It may be compared with the 1832 edition of the liberal [Sir] J. P. Kay [Shuttleworth], *The Moral and Physical condition of the Working Classes employed in the Cotton Manufacture of Manchester* (Cass, 1969). The somewhat ambivalent views of the surgeon Peter Gaskell, originally expressed in *The Manufacturing Population of England* (1833), were expanded in *Artisans and Machinery* (1836; Cass, 1969). Dr Charles Wing wrote his *Evils of the Factory*

System (1837; Cass, 1967) as a convinced opponent of child labour and largely reprinted Parliamentary evidence.

The evidence given to Peel's 1816 Committee (*PP* (1816), iii), Sadler's Report of 1832 (*PP* (1831–2), xv) and the 1833 Commission's first Report (*PP* (1833), xx) has been reprinted (Cass, 1968–9; Irish U.P., Shannon, 1968–9). The Commission's later Reports (*PP* (1833), xxi, (1834), xix, xx), the 1840 Committee's Reports on the operation of the 1833 Act (*PP* (1840), x, (1841), ix) and the Inspectors' Reports have also been reprinted (Irish U.P.).

Other sources on the 'reform' side are John Fielden, *The Curse of the Factory System* (1836; intro. J. T. Ward, Cass, 1969); Mrs Frances Trollope's novel *The Life and Adventures of Michael Armstrong, the Factory Boy* (1840; Cass, 1968), which was partly based on a northern tour in 1839; the exaggerated but widely read *Narrative of the Experience and Sufferings of William Dodd, a factory cripple* (1841) and Dodd's *The Factory System Illustrated* (1842), reissued in a single volume (intro. W. H. Chaloner, Cass, 1969); and [James Myles ed.], *Chapters in the Life of a Dundee Factory Boy* (Dundee, 1850; John Scott, Dundee, 1951).

Some impression of hostile viewpoints may be obtained from Andrew Ure, *The Philosophy of Manufactures* (1835; Cass, 1969) and W. Cooke Taylor, *Notes, of a Tour in the Manufacturing Districts of Lancashire* (1842; Cass, 1968). Economists' attitudes are re-examined in K. O. Walker, 'The Classical Economists and the Factory Acts', *JEH* i (1941); L. R. Sorenson, 'Some Classical Economists, Laissez Faire and the Factory Acts', ibid., xii (1952); and (most effectively) Mark Blaug, 'The Classical Economists and the Factory Acts: a Re-examination', *Quarterly J. of Economics*, lxxiii (1958).

The most reliable biography of Ashley remains Sir Edwin Hodder's *The Life and Work of the Seventh Earl of Shaftesbury, K.G.* (3 vols, Cassell, 1886). Oastler's career is superbly described in Cecil Driver, *Tory Radical: The Life of Richard Oastler* (O.U.P., New York, 1946). The involvement of the Church is best examined in Canon J. C. Gill's books *The Ten Hours Parson* (S.P.C.K., 1959) and *Parson Bull of Byerley* (S.P.C.K., 1963) and is dealt with more slightly in Canon C. J. Stranks, *Dean Hook* (Mowbray, 1954) and R. G. Cowherd, *The Politics of English Dissent* (New York U.P., 1956; Epworth Press, 1959).

Shorter biographies are provided in Frank Beckwith, 'Robert Baker', *Univ. of Leeds Rev.*, vii (1960); W. R. Lee, 'Robert Baker: The First Doctor in the Factory Department', *British J. of Industrial Medicine*, xxi (1964); W. H. Chaloner, 'Mrs Trollope and the Early Factory System', *VS* iv (1960); G. D. H. Cole, *Chartist Portraits* (Macmillan, 1941; intro. Asa Briggs, 1965) on Doherty, Fielden, Oastler and Stephens; J. T. Ward, 'Revolutionary Tory: The Life of J. R. Stephens', *TLCAS* lxviii (1958), 'M. T. Sadler', *Univ. of Leeds Rev.*, vii (1960), 'Matthew Balme (1813–1884) Factory Reformer', *Bradford Antiquary*, xl (1960), 'Squire Auty', ibid., xlii (1964), 'Two Pioneers in Industrial Reform' [John Wood and William Walker], *Bradford Tex. Soc. J.* (1964) and [on Ferrand] 'Young England', *HT* xvi (1966).

The movement has been re-examined periodically since the Victorian works of Kydd, Grant and Croft. B. L. Hutchins and Amy Harrison, *A History of Factory Legislation* (3rd ed. 1926; Cass, 1969) is comprehensive in scope but sketchy in detail. M. W. Thomas, *The Early Factory Legislation* (Thames Bank, Leigh-on-Sea, 1948) meticulously examines the operation of the Acts, primarily through the Inspectors' papers. N. J. Smelser, *Social Change in the Industrial Revolution* (Routledge, 1959) includes a fascinating but incomplete sociological examination of some aspects. J. T. Ward, *The Factory Movement, 1830–1855* (Macmillan, 1962) is a detailed history of the agitations. Local studies include

J. T. Ward, 'Bradford and Factory Reform', *Bradford Tex. Soc. J.* (1961), 'Some Industrial Reformers', ibid. (1963), 'Leeds and the Factory Reform Movement', *Pub. Thoresby Soc.*, xlvi (1961), 'The Factory Reform Movement in Scotland', *Scott. Hist. Rev.*, xli (1962) and 'The Factory Movement in Lancashire', *TLCAS* lxv–lxvi (1969).

Political attitudes are examined in D. Roberts, 'Tory Paternalism and Social Reform in Early Victorian England', *AHR* lxiii (1958); W. O. Aydelotte, 'The House of Commons in the 1840s', *History*, xxxix (1954), 'Voting Patterns in the British House of Commons in the 1840s', *Comp. Studies in Society and History*, v (1963), 'Parties and Issues in Early Victorian England', *J. British Studies*, v (1966) and 'The Conservative and Radical Interpretations of Early Victorian Social Legislation', *VS* xi (1967). Professor Aydelotte generally opposes the traditional account of Tory involvement, at least in Parliament; cf. Jenifer Hart, 'Nineteenth-Century Social Reform: A Tory Interpretation of History', *Past and Present*, 31 (1965) and S. C. Deb, 'British Factory Movement in the Early Nineteenth Century', *Indian J. Economics*, xliv (1963).

The most celebrated liberal 'attack' is W. H. Hutt, 'The Factory System of the Early Nineteenth Century', *Economica*, vi (1926), reprinted in F. A. Hayek (ed.), *Capitalism and the Historians* (Routledge, 1954). For the standard Marxist work, see Friedrich Engels, *The Condition of the Working-Class in England in 1844*, trans. Mrs F. K. Wischnewetzky (Sonnenschein, 1892), reprinted in *Karl Marx and Frederick Engels on Britain* (Foreign Languages Publishing House, Moscow, 1953; Lawrence & Wishart, 1954); trans, and ed. W. O. Henderson and W. H. Chaloner (Blackwell, Oxford, 1958).

NOTES

1. *The Times*, 7 Sept 1861.

2. G. S. Bull, *Richard Oastler: A Sermon preached in St James' Church, Bradford, Sept 1st 1861* (Bradford, 1861), pp. 12, 16; N. W. Senior, *Letters on the Factory Act, as it Affects the Cotton Manufacture* (1837), pp. 12, 16

3. *Leeds Mercury*, 8 Sept 1832; *Speeches of the Rt Hon. T. B. Macaulay, M.P.* (1854), p. 451.

4. Roebuck to Shaftesbury, 24 Mar 1860 (Sir Edwin Hodder, *The Life and Work of the Seventh Earl of Shaftesbury*, 3 vols (1886), ii, 375).

5. 'J.C.', *The Weaver's Pocket-Book: or Weaving Spiritualized* (Dundee, 1766), pp. 147–8, 149.

6. John Aikin, *A Description of the Country from thirty to forty Miles round Manchester* (1795), pp. 219–20; *PP* (1816), iii, 139–40.

7. *The Home*, 3 May 1851; Richard Oastler, *A Letter to the Archbishop of York* (Huddersfield, 1836), pp. 13, 15, 16, *Convocation: The Church and the People* (1860), p. 12.

8. Richard Oastler, *Speech delivered in the Primitive Methodist Chapel, Bowling Lane, Bradford, . . . on 14 January 1833* (Leeds, 1833), p. 2; *A Letter to Those Sleek, Pious, Holy and Devout Dissenters, Messrs Get-All, Keep-All, Grasp-All, Scrape-All, Whip-All, Gull-All, Cheat-All, Cant-All, Work-All, Sneak-All, Lie-Well, Swear-Well, Scratch-Em and Company, The Shareholders in the Bradford Observer* (Bradford, 1834), p. 29; *Yorkshire Slavery: The 'Devil-To-Do' Amongst the Dissenters in Huddersfield* (Leeds, 1835), p. 7; *Fleet Papers*, 3 June 1843.

9. S. T. Coleridge, *Two Addresses on Sir Robert Peel's Bill* (1818); Jack Simmons, *Southey* (1945), p. 153; William Wordsworth, *The Excursion* (1814).

10. Samuel Fenton's diary (Leeds City Reference Library Ms 923.2/SA 15 L), 22 Jan 1829. See *Memoirs of the Life and Writings of M. T. Sadler* (1842).

11. Lord Lamington, *In the Days of The Dandies* (1890), pp. 92–3.

12. Lord Morley, *The Life of Richard Cobden* (1910 ed.), p. 301; G. M. Trevelyan, *The Life of John Bright* (1913), p. 74; Marx in *New York Daily Tribune*, 15 Mar 1853, reprinted in *Karl Marx and Frederick Engels on Britain* (Moscow, 1953), p. 368.

13. Richard Oastler, *Facts and Plain Words on Every-Day Subjects* (Leeds, 1833), p. 55; W. B. Ferrand, 'Letter to the Duke of Newcastle' (*The Home*, 27 Mar 1852), 'To the Farmers, Operatives and Friends of Native Industry in the West Riding', 16 Jan 1846 (Ferrand MSS, by courtesy of the late Col G. W. Ferrand, O.B.E.).

14. Quoted in *Church of England Quarterly Review*, xc (1852), p. 502.

15. R. H. Greg, *The Factory Question* (1837), pp. 68–9.

16. *The League*, 23 Dec 1843, 23 Mar 1844, 13 June 1846; *Dundee Advertiser*, 26 May 1846.

17. *Leeds Mercury*, 16 Oct 1830.

18. *Leeds Intelligencer*, 24 Nov, 20 Oct 1831.

19. Oastler to Daniel, 14 Mar 1832 (Collection of the late Professor Cecil Driver, by courtesy of Mrs C. M. Lyman); Richard Oastler, *The Unjust Judge* (Leeds, 1836), pp. 11–12, *The Law or the Needle* (1836), *passim*, *A Letter to those Millowners who continue to oppose the Ten Hours Bill* (Manchester, 1836), p. 3.

20. Oastler to Owen, 22 Nov 1833 (Owen collection, Holyoake House, Manchester, 668); *Mr Bull and the Regeneration Society* (n.p., 1834), pp. 2–3.

21. *Poor Man's Advocate*, 10 Mar 1832; *Ashton and Stalybridge Reporter*, 24 July 1858; *Manchester and Salford Advertiser*, 12 Dec 1835; *Ashton Chronicle*, 21 July 1849.

22. *Dundee Advertiser*, 14 Apr 1831, 23 Feb 1832; *Aberdeen Journal*, 17 July 1833; *Edinburgh Evening Courant*, 28, 31 Dec 1846; *Glasgow Saturday Post*, 19 Dec 1846; *Renfrewshire Advertiser*, 19 Dec 1846; *Glasgow Courier*, 10 Mar 1832, 12 Dec 1846; *Fleet Papers*, 15 Oct 1842.

23. *Leeds Mercury*, 8 Sept 1832; Oastler to John Foster, 23 June 1833 (Goldsmiths' collection, London University Library); *Keighley News*, 9 Apr 1870.

24. *Leeds Mercury*, 27 Feb 1875; Balme collection (Bradford City Library); *Bradford Observer*, 28 May 1870; *Huddersfield Examiner*, 13 May 1876; *Keighley News*, 13 Sept 1952.

25. Fielden MSS (by courtesy of the late Professor David Owen).

26. *Manchester Guardian*, 20 Feb 1847.

27. *The Champion*, ii (1850), 7, 14 (n.d.).

28. Richard Oastler, *The Huddersfield Dissenters in a Fury* (Leeds, 1835), p. 4.

29. *Poor Man's Guardian*, 29, 15 Aug 1835.

3. The Anti-Poor Law Agitation

M. E. ROSE

OF all the legislation for social reform which the early nineteenth century produced, few Acts aroused such passionate hostility as did the Poor Law Amendment of 1834, the New Poor Law. The Act was based on the recommendations of a Royal Commission which had been set up in 1832 to find some final solution to the poor law problem. Not only was the cost of poor relief under the old system increasing, but also, it was alleged, the methods of relief, particularly that of making up the wages of ill-paid labourers with large families out of the poor rates, were demoralising the rural labourers. Final proof of such demoralisation seemed to come in the shape of the agrarian riots which spread across much of southern and eastern England in 1830. Alarmed, the landed classes pressed the Government to take action, and the Government, embroiled in the controversy over the Reform Bill, passed the question of poor law reform over to the Royal Commission.

Early in 1834 the Royal Commission reported. The Report was the work of its two most prominent members, Nassau Senior, a former professor of economics, and Edwin Chadwick, a young lawyer who had been secretary to Jeremy Bentham until the philosopher's death in 1832, and who had imbibed many of his former master's ideas on administration. The Report strongly condemned the existing system of poor relief and put forward a number of suggestions for reform. The most important of these were, first, that all relief to the able-bodied poor be given only in a 'well-regulated' workhouse and not in the form of out-relief doles. In this way, poor relief would incorporate the principle of 'less eligibility', by which the condition of the labourer on poor relief would be less comfortable than that of the worker who lived independently of the rates. Thus only those who were genuinely destitute would apply for relief and enter the workhouse. The second, and most important, suggestion was that a central authority for poor relief should be established with powers of control over the local authorities who distributed relief to the poor. This arrangement, it was hoped, would ensure some measure of national uniformity in poor relief methods.

Although some members of the Cabinet disliked the principle of administrative centralisation embodied in the Report, the Government drafted a Bill which created a Poor Law Commission of three members with powers to group parishes into Unions for poor relief purposes. Administration in the Unions was to be carried out by elected boards of guardians under the supervision and control of the Poor Law Commission. The task of establishing a 'less eligibility' system of relief was left to the new central authority, whose powers over the local authorities were far weaker than Edwin Chadwick wished.

The Bill passed through its parliamentary stages with relative ease and received the royal assent in August 1834. The main opposition in the House of Commons came from the ageing Radical William Cobbett, who spent the last year of his life in furious attacks on the 'Poor Man's Robbery Bill', as he called it, and from John Walter, M.P. for Berkshire and proprietor of *The Times*. To the alarm of the Government, *The Times* took up its proprietor's attack against the Bill, and became one of the most formidable and consistent critics of the New Poor Law. Senior rather contemptuously dismissed this opposition as 'a silly paragraph in the *Times*, which speaks only the sentiments of Mr Walter, who wishes to sit for Berkshire as the poor man's friend, and some ravings of Cobbett's'.[1]

Such a comment was premature in the extreme. Opposition to the New Poor Law was to continue and to increase in intensity. In a sense, there was continuous agitation against the New Poor Law from its creation in 1834 until the demise of the boards of guardians in 1929, from Cobbett in the 1830s to George Lansbury in the 1920s. This continuing opposition and criticism was responsible for many of the amendments of the 1834 system, for that 'history of leftward deviations' which marked its life.[2] Paradoxically, however, the Anti-Poor Law Movement, which is the subject of this chapter, was one of the shortest-lived of early nineteenth-century protest movements. It reached its height in the years 1837 and 1838 in the manufacturing areas of Lancashire and the West Riding of Yorkshire. By 1839, although hostility to the Poor Law did not abate, the organised movement of protest was being rapidly swallowed up in the wider campaign for the People's Charter.

Perhaps because of these chronological and geographical limits, the Anti-Poor Law Movement lacks its own separate history. Poor Law

historians have concentrated mainly on the administrative aspects of the
New Poor Law, and have dealt only briefly with the organised opposition to it.[3] The best discussions of the anti-Poor Law campaign have
come from historians of the Factory Movement and of Chartism who
have realised the importance of anti-Poor Law feeling in the development of these movements. J. T. Ward has shown how the anti-Poor Law
campaign was born out of the Ten Hours Movement, and then absorbed
in its turn by Chartism.[4] Biographers of the Ten Hours Movement's
northern leaders have described the part played by their subjects in the
struggle against the New Poor Law.[5] R. G. Gammage, the earliest
historian of Chartism, had little to say about the anti-Poor Law campaign, but the French historian Dolléans discussed the effect of the New
Poor Law at some length and came to the conclusion that 'the abolition
of the old system of relief was to be one of the most powerful factors in
the Chartist agitation'.[6] Perhaps the most perceptive description of
the Anti-Poor Law Movement is to be found in Mark Hovell's history
of Chartism. He saw very clearly the dual nature of the protest against
the New Poor Law. 'It was a conservative opposition to a radical
measure, and it was a popular outburst against what was conceived as a
wanton act of oppression', he wrote.[7]

Tories like Richard Oastler, the Factory Movement's charismatic
leader, George Stringer Bull, curate of Bierley near Bradford, or
Samuel Roberts, the Sheffield silver plater, that 'Sheffielder of the old
school' as he proudly described himself, saw the New Poor Law as yet
another threat to the old paternalist society to which they looked back
with sentimental affection. The new system would spell an end to
parochial responsibility for the poor, in which the overseer under the
fatherly eye of the local justice of the peace had attended to the wants of
his neighbours in the parish. Poor Law administration of this type,
which Samuel Roberts described as being 'like the conducting of an
extensive family', was to be replaced by an impersonal bureaucratic
system in which the local authorities would have to obey the dictates of
a central authority, a system which Roberts condemned as 'this Regent
Street, Frenchified, lath and plaster structure'.[8] Society, and particularly the security of property, rested, in their view, on the fact that
the poor were the first charge on the estates of the wealthy. If the poor
were to be denied this right, then they would rebel and anarchy would
result. 'It lays the axe to the root of the social compact; it must break
up society and make England a wilderness', Oastler said of the New
Poor Law.[9] He, and Tories who felt like him, were bewildered by the

support given to the Poor Law Amendment Act in Parliament by leading members of the Tory party such as the duke of Wellington and Sir Robert Peel.

At the other end of the political spectrum, many Radical working men saw the Poor Law as another instalment in the catalogue of Whig treacheries which had begun with the Reform Act betrayal of 1832 and continued in the Factory Act of 1833 and the attack on trades unions culminating in the prosecution of the Dorchester labourers in 1834 and the Glasgow cotton-spinners in 1837. Meetings of trade societies were summoned in Manchester and Sheffield to discuss the new poor relief system, and heard dire warnings that its whole intention was one of reducing wages. As if in proof of this, the Poor Law Commission was busily engaged in 1835 and 1836 in trying to arrange the migration of impoverished labourers and their families from the villages of southern and eastern England to the factories of Lancashire, Cheshire and the West Riding. 'The New Poor Law Act was passed', pronounced the Chartist Bronterre O'Brien '. . . to place the whole of the labouring population at the utter mercy and disposal of the monied or property owning classes.'[10] Thus northern Radicals found it hard to understand why Radicals like Francis Place favoured the Poor Law Amendment Act. 'Were it not for his bigotry to the accursed Poor Law we should point out Francis Place as one of the finest specimens in Europe of a republican philosopher', announced the *Northern Liberator*, an ultra-Radical Newcastle paper.[11]

Hostility to the New Poor Law cut across party and 'class' divisions. It cannot be explained in terms of Tory versus Liberal, middle classes versus working classes or progressives versus reactionaries. The anti-Poor Law cry could unite men of high and low estate and thus pose, if only briefly, a serious threat to the established order. It is the aim of this chapter to examine the causes of this hostility, the methods by which it was exploited, the degree of success which the Anti-Poor Law Movement achieved, and the reasons for its early disappearance.

It would be wrong to imagine that hostility to the New Poor Law was confined to the industrial areas of northern England, and particularly to Lancashire and the West Riding. The Poor Law Commission encountered a good deal of opposition when they were introducing the New Poor Law into the rural areas of southern and eastern England in 1835 and 1836. They tended to play this down in their annual reports as being the work of self-interested or semi-criminal elements in the population.[12] There were, however, several spontaneous riots against the new system, whilst other outbreaks of rural violence, such as the mysterious Courtenay rising in Kent in June 1838, reflected in part a simmering hostility to the New Poor Law.[13] Local philanthropists in these areas, particularly clergymen, were inspired to petition the Poor Law Commission or write letters to *The Times* protesting against alleged cruelties. In Wales the Poor Law Commissioners and their Assistants met with a good deal of hostility from local officials, and the New Poor Law was one, though by no means the sole, cause of the 'Rebecca Riots' of 1839 and 1842.[14] Many London parishes complained bitterly about the authority of the Poor Law Commission, and succeeded in retaining a fair degree of autonomy.

Yet, with the exception of the Rebecca Riots, much of this protest was unorganised. Some protest meetings were held in East Anglia, largely under the influence of the Reverend Frederick Maberley, rector of Great Finborough and a violent critic of the New Poor Law. Rate-payers in several London parishes held meetings of protest against the interference of the Commissioners. Nevertheless, when Earl Stanhope launched a Metropolitan Anti-Poor Law Association in February 1838, it was the example of the South Lancashire Anti-Poor Law Association, founded in November 1837, to which he looked in the hope that other parts of the country would follow the example of Lancashire and the West Riding by founding their own associations, whose protests could be co-ordinated by the London association. One such association was founded at Newcastle, and there was talk of a Midlands association based on Birmingham, and a Western association based on Bristol. Nothing seems to have come of these, and the Metropolitan Association did not fulfil Stanhope's ideal of becoming the centre of a national network of anti-Poor Law associations. The most violent, highly organised opposition to the work of the Poor Law Commission came from the manufacturing towns and villages of Lancashire and the West Riding of Yorkshire.

The reasons for this geographical concentration of resistance are not far to seek. In the first place, ratepayers and local Poor Law adminis-trators in these districts were particularly infuriated by the threat of interference in their affairs by three officials sitting in Somerset House in London. Over the past thirty or forty years many townships had been engaged in the reform of their Poor Law administration. Select vestries, small committees of leading inhabitants, had been established. They met regularly to discuss relief policy and keep a check on the conduct of the overseer. In many places, salaried assistant overseers had also been appointed to help the unpaid, part-time overseer perform the duties of collecting the poor rate and relieving the poor, duties which were becoming more arduous because of the rapid growth of population. Improved administration had brought with it a stricter policy with regard to the distribution of relief. It had also, the local administrators claimed, brought with it a fall in the cost of relieving the poor. This fall in expenditure continued during the economically prosperous years of 1835 and 1836. The overseers of Little Bolton, for example, claimed 'a reduction of twenty per cent effected by themselves and without the interference of the Poor Law Commission'.[15] Indeed, the fact that the Commissioners began their work in southern England after 1834 seemed to imply that they were going to leave the well-administered, low-rated northern parishes alone. Thus many ratepayers, parish officers and magistrates were amazed and annoyed when Assistant Commissioners appeared in their townships late in 1836 and announced that they were to be grouped into Unions. Assistant Commissioner Alfred Power reported to Somerset House that not only was hostility to the New Poor Law general among the operative classes but that adverse feelings were also being entertained by 'a considerable number of respectable and influential persons'.[16] The sentiments of a resolution passed by a ratepayers' meeting at Kirkheaton, near Huddersfield, in August 1838 were shared by many other townships:[17]

It has been determined unanimously by the ratepayers of the above township that we will keep our own poor as we have a good poor house and everything in good order and as we do not understand the New Poor Law we are determined to go on in the old way.

Not only was it felt that there was no need for the Poor Law Commission to interfere in the affairs of these townships, it was also argued, with some degree of truth, that the New Poor Law had been designed to meet a problem of rural, agrarian poverty and was therefore totally unsuited to an urban, industrial situation. No workhouse could possibly accommodate the thousands of able-bodied men thrown out of work by a downward swing of the trade cycle. Unemployed factory employees and underemployed handicraft workers could be relieved more humanely and cheaply with a dole of a few shillings a week. If taken into the workhouse, their homes would be broken up, their tools and other possessions sold, and the whole cost of their maintenance would have to be borne by the rates. When economic prospects improved, it would be difficult for them to find employment. In addition, many overseers and

select vestry members were strongly opposed to mixing honest working
men with idle loafers and vagrants, whether in a workhouse or in some
form of outdoor labour test. Their local knowledge, they claimed, enabled
them to know the deserving from the undeserving poor. Thus they
should be allowed to relieve these different types as they thought fit and
not have their hands tied by regulations drawn up by distant
commissioners in London.

Naturally, the anti-Poor Law agitators played on such feelings to stir
up hostility to the New Poor Law. The Poor Law Commissioners were
portrayed as being desirous of destroying all rights of local self-government. All the Commissioners wanted, a speaker told a Newcastle
meeting, 'was to get their clutches fastened on the North as well as on
the South of the Island in order to satiate their lust of power and patronage'.[18] Another speaker warned a Sheffield audience that the new
boards of guardians would be 'the tools of the Commissioners as the
cutler's hammer was his'.[19] 'The Guardians under this Act dare not
give one spoonful of porridge more to the inmates of a workhouse than
their three great masters choose to order', thundered 'Parson' Bull.[20]
Banners at anti-Poor Law demonstrations were embroidered with such
texts as 'We can manage the affairs of the poor without the aid of
commissioners' and 'We will not be governed by three infernal lick
spittles'.[21]

A considerable section of influential opinion in Lancashire and the
West Riding was hostile to the New Poor Law. Magistrates like W. B.
Ferrand of Bingley or John Fielden of Todmorden played a prominent
part in the activities of the Anti-Poor Law Movement, while others like
Matthew Thompson and J. G. Paley of Bradford were to be seen on
the platform at anti-Poor Law meetings. In the Huddersfield Union the
magistrates refused to help in the difficult task of launching the new
system of administration, while at Halifax several magistrates were said
to have 'no faith in the New Poor Law'.[22] Clergymen such as the
Reverend Thomas Allbutt, vicar of Dewsbury, or the Reverend
Patrick Brontë, rector of Haworth, took the chair at their townships'
anti-Poor Law meetings. Even Whig Liberal magistrates who strongly
disliked the leaders and methods of the Anti-Poor Law Movement,
distrusted the centralising aspects of the new system. William Ellis of
Bingley, Edward Baines, proprietor of the *Leeds Mercury*, and Edmund
Ashworth, the Bolton cotton manufacturer, all expressed the view that
interference by the Poor Law Commission was not welcome in their
area. Whig candidates at the parliamentary elections of 1837 and 1841

were forced to admit that the Act of 1834 had not been intended for the north of England and to promise to work for its modification as far as that part of the country was concerned.

Not only did the Poor Law Commission find strong middle-class opposition to their schemes in Lancashire and the West Riding, they also found the great majority of the working classes united against them. The Poor Law Commissioners had chosen a bad time to move north of the Trent. Edwin Chadwick had urged them to begin operations in the northern manufacturing districts in 1835 and 1836 while economic conditions were favourable and employment high. The Commissioners had ignored the advice of their secretary, whom they were rapidly coming to dislike and distrust. By the time the Assistant Commissioners arrived to form Unions in the northern counties, the trade cycle had turned downwards and the industrial economy was slipping into another depression. Factory workers found their wages reduced by short-time working; handicraft workers saw their earnings fall through a lack of orders. The spectre of unemployment was advancing down the Pennine valleys and with it the prospect of having to apply to the parish for relief. If the New Poor Law Unions were formed, however, their appeal might be not to the parish overseer, whom they knew, but to a board of guardians controlled by inhuman bureaucrats in London. Their cry for relief might go unheard unless they were willing to enter the workhouse, the dreaded New Poor Law 'Bastille', as they christened it. Here they believed that they would be separated from their wives and children, and treated more severely than criminals in gaol.

Anti-Poor Law agitators did nothing to allay their fears on this score. 'Shortly you are to have its influence cast over you', R. J. Richardson, secretary of the South Lancashire Anti-Poor Law Association, warned an audience at Bury, 'then will you feel its baneful effects upon your shoulders, and within your hungry bellies, . . . your wives locked up in bastilles, and your children separated by iron gratings.'[23] Speeches, pamphlets and newspaper articles carried grim stories of the cruelties allegedly practised on paupers in the workhouses of southern England. Some of these were highly coloured in the extreme. Feargus O'Connor's story of a starving workhouse boy who had gnawed his fingers down to the first joint, and 'Parson' Bull's revelation that a young woman had been 'flogged like a soldier' in a workhouse were both shown to be untrue. Nevertheless such tales persisted and culminated, early in 1839, in the allegation that the Poor Law Commission, or someone close to them, had put out a pamphlet, under the pseudonym of 'Marcus', which advocated the painless extinction of babies as a means of keeping population growth in check. A 'People's Edition' of the pamphlet, with the lurid title *A Book of Murder* was put out and widely advertised in anti-Poor Law newspapers. The close connection which existed between the New Poor Law and the fears of overpopulation aroused by the writings of Malthus was enough to give the allegation a faint ring of truth, and the Poor Law Commissioners were hard put to it to deny their authorship.

Not only did the Poor Law Commission find strong opposition to the New Poor Law among all classes of society in the manufacturing districts of Lancashire and the West Riding, they also found that opposition to be well organised. 'Parson' Bull described the northern workers as 'a reading people, and a thinking people', who had been 'taught to take a great interest in all political matters'.[24] Since 1830 many of them had received such education from the Ten Hours Movement, which had spread a network of Short-Time Committees over the factory districts. In 1837 this organisation stood ready to be mobilised against the New Poor Law. The Short-Time Committees of Huddersfield, Halifax, Bradford and Keighley announced a delegate meeting at Bradford in March 1837 to discuss both the Ten Hours Bill and the organisation of a West Riding demonstration against the Poor Law. Membership of the Ten Hours Movement almost automatically implied hostility to the Poor Law, and resistance tended to be strongest in areas where the campaign for factory reform had struck deepest. 'I believe you cannot be aware of the perfect state of organisation into which the district has been put', a correspondent in Huddersfield told the Poor Law Commission in 1837, 'an association is formed having for its avowed object direct opposition to the law. Delegates are appointed and contributions levied for the purpose of paying the wages of itinerant agitators and for securing the return of Guardians pledged to oppose your orders.'[25] In the West Riding the activities of these township committees were co-ordinated by a West Riding Anti-Poor Law Committee whose chairman, William Stocks, a Huddersfield yarn-dealer, was an experienced Ten Hours campaigner. In Lancashire, the South Lancashire Anti-Poor Law Association was founded at Manchester in November 1837 under the leadership of Reginald John Richardson, a Salford stationer, who was later to play a prominent role in the Lancashire Chartist movement. The South Lancashire Association sent out delegates to organise anti-Poor Law committees in the factory towns of Lancashire and Cheshire. By 1838 there were thirty-eight of these in an area bounded by the Ribble in the north and Cheshire in the south, and the Association was said to be spreading its influence into the Potteries.

The chief weapon used by the anti-Poor Law organisation to stir up resistance was the public meeting. Throughout 1837 and 1838 townships held their own protest meetings, often chaired by the local parson or some prominent inhabitant, and addressed both by local speakers and by itinerant orators sent by the South Lancashire Association. Resolutions condemning the New Poor Law were passed and petitions against it drawn up to be forwarded to Parliament for presentation by M.P.s favourable to the cause, such as John Fielden or John Walter. These local meetings culminated in great open-air demonstrations like that organised by the West Riding Committee at Hartshead Moor on Whit Tuesday, 1837. Thousands gathered on the moor to hear violent denunciations of the New Poor Law from the lips of such experienced orators as Richard Oastler, 'Parson' Bull and Joseph Rayner Stephens, the dissident Wesleyan preacher from Ashton-under-Lyne.

To spread its protest to a wider audience, the Anti-Poor Law Movement made considerable use of the printed word. In most northern towns a newspaper could be found which was hostile to the Poor Law, whether its politics were Tory like the *Leeds Intelligencer* or the *Bolton Chronicle*, or Radical like the *Sheffield Iris* or the *Northen Liberator*. Such papers printed extensive reports of anti-Poor Law meetings, editorials and articles condemning the New Poor Law, and letters from such frequent and often long-winded correspondents as Richard Oastler and Samuel Roberts. *The Times* gave national coverage to activities in the north, and the Press support for the campaign was further strengthened by the founding of the *Northern Star* at Leeds in November 1837. In its early issues the *Star*, like its proprietor Feargus O'Connor, was fully involved in the attack on the New Poor Law. To supplement the articles and letters in newspapers, numerous pamphlets were produced by the anti-Poor Law agitators. Perhaps the Movement's leading pamphleteer was the ageing Samuel Roberts, who produced such works as *England's Glory, or the Good Old Poor Laws, Living Tobacco Stoppers or the Luxury of Oppression* and *The Bone Gnawing System*, their titles leaving the reader in no doubt as the nature and style of their contents.

As has been seen, the arguments advanced in the speeches and writings of the Anti-Poor Law Movement appealed to the classes hostile to the new system. Thus the New Poor Law was shown to be an unconstitutional interference with the historic rights of local self-government, as well as being a measure which would degrade and humiliate the working classes. Over these arguments the anti-Poor Law campaign, like most early nineteenth-century pressure groups, spread the gloss of religion. 'Do not affect to lay unction to your consciences by affirming that it is a political subject. It is most decidely a moral and religious one!' Samuel Roberts warned the clergy of Sheffield.[26] The campaign was portrayed as a crusade for the 'divine rights' of the poor against the 'Devil King Law'. Orators and pamphleteers used the most glowing, violent language they could muster, and relied more on Biblical than statistical evidence. 'The Bible containing the will of God – this accursed Act of Parliament embodies the will of Lucifer. It is the Sceptre of Belial establishing its sway in the Land of Bibles!! DAMNATION! ETERNAL DAMNATION to the accursed Fiend!' cried Oastler.[27]

Such violent language called forth an equally violent determination to resist the extension of the new system to the area. The best means of doing this seemed to be to obstruct the new boards of guardians so as to prevent them from carrying out their duties. On some boards this was achieved by securing the election of members opposed to the Poor Law, aided in some cases by local magistrates who were *ex officio* members of the board. At Huddersfield the board refused to proceed to the election of a clerk. At Rochdale the guardians refused to take over administration of relief from the township overseers. Overseers might also be persuaded to hinder the progress of the new Unions by refusing to hand over the poor rates they had collected to the guardians, while some ratepayers refused to pay their poor rates. Outside the board-rooms working men were roused to violence by the harangues of anti-Poor Law orators. At Huddersfield, crowds gathered outside the meeting-place of the guardians, and on one occasion invaded the board-room, led by Oastler, to prevent the transaction of further business. Assistant Commissioner Alfred Power was assaulted at Bradford and Keighley. Guardians who favoured the New Poor Law were rolled in the snow by women at Elland, and some of them had their houses broken into and furniture smashed by a mob at Todmorden. Rioting occurred when the guardians attempted to carry out their duties at Bradford in 1837 and at Dewsbury and Todmorden in 1838, and this was serious enough to warrant the sending of troops and squads of Metropolitan police.

The widespread, organised and at times violent opposition which greeted their attempt to carry the New Poor Law northwards in 1837 alarmed the Poor Law Commission. They had planned to carry out their work in the northern counties in two stages, first forming Unions and getting boards of guardians elected merely for the purpose of carrying out the provisions of the Registration Act of 1836, under which each Poor Law Union was to form a superintendent registrar's district and the guardians were to appoint the registrars of births and deaths. At a later date the guardians would take over the administration of poor relief from the parish overseers. Even the first stage of this plan met with difficulty, particularly at Huddersfield where the guardians refused even to elect a clerk. The second stage brought the riots at Bradford and Dewsbury, and a point-blank refusal from the Rochdale board of guardians.

Given the strong and excitable feelings existing in the area, the Poor Law Commission was hesitant to use even the weak powers of compulsion it possessed. On the advice of the Home Secretary the Huddersfield guardians were allowed to postpone their takeover of poor relief duties for twelve months. Plans for the formation of a Union based on Barnsley were postponed until hostility in the area had abated. The Rochdale guardians maintained their defiance of the central authority until 1845. Even where boards of guardians had assumed control over poor relief, the Poor Law Commission, on the advice of its assistant commissioners, allowed the widest possible discretion in giving relief to the guardians. The orders which were issued from Somerset House to boards of guardians in Lancashire and the West Riding in 1838 merely enjoined the guardians to continue to grant relief as under the Act of 1601. There was no mention of 'less eligibility' or the workhouse test. 'Lord John Russell is a day after the fair', Joseph Rayner Stephens told an audience in 1838, 'WE HAVE NO POOR LAW.'[28]

The Anti-Poor Law Movement had scored an initial, local success, and yet at the height of this success it began to fade away. By the spring of 1839 the *Northern Star* was urging the formation of new committees and the drafting of more petitions. Sheffield's Anti-Poor Law committee was split by a quarrel in 1838. R. J. Richardson abandoned the South Lancashire Association in the same year, and the opposition in Lancashire was severely weakened. There was some revival of meetings and committees in 1841 to oppose the renewal of the Poor Law Commission's powers, and again in 1844, when a further Poor Law Amendment Bill was before Parliament. Individuals like W. B. Ferrand, Samuel Roberts and Richard Oastler continued to attack the New Poor Law with tongue and pen. Yet this activity lacked the breadth, organisation and power of that of 1837 and 1838. It remains to consider why the Anti-Poor Law Movement's life was so short.

One obvious cause for the waning of anti-Poor Law organisations in 1838 was the powerful alternative attraction of the Chartist movement. The Poor Law campaign had reached something of a position of stalemate. While the full rigours of the new system had been excluded from northern manufacturing districts, the hated Act itself remained unrepealed. Despite the shoals of petitions dispatched to Westminster from northern meetings, John Fielden's motion for repeal had been defeated in February 1838 by 309 votes to 17. A select committee of the House of Commons, after examining numerous witnesses, reported that with minor exceptions the new system was working well. In such a position there were obvious attractions in the argument that priority should be given to the agitation for universal suffrage. Once the working classes had the vote, the New Poor Law, like all other bad laws, could be repealed without further ado. Banners and motions advocating universal suffrage began to make their appearance at anti-Poor Law meetings. Such activity opened a split between the conservative and radical elements in the anti-Poor Law campaign. Radical working men were already beginning to chafe under the paternalistic attitudes of some of the campaign's leaders. Sheffield artisans left the town's anti-Poor Law committee in protest against the 'drill sergeant' attitudes of Samuel Roberts. At a meeting in London called to consider the formation of the Metropolitan Anti-Poor Law Association, the Chartist leader, Henry Vincent, attacked the attitude of John Walter, whom he accused of writing down working men in the morning and coming to sympathise with them in the evening. The struggle for the Charter seemed to offer far greater prospects to the independent-minded working man than the more limited campaign against the New Poor Law. Radical newspapers, particularly the *Northen Liberator* and the *Northern Star*, began to give increasing space to the activities of the Chartists to the exclusion of those of the Anti-Poor Law Movement.

Loss of support of Chartism infuriated the anti-Poor Law Tories to whom democracy was as distasteful as bureaucracy. 'Parson' Bull stated that he 'did not choose to be mixed up with persons who appeared to me by the promulgation of certain strong political sentiments to be promoting views unfavourable to the permanency of the constitution of the country and to the general good'.[29] Both Oastler and Dr Matthew Fletcher, a prominent member of the South Lancashire Association, alleged that certain elements in the Chartist movement had been encouraged by the Government to undermine the anti-Poor Law campaign. The alliance between Tories and Radicals on the Poor Law question had always been a somewhat uneasy one. At the 1837 election the Radical *Sheffield Iris* had warned its readers not to be fooled into. voting for Tory candidates because they were hostile to the Poor Law. It reminded them of other issues such as corn laws or church rates on which Tory and Radical opinions were oceans apart.

Undoubtedly the rise of Chartism took much of the sting out of the anti-Poor Law Movement. Yet there is good reason to think that even without this rival attraction, its existence would have been a brief one. To some extent the campaign was destroyed by its own success. By 1838 the poor law was being administered in Lancashire and the West Riding much as it always had been. Working men found that when they or their relatives applied for relief it was usually given in the same way as before. There was no mass incarceration in grim 'Bastilles'. Thus, their immediate anxieties relieved, anti-Poor Law propaganda had less of an impact on them. The middle classes also discovered that their immediate fears were not realised. Central control proved to be far less rigid than they had believed. The parish and its officers still retained considerable freedom of action. Indeed some northern parishes were not even grouped into Unions for another decade or more. The Poor Law Commission had no power to dissolve incorporations of parishes under Gilbert's Act of 1782 without the consent of a majority of the guardians of the incorporation. Thus considerable areas of the country could not be organised into viable New Poor Law Unions.

Even those who did come under the New Poor Law system found that there were subtler, more effective ways of opposing Somerset House than by incendiary speeches and inflammatory pamphlets which might lead to riots and destruction of property. As has been seen, boards of guardians in northern Unions were left with considerable discretionary powers of relief administration. These powers they were determined to maintain, and it was by coaxing and cajoling rather than by legislative fiat that the central authority achieved any degree of conformity to its orders. When it did try to circumscribe these discretionary powers by the Relief Regulation Order of August 1852, it brought down on its head a new movement of protest. This time, however, the protest was organised almost solely by boards or guardians and was successful in getting the order considerably modified. 'The difficulties to be feared from almost any degree of popular excitement are not so great as those to be encountered from an adverse and factious

Board of Guardians', Alfred Power, their assistant commissioner in Lancashire and the West Riding, warned the Poor Law Commissioners in 1839.[30]

Thus, although attacks on the Poor Law were to continue for a century, the Anti-Poor Law Movement was at its height for less than two years. Although protests were heard throughout the country, highly organised protest was largely confined to the industrial areas of Lancashire and the West Riding. Despite these confines, however, the Anti-Poor Law Movement is of interest to the student of early nineteenth-century political movements. The speeches and writings of its leaders contain excellent examples of that strain of semi-prophetical violence in which the platform orator, steeped like his audience in the bloodthirsty imagery of the Old Testament, frequently indulged.[31] This strain was continued in the northern Chartist movement which absorbed the anti-Poor Law campaign. Secondly the anti-Poor Law agitation shows how much early nineteenth-century protest cut directly across party and class lines. Tory and Radical, squire and artisan could unite, if only briefly, in opposition to the Act of 1834. Those who looked back to a golden age in the past and those who looked forward to a brave new world in the future felt their vision to be threatened by the operations of the Poor Law Commission. Finally, the support which the movement obtained reveals very clearly the deep distrust of centralised government which existed in early Victorian England, and which thwarted many of the projects of social reformers like Edwin Chadwick. 'If, Sir, you really do wish to benefit us', wrote Samuel Roberts to Edwin Chadwick, 'only be so good as to desire your employers to request their employers to LET US ALONE.'[32] The cry of 'let us alone' lay at the heart of the attack on the New Poor Law of 1834.

BIBLIOGRAPHICAL NOTE

The best introduction to the history of the Poor Law in this period is to be found in Sidney and Beatrice Webb, *English Local Government: English Poor Law History, part ii: The Last Hundred Years* (p.p. 1929; Cass reprint, 1963) i. The same authors' *English Poor Law Policy* (Longmans, 1910; Cass, 1963) contains a useful breakdown of the Royal Commission's recommendations and the Poor Law Commission's policy with regard to the various categories of pauper.

Mark Blaug, 'The Myth of the Old Poor Law and the Making of the New', *JEH* xxiii (1963) and 'The Poor Law Report Re-examined', ibid., xxiv (1964) are critical of the work of the Royal Commission of 1832–4 and particularly of its attitude to the pre-1834 Poor Law system. The work of some of the early Assistant Commissioners and their difficulties with recalcitrant boards of guardians are described in David Roberts, *Victorian Origins of the Welfare State* (Yale U.P., New Haven, 1960).

A detailed account of the Anti-Poor Law Movement is to be found in J. T. Ward, *The Factory Movement, 1830–1855* (Macmillan, 1962). Dr Ward shows very clearly how the Anti-Poor Law Movement in northern England emerged out of the Ten Hours movement and was in turn swallowed up by Chartism. M. E. Rose, 'The Anti-Poor Law Movement in the North of England', *Northern History*, i (1966) describes the agitation in Lancashire and the West Riding. Rhodes Boyson, 'The New Poor Law in North-East Lancashire, 1834–71', *TLCAS* lxx (1960) shows how Lancashire boards of guardians modified the New Poor Law to suit their own circumstances, regardless of the central authority.

David Roberts, 'How Cruel was the Victorian Poor Law?', *HJ* vi (1963) has pointed out some of the exaggerated statements made by critics of the New Poor Law, although Ursula Henriques, 'How Cruel was the Victorian Poor Law?', ibid., xi (1968) argues that the advocates of the 1834 system were, if not deliberately cruel, frequently insensitive. A collection of anti-Poor Law propaganda is to be found in G. R. Wythen Baxter, *The Book of Bastilles* (Smith & Elder, 1841).

There are good biographies of most of the leading figures in the struggle over the New Poor Law. S. E. Finer, *The Life and Times of Sir Edwin Chadwick* (Methuen, 1952) and R. A. Lewis, *Edwin Chadwick and the Public Health Movement, 1832–1854* (Longmans, 1952) describe Chadwick's influence on the Royal Commission of 1832–4 and his struggle to get his ideas on poor law policy adopted in face of the opposition both of the Poor Law Commissioners and of the opponents of the New Poor Law. Cecil Driver, *Tory Radical: The Life of Richard Oastler* (O.U.P., New York, 1946) gives a brilliant portrait of the leading campaigner in the Anti-Poor Law Movement. J. C. Gill, *The Ten Hours Parson* (S.P.C.K., 1959) describes the part played by 'Parson' Bull in the struggle against the New Poor Law; the same author's *Parson Bull of Byerley* (S.P.C.K., 1963) has little to add on this aspect of Bull's life. D. Read and E. Glasgow, *Feargus O'Connor, Irishman and Chartist* (Arnold, 1961) give an account of O'Connor's brief but important role in the anti-Poor Law campaign. J. R. Stephens's life was written by G. J. Holyoake, *Life of Joseph Rayner Stephens* (Williams & Norgate, 1881), but much useful and interesting information has been added to that contained in the earlier biography by J. T. Ward, 'Revolutionary Tory: The Life of J. R. Stephens', *TLCAS* lxviii (1958). Samuel Roberts and R. J. Richardson have yet to find their biographers, but there is a collection of Roberts's pamphlets on the Poor Law and other subjects in the local pamphlets collection of the Sheffield City Library.

Of the historians of Chartism, Mark Hovell, *The Chartist Movement* (Manchester U.P., 2nd ed., 1925) gives by far the best analysis of the Anti-Poor Law Movement. Asa Briggs (ed.), *Chartist Studies* (Macmillan, 1965) discusses more briefly the influence of the anti-Poor Law agitation on the Chartist movement.

NOTES

1. Quoted in Sir George Nicholls, *A History of the English Poor Law* (1904), iii (by T. Mackay), p. 127.
2. H. L. Beales, *The Making of Social Policy. L. T. Hobhouse Memorial Trust Lecture, 1945* (1946), p. 12.
3. S. and B. Webb, *English Local Government: English Poor Law History*, part ii: *The Last Hundred Years* (1929), i, 116–19, 153–64, 172–6; Nicholls,

op. cit., ii, chs 16, 17; Mackay, op.cit., iii, chs 11, 12. Since Sir George Nicholls was a member of the Poor Law Commission after 1834 and Thomas Mackay was a strong advocate of 'the policy of the Act of 1834', their treatment of the anti-Poor Law agitation was hostile and contemptuous.

4. J. T. Ward, *The Factory Movement, 1830–1855* (1962), chs 7, 8.

5. C. Driver, *Tory Radical: The Life of Richard Oastler* (New York, 1946); J. C. Gill, *The Ten Hours Parson* (1959); G. J. Holyoake, *Life of Joseph Rayner Stephens* (1881); J. T. Ward, 'Revolutionary Tory: The Life of J. R. Stephens', *TLCAS* lxviii (1958).

6. R. G. Gammage, *The History of the Chartist Movement* (1854); E. Dolléans, *Le Chartisme, 1830–1848* (Paris, 1912–13), i, 173.

7. Mark Hovell, *The Chartist Movement* (Manchester, 1925 ed.), p. 79.

8. *Sheffield Iris*, 24 Jan 1837, 21 Sept 1841.

9. Richard Oastler, *Damnation! Eternal Damnation to the Fiend – Begotten, Coarser Food, New Poor Law, A Speech* (1837).

10. *Northern Star*, 24 Feb 1838.

11. *Northern Liberator*, 30 Dec 1837.

12. Poor Law Commission, 2nd Annual Report (1836), appendix B.

13. P. G. Rogers, *Battle in Bossenden Wood* (1961).

14. D. Williams, *The Rebecca Riots: A Study in Agrarian Discontent* (Cardiff, 1955).

15. *Bolton Chronicle*, 10 June 1837.

16. PRO, Assistant Commissioners' Corr., MH 32/63: Alfred Power to Poor Law Commission, 10 May 1837.

17. PRO, MH 32/57: enclosure in Assistant Commissioner Mott's corr., 16 Aug 1838.

18. *Northern Liberator*, 31 Mar 1838.

19. *Sheffield Iris*, 9 May 1837.

20. *Bradford Observer*, 2 Feb 1837.

21. *Sheffield Iris*, 23 May 1837.

22. PRO, MH 12/14974: A. Power to P. L. Commission, 7 Feb 1838.

23. *Northern Star*, 6 Jan 1838.

24. *PP* (1837–8), xviii, q. 6275.

25. PRO, MH 12/15063: George Tinker to P. L. Commission, 8 June 1837.

26. S. Roberts, *A Solemn Appeal to Ministers of the Gospel of Every Denomination on the Subject of the Poor Laws* (n.p., 1837).

27. Oastler, *Damnation*.

28. *Northern Star*, 16 Oct 1838.

29. *PP* (1837–8), xviii, q. 6258.

30. PRO, HO 73/55: A. Power to P. L. Commission, 21 Sept 1839.

31. See G. S. R. Kitson Clark, 'Hunger and Politics in 1842', *JMH* xxv (1953).

32. S. Roberts, *Letter to Edwin Chadwick, Esq., on his Coming to Sheffield* (Sheffield, 1843).

4. Trade Unionism

W. H. FRASER

THE 'sustained intensity of excitement'[1] through which Britain passed in the early 1830s was nowhere more apparent than among trade unions. Sidney and Beatrice Webb in *The History of Trade Unionism* called the years between 1829 and 1842 'the revolutionary period' and few would quarrel with such a description of that time of ferment and self-examination, when trade unions adjusted to the legality they had achieved by the repeal of the Combination Acts in 1824. Where historians have differed is over the stress to be laid on particular aspects of the trade unionism of this period. The Webbs, interested in the development of the institutions of modern unionism, considered that there was little of lasting value in the activities of the 1830s. Socialist historians, on the other hand, have viewed the developments in the context of the history of socialism and the creation of a 'working-class movement'. They find evidence of a growing class-consciousness and an acceptance of many 'socialist' tenets by trade unionists, only crushed by economic distress, Government repression and the apostasy of what one historian has called 'the servile generation'[2] of trade union leaders who came to the fore after 1850. Most of these works exaggerate the homogeneity of the trade unions (and of other working-class movements) of the period.

Recent studies have, however, pointed to the more fruitful approach of examining trade union developments against the background of the complex process of industrialisation.[3] Although Britain had been undergoing rapid industrial expansion since the last quarter of the eighteenth century, in 1830 the process was far from complete. Industrialisation was bringing about a drastic alteration in the structure of industry and of society, but the timing of it varied from area to area; so too did the response to change on the part of the workers.

In 1830 the factory system was not universal. In Lancashire and south-west Scotland technological innovation had forced spinners into factories, but they remained only a minority of cotton workers. There were more cotton handloom weavers than all textile factory operatives put together and their number was only just beginning to decline. Handlooms outnumbered power-looms by five to two. These out-workers were suffering less from the introduction of powered machinery than from an overcrowded labour market. The prosperity of many handloom weavers during the war years had encouraged a steady flow of new workers into the trade. Weaving was the easiest to learn of all trades and the basic skills could be acquired in a matter of weeks. The increase in numbers brought falling earnings. Now power-loom competition aggravated their plight. Women and girls worked the new machines and so the displaced handworker could not move into the power-loom branch.

The workers in factories, although financially better off than the outworkers, had to adjust to the new disciplines of power-driven machines. Masters and foremen imposed, by means of fines, corporal punishment and later piecework payments, a regular day and steady work. High wages, however, attracted new workers and by the end of the 1820s the spinners, too, were beginning to feel the effects of increased numbers and a downward pressure on wages.

Technological change was later in coming to the woollen and worsted industries of Yorkshire, but in 1830 these industries were already in the midst of a transition from hand to power production. Worsted-spinning was predominantly a factory industry before 1830, and in the thirty years following hand-weaving and hand-combing were wiped out. Attempts by handworkers to halt, or any rate slow down, the introduction of new machinery by means of riot and strikes resulted mainly in the speeding up of its adoption by employers.

Traditional handicrafts persisted in all towns. Tailoring, shoemaking, cabinet-making, painting, baking or building remained largely untouched by technical change. In the specialist metal trades of Birmingham and Sheffield workers in brass and fine steel remained centred in small workshops and for another three or four decades continued using hand-tools. But, like the handworkers in the north, the position of the skilled craftsmen was being weakened by the influx of new workers who had served no formal apprenticeship. The repeal in 1813 of the clauses in the Elizabethan Statute of Artificers which had insisted upon a seven years' apprenticeship had opened the way for the entry of unapprenticed and semi-skilled workers into the formerly protected crafts. These new men would work irregular hours at irregular rates. The result was the creation of two levels of trade, 'honourable' and 'dishonourable'. The first consisted of trade society men who had served a full apprenticeship, working usually in small workshops and maintaining the traditional rates and customs of the craft. The second consisted of 'unskilled' men and women, working in large workshops or as outworkers, at low rates and for long hours ignoring any traditional craft restrictions. Pressure of numbers was, therefore, lowering the status, eroding the independence and destroying the craft of the skilled artisan.[4] Some urban craftsmen were being affected by mechanisation: for example, a section of the bookbinders, the beaters, were being replaced by rolling machines. But largely it was the influx of 'dishonourable' or 'illegal' members which most hurt the craftsman's position.

I

Trade unions evolved to deal with specific problems being faced by workers in particular industries. With so many workers feeling the effects of new men working at reduced rates, one of the major tasks undertaken by unions was to try to control entry into a trade. This could be done either by enforcing traditional craft apprenticeship regulations or, as in the case of new trades like mule-spinning, creating an artificial 'apprenticeship' system, restricting entry into the ranks of spinners to those who had passed through various lower stages as a spinner's assistant or piecer. Both of the 'national' conferences of cotton-spinners held on the Isle of Man in 1829 and at Manchester in 1830 stressed the need for control over numbers. Spinners were to be allowed to train only their own families and poor relations of mill-owners. The Glasgow spinners went further and tried to prevent mobility by excluding those who had not started as a piecer in Glasgow.

The unions were limited in the weapons they could apply. Strike action was often ineffective since it provided employers with an opportunity to bring in even more new hands. One method was to pay a weekly wage from union funds to superfluous workers to prevent their taking work at a level under the approved rate and thus bringing down wages. Another method was to frighten off new men or non-society men by violence and intimidation. Cotton-spinners in Scotland resorted to vitriol-throwing and murder, while among artisans the most effective method was the destruction of a man's tools or his handiwork. The outworkers, weavers in Lancashire and Yorkshire and framework-knitters in Nottinghamshire and Leicestershire, however, never managed to establish really effective unions to halt the steady decline in their earnings. There were always too many ready to accept pitifully reduced wages.

Trade unions had also to cope with the relentless advance of machinery. In cotton-spinning, larger machines were coming into use and smaller machines were being 'doubled'. The result was extensive dismissals and harder work. The unions were determined to restrict the introduction of larger machines and to improve the position of the spinner by retaining the piece-rates payable on the old machines. Most of the major cotton strikes between 1824 and 1837 – at Hyde in 1824, Manchester in 1829, Ashton in 1830 and Glasgow in 1837 – were over the conditions governing the introduction of large machines. By 1837 further technical improvements were affecting the spinners' status, with the introduction of the self-acting mule, which required almost no skill to operate. More 'new men' were attracted into the trade. The hand-mule spinners looked down on the self-actor minders and this inhibited union development among the factory operatives for more than two decades after 1830.

Differences in the position of the two main groups of workers – the industrial proletariat and the skilled artisans – can be illustrated by comparing the objectives of two early attempts at combining workers of different trades in a general union in 1818. In Lancashire, the union of largely factory-based workers, 'the Philanthropic Society', was intended to help redress 'the Distressed State and Privations to which the Working Class of Society are reduced, by their avaricious Employers reducing wages to less than sufficient to support nature or purchase the bare necessities . . .'. On the other hand, the union of London artisans, known as 'the Philanthropic Hercules', existed 'for the mutual support of the Labouring Mechanic and the Maintenance of the Independence of their trade against the infringements too generally made upon their just Rights and Rewards, by the hands of Avarice and Oppression'.[5] The industrial worker of the north was striving for subsistence for himself and his family and was organised against the employer. A new type of master was beginning to appear: the second generation man who had never himself worked at the loom – the 'polished dandy who has been taught at great expense, at boarding schools or colleges, that he is not to work for his bread'.[6] The urban craftsman was less concerned with confronting his employer. The distinctions between master and journeyman remained blurred among this section of workers. There was still a great deal of movement up and down between the two levels. The artisan was concerned about maintaining the privileges of his trade, his craft status, his 'independence' and his 'rights'. Both groups, however, used the most effective means of protest available to them – trade union organisation.

II

The roots of most trade unions lay in friendly societies, in the local trade clubs formed to insure through savings against sickness, old age and death. These, in turn, had often arisen from the contacts of convivial drinking or as a remnant of medieval craft solidarity. Early nineteenth-century trade societies retained many of these features. However, industrialisation forced unions to concern themselves with conditions of employment. Loose federations of trade clubs had been formed during the eighteenth century to cater for the artisan 'tramping' from town to town in search of employment.[7] Others were based upon the simple formula that 'unity is strength' and were intended to provide mutual assistance in times of industrial strife and to prevent the importation of blackleg labour from one area to another. In time this practice extended to trade societies in different industries. From at least 1815 there were regular meetings of trades' delegates in London and other cities to provide financial aid to workers on strike or locked out. Attempts at a more permanent organisation in 1818 proved abortive; but, in London, John Gast, a shipwright of Deptford, was particularly active in trying to draw different trade societies together. A committee of trades' delegates, led by him, 'kept up a persistent agitation against any re-enactment of the Combination Laws' during 1824–5 and issued its own newspaper.[8] It was, however, in Lancashire that the most successful attempts took place. There, trade unions had to deal with a small number of employers within a limited area and, therefore, the possibilities of working together were greater.

Between 1825 and 1828 a severe trade depression had crushed the nascent trade unions that had burst on the scene following the repeal of the Combination Acts. When the economic position began to improve, unionism was revitalised. So-called 'national unions', loosely linking local trade clubs, began to appear. In the summer of 1827 the first national union of carpenters was formed, and two years later there was a 'National Society of Bricklayers'. Also in 1829, delegates from the cotton-spinners of Ireland, Scotland and England met at Ramsay in the Isle of Man and formed the Grand General Union of Operative Spinners of the United Kingdom. In the same year the Scottish ironmoulders united in the Scottish Iron Moulders' Friendly Society, and in 1830 the printers of Lancashire established the Northern Typographical Union. Even the miners, cut off in their own communities, often tied by annual contracts to their colliery and employed in an industry that had yet to undergo a major technological revolution, were feeling the pressure of a massively increased demand and were organising to cope with it. In Northumberland and Durham Thomas Hepburn's union won a twelve-hour day and a guaranteed minimum of 1s a day.

The trend appeared to be towards 'national' unions and towards general unions: the former bringing local clubs of one particular trade into a loose union, the latter linking societies of different trades in one union. These attempts were based largely on the need for mutual support to strengthen bargaining positions. Even the Home Secretary, Lord Melbourne, recognised this, when he wrote in October 1831:[9]

> It is coming to be admitted by the workmen themselves . . . that the unions have generally failed. . . . At present their language is an admission that their partial and local unions have failed; that in such circumstances the masters are sure to get the better, and have done so; that they must have a general and national union.

The Lancashire cotton workers led the way.

Attempts following the Isle of Man Conference to create a viable federation of cotton-spinners covering England, Scotland and Ireland were not really successful, and the Grand General Union became little more than a loose federation of Lancashire societies. Feeling strengthened by the Grand Union, the Manchester spinners, in October 1830 initiated an agitation to recover the wage cuts of the preceding years. The method used was the 'strike in detail', by which the union withdrew workers from only one or two mills at a time and supported the strikers by levies on those still at work. The employers of Ashton and Stalybridge responded with a general reduction of wages. A call for a general strike was rejected by the Irish and Scottish spinners at the Manchester Conference and the strikers were gradually forced back to work. This was effectively the end of the Grand General Union, and the Lancashire spinners' societies did not recover from the defeat until the mid-thirties. They turned their attention instead to the ten-hour agitation.

Meanwhile, however, the secretary of the Manchester cotton-spinners, John Doherty, had inaugurated a wider general union, the National Association of United Trades for the Protection of Labour. Doherty saw trade unions as a means of altering the structure of society.

He propagated co-operative schemes in the pages of the various journals he edited, first the *United Trades' Co-operative Journal*, then the *Voice of the People* and later the *Poor Man's Advocate*. But for most of his fellow-spinners the Association merely offered further support for their own position. It was the refusal of the Lancashire spinners to give aid to strikers in the Midlands which ultimately brought about the disintegration of the National Association in 1832.

Other areas followed the example of Lancashire. In Sheffield, for instance, there was a 'Trades General Union' and in Scotland a 'Glasgow and West of Scotland Association for the Protection of Labour'. These grew independently in some cases, but in others, such as in the textile areas of the Midlands and in the Staffordshire potteries, missionaries from Lancashire planted the seed. The missionaries were not always successful in persuading new unions to affiliate to the Manchester body.

Effective unionism among the Yorkshire woollen workers revived during 1830 and 1831, in part because of the short-time movement, but mainly as a result of an attempt to raise wages and regulate the terms on which machinery was introduced. A major strike lasting thirty-three weeks between February and October 1831 broke out among the weavers at Benjamin Gott's mill at Leeds, and this further encouraged the development of unionism in Yorkshire. From the weavers unionism spread to the finishing trades and both groups combined in a 'Leeds Clothiers' Union'. This in turn seems to have become the nucleus of a general union of trades, the 'Leeds Trades' Union', which extended throughout Yorkshire and was reputed to have linked up with a union of workers in the worsted industry.[10]

The National Association and the Leeds Trades' Union were loose federations linking trade societies that largely retained their autonomy. The same was true of some of the 'national' unions that emerged. The Operative Builders' Union, formed at Manchester in 1831, was a federation of existing unions and retained craft divisions between masons, slaters, joiners, painters, plasterers and bricklayers. Its declared purpose was 'to advance and equalise the price of labour in every branch of the trade', but it was particularly opposed to the spread of the contract system, whereby a general contractor came between the buyer and the journeymen. The contractor would take the responsibility for all aspects of building, thus eliminating the man who would work as a master when he could get a contract and restricting the opportunities for a journeyman to move to the rank of master. The complaints of the builders were mainly directed against loss of independence and loss of opportunity, and small masters predominated in the union.

II

In the early 1830s the fundamental concerns of trade unions remained what they had been at least since 1815 – wages and conditions of work. However, inextricably bound up with unionism in these years is the complex and often confused ideology of Owenism, which was an amalgam of numerous ideas and theories that during the 1820s had been built upon the philosophy of Robert Owen. Starting from the position that man's character was entirely shaped by his environment, Owen condemned the competitive system upon which modern industry was based and advocated a society based upon co-operation. Others such as George Mudie, John Minter Morgan, William Thompson and John Francis Bray enlarged upon and propagated his ideas. These in turn linked up with specifically anti-capitalist theories, such as the notion that the entire produce of labour ought to belong to the labourer, put forward especially by Thomas Hodgskin. Although Owen himself believed that the interests of the 'producing classes' were identical, the imprecision of his ideas allowed others to use and adapt them. Owenism covered a wide spectrum of views and was varied in its appeal to different sections of the community.

Attacks on competition appealed to those skilled craftsmen whose position was being undermined by an unrestricted increase in numbers. These same workers were able to think in terms of setting up in business on their own and co-operation could provide the solution to shortage of capital and restore lost independence. Co-operative schemes appealed also to the factory operatives and the outworkers as a means of employing surplus labour. For all sections there was the vague promise of a new society, of the millennium.

The establishment of co-operative communities was central to Owenite teaching, but during the 1820s there developed, in London and many other parts of the country, co-operative trading stores. The profits were intended to finance the establishment of communities, but in fact very few of these stores came near to the Owenite ideal.[11] However, they provided a network of Owenite centres throughout the country and it was through the stores that contact was made with trade unions and Owenite ideas were propagated. John Finch in Liverpool, William Pare in Lancashire and the Midlands, Alexander Campbell in

Glasgow and Lawrence Pitkeithley in York shire were among those who preached co-operation to trade unions. Unionism and co-operative production became intertwined. A scheme for general union drawn up in Glasgow clearly laid down 'that the great and only object of the whole Union should be to give employment to the idle or superfluous hands belonging to the different trades who contributed to the general fund'.[12] Doherty was an Owenite of sorts and urged the adoption of 'that beautiful system' in the pages of the numerous papers he edited.[13] And in London there was a direct link of personnel between the British Association for Promoting Co-operative Knowledge and the Metropolitan Trades' Union.

Before 1832 Robert Owen's own contact with working-class leaders was negligible. He had issued an *Address to the Working Class* in 1819, which sought to dissuade them from class hostility, but had not looked to the working class for support for his schemes. On his return from community-building in the U.S.A., however, Owen found that the co-operators looked to him as their mentor. He was not altogether happy at this. He felt that the trading associations were not sufficiently concerned with the regeneration of society, and declared 'that their mere buying and selling formed no part of his grand "co-operative scheme"'.[14] Schemes for equitable labour exchanges did appeal to him, however, where the middleman was entirely eliminated and producers directly exchanged their goods. The new standard of value was to be the time spent in production and 'labour notes' were issued indicating labour-time. A National Equitable Labour Exchange was opened in London in 1832 with Owen as Governor and the example was followed in other towns, but the scheme never achieved the stability and respectability which would have allowed its ultimate success. During 1834 the exchanges collapsed.

In their short existence the labour exchanges extended the contact between Owenites and trade unions. Some co-operators eyed the funds of trade unions, but generally found the unionists cautious. However, Owen coveted not their money but their numbers, and came to see the unions as a base upon which he might build his new society and through which the millennium might be achieved. During the autumn of 1833 he moved through the Midlands, Yorkshire and Lancashire trying to win over the northern unions and, as R. H. Tawney wrote, 'His reputation, his personality and his prodigious propagandist powers brought thousands to his feet',[15] as he held out the prospect of changing society within a matter of months.

At a meeting of the Grand Lodge of the Operative Builders' Union, 'the Builders' Parliament' as it was called, held in Manchester in September, he won over the Union to a scheme for a Building Guild that would build directly for the public – thus eliminating general contracting. In Staffordshire he succeeded in persuading the Potters' Union to embark on a scheme for co-operative production. He then tried to outbid Oastler and the ten-hour men for the leadership of the Factory Reform Movement by joining with John Fielden in demanding an eight-hour day. Their 'Society for Promoting National Regeneration' secured the support of many Lancashire reformers, including Doherty, inflamed industrial relations in the Lancashire cotton industry and triggered off a strike at Oldham. Oastler's ten-hour campaign suffered from the Society's activities and subsequent collapse.

IV

1833 is the 'annus mirabilis' of nineteenth-century trade unionism. Conditions for expansion – full employment and good harvests – existed and throughout 1833 a steady growth in numbers took place. The Operative Builders' Union reached 40,000 members and the Potters' 8800.[16] New unions continued to appear. For example, the National Union of Cabinetmakers formed at Liverpool in March, spread to Scotland. Even groups of unskilled workers and of women workers were organised. The Friendly Society of Agricultural Labourers was established in October. But generally, the expansion was confined to the skilled trades, to those that already had some form of organisation.

The expansion of unionism naturally brought a hostile reaction from employers. In July the *Leeds Mercury* warned that 'a great struggle between the master manufacturers and the Trades Union in the different branches of the woollen trade is at hand.'[17] But it was among the building trades that the main clash came. Starting in Lancashire, strikes spread to Birmingham. The masters presented the 'document' in which the men were asked to renounce their membership of the Union. The Owenites tried to secure the leadership and, in the state of crisis created by the strikes, were able to do so. Two Owenite architects from Birmingham, Joseph Hansom and Edward Welch, moved to Manchester and were successful in winning over the union leadership there, and thus preparing the ground for Owen's victory at the Builders' Parliament in September.

Owen sought to amalgamate the unions and the exchanges. In October he proposed a 'Grand National Moral Union of the Productive Classes', in which trade unions were to form the base of a 'pyramid of production' and the exchanges were to distribute the co-operatively produced goods.[18] But the unions went for immediate and practical goals. There were strikes in Leeds, Liverpool, Manchester, Sheffield, Huddersfield and Leicester, culminating in a great strike and lock-out at Derby. Between August 1833 and June 1834 the Potters alone spent more than £6000 'in futile strikes'.[19] The Derby 'turn out' became the focus of the struggle. Help flowed into Derby from all over the country. The enthusiasm it engendered stimulated union growth, but at the same time lock-outs by employers spread. The strain on the finances of unions was colossal. Once both employers and the Government had determined upon the issue defeat was only a matter of time.

Many unions were already beginning to succumb to the pressure from hostile employers before the best-known of the general unions, the 'Grand National Consolidated Trades' Union of Great Britian and Ireland' was established in February 1834. It was less the culmination of the general union movement, as so often assumed, than merely the London section. It was firmly based on the London crafts. The initiative came from the London tailors, and although the first meeting included delegates from Birmingham, Wolverhampton, Derby, Worcester and Bradford, the Grand National never included any of the important provincial unions. It remained London-based and London-centred, never providing the national leadership then so badly required. It was not even completely devoted to Owenism. A few of the leaders were trying to convert it to the struggle for moral regeneration, but for the tailors the goals remained strictly practical: to get general rules for their trade; to procure an equalisation of hours and wages; and to restore some of the 'morality of trading' which 'excessive competition' had undermined.[20]

Although Owenite missionaries did communicate with different parts of the country, there was no really effective link-up. There was weakness and divided leadership at the top. The harsh sentences imposed upon the agricultural labourers of Tolpuddle terrified many activists. Employers redoubled their pressure and numbers began to melt away with great rapidity. Owen had already lost interest. With his splendid autocracy, he transformed the Grand National into the amorphous 'British and Foreign Consolidated Association of Industry, Humanity and

Knowledge', which had the imprecision and grandiosity that he loved in his organisations.

To make sense of the events of 1833–4 it it necessary to differentiate between Owen's views, those of some of his followers and those of the unions themselves. Owen needed a structure upon which to build his 'new moral world', and the expanding trade unions presented themselves to him as such a structure. He was willing to use them. His writings indicate that he had almost no insight into the real demands of trade unionists. He dealt exclusively in generalities and this largely accounts for the initial success. However, as trade unions faced suppression through lock-outs and the 'document', he failed to get away from generalities which were not irrelevant to unionists. After two months of a lock-out he could still tell the Derby trade unionists that 'he was quite sure before the end of another week a Union would be formed amongst the masters and men to confer together, and harmony and success would attend their future connexion'.[21] Owen's aim was the unity of 'all the intelligent, well-disposed, and superior minds among all classes of society'.[22] The defeat of the unions meant little to him: he altered the name and moved on.

Some of Owen's followers did try to develop a consistent theory of trade union action, rejecting generalities and addressing the workers in the language of class war. In the early stages they had control of the Owenite newspapers and were able to press their views. According to James Morrison, the editor of the *Pioneer*, the organ first of the Builders' Union and then of the whole movement, 'the question to be decided is shall labour or capital be uppermost' and, with James Elishma Smith, he advised:[23]

> Your present object must be to change *your wages* into a fair *share of the profits* of the productive concern in which they are employed. This is the object of Trades' Unions, if they have any rational object at all. . . . I would banish the word wages from the language, and consign it, with the word slavery to histories and dictionaries.

Owen condemned such a lack of 'the spirit of peace and charity by which alone the regeneration of mankind can be effected',[24] and gradually ousted both Morrison and Smith, after which the Press lost what relevance it had for trade unionists.

But what of the trade unionists? It is impossible to estimate how far they accepted the views of either Owen or the *Pioneer*. Among both trade unionists and co-operators Owen's anti-religious views frequently proved a stumbling block. The Glasgow trades, trying to form a general union in 1830, went out of their way to deny any association with Owen. In the Potteries he was opposed by the strong Methodist element in the region. Among the builders there was a significant group called 'the Exclusives' who wished the builders to retain their craft divisions and rejected the intervention in their proceedings of non-unionists such as Owen. The objectives of most trade unions remained what they had always been, partly defensive, partly militant: fighting for reductions in hours or against deterioration in conditions of work, moving for advances and improvements when times were favourable. Too many looked to the Union '*only* as a great power that will enable them to strike for a temporary advance in wages', complained the Grand Master of the Operative Cordwainers, rather than as the means of 'instituting such measures as shall effectually prevent the ignorant, idle and useless part of society from having that undue control over the fruits of our toil, which . . . they at present possess'.[25] Few unionists were willing to wait for the general strike to overthrow the existing system, as Morrison and Smith desired, or to wait for harmony betweeen employers and men brought about by moral regeneration, as Owen wanted.

Certainly much of the leadership was Owenite, but this should not be exaggerated. Doherty's schemes seemed too ambitious to many cotton-spinners. Hansom and Welsh, in Birmingham, did not take over the the leadership of the builders there until the crisis arose in August. By end of 1833 both had lost touch with the Union. The position of the Owenite potters was always precarious. The statements issued by strik-ing unionists during 1833–4 frequently contained Owenite phraseology, but beneath it there remained the basic demands for equalisation of wages, restoration of wage cuts, shorter hours, the 'morality of trading', the end of general contracting. Co-operative production schemes were adopted almost exclusively as a means of keeping idle workers out of the labour market. Francis Place and William Lovett, who were both involved in the movements of these years, were agreed that the principal object of the unions was 'to obtain a fair standard of wages'.[26]

Estimates of the number of workers involved in the various trade unions of this period vary greatly. J. L. and B. Hammond wrote of 'over a million members attached to the Consolidated', and according to the Webbs it had half a million members within weeks of its formation.[27] Both were exaggerating the extent of consolidation. The researches of Dr Oliver have revealed just how far the Grand National was a London body and suggest that a realistic figure for membership would be well below the 40,000 who took part in the demonstration against the sentences on the 'Tolpuddle Martyrs'. In April 1834 there was a paying membership of just over 16,000, while a little later there was little more than 7000.[28] At any rate fluctuations were so great, and differences between paying membership and attached membership so wide, that any estimate of union membership at one particular time must be impossible.

Owenite involvement in trade unions is not entirely without significance. Unions were persisting with traditional objectives and methods, but the Owenites had generated enthusiasm, they had provided a link between various formerly unconnected sections, and they encouraged a belief that there was an alternative to the existing system. All of these continued. As Professor Briggs has pointed out, the demand for a general union 'was directly related to the story of the emergence of a self-conscious "working class" ',[29] and Doherty, with those who followed him, did succeed in his declared objective, 'to inspire the labouring classes with a due sense of their own importance'.[30]

V

Placed as it is between the two political movements of the parliamentary reform campaign and Chartism, the 'explosion' of trade unionism in 1833–4 lends itself to a 'pendulum' explanation: that the working class adopted political objectives up to 1832 and when the Reform Act of that year proved to be a 'delusive, time serving, spacious and partial measure',[31] turned to industrial action. When that failed they reverted to the political demands of the sixpoints of the Charter. As a generalisation the view has some value, but requires careful qualification. Political action and industrial action were never mutually exclusive and often interconnected. Both methods were intended to achieve an improvement in the conditions of the working class: circumstances caused only the emphasis to change. The foundations of trade union expansion were laid during 1831–2, and during the Chartist years there was plenty of industrial action.

Many trade unions, complete with banners and regalia, took part in the various reform demonstrations of 1831–2, but they in no sense became 'political' bodies. Many working-class leaders did expend a great deal of energy on the campaign for the extension of the franchise. In Glasgow political activities delayed the development of general unions. There was dissension, especially among the London artisans, on how much hope could be placed on political solutions. Owen himself completely rejected political objectives, and it never occurred to him that there could be any way to achieve his goal other than his own. He had, as E. P. Thompson has written, 'a vacant place in his mind where most men have political responses'.[32] In this he was followed by many Owenites, but not by all. Doherty, for example, saw the unions as a means of 'by force' compelling the Government 'to do what was right', and he warned Francis Place 'that the people ought no longer to be shuffled off with a Bill which could do them no good'.[33] In few cases did the bulk of unionists make any conscious choice between methods. They used that which was likely to be most effective at the time.

Similarly, during the Chartist years there were no hard and fast divisions. The Owenite Alexander Campbell found that the members of the Chartist associations regarded themselves as '*political* socialists', and he explained 'that their ultimate object is [to] arrive at our views but they think it necessary first in order to obtain the practicability of our principles first to be put in possession of what they call their political rights . . .'.[34] Certainly many individual trade unionists were active Chartists. The London Working Men's Association emerged from the National Union of the Working Classes, and in Manchester R. J. Richardson, who had been secretary of the Manchester Operative Trades' Union, became secretary of the new Manchester Political Union and a Chartist. At the first monster meeting on Kersal Moor in September 1838 trade unionists were prominent, and this alliance of political and industrial organisations continued. On the other hand, in Sheffield the 'Organised Trades' withdrew their support from the Chartists when the Government moved against the leaders. In Scotland one of the most important Chartist leaders was William Pattison, the general secretary of the Journeymen Steam Engine Makers' Union.

Individual unions, however, rarely discussed politics at their meetings. Any political involvement inevitably caused disharmony. But the Charter provided the focus of a multitude of discontents and, as with the Owenites, Chartists could provide leadership at a time of crisis. They were prominent, for example, during the strikes and riots of 1842 in Lancashire and the Midlands. Unions, however, remained wary of getting involved in politics.

VI

The collapse of all the general unions followed rapidly on the fall of the Grand National. The 'exclusives' came forward to salvage what they could from the wreckage. Among the builders only the stonemasons' organisation survived. The potters, however, fought on for another two years in defence of their union and for improved terms of employment. The Manchester spinners reorganised and those in Scotland remained active. Nor was united action abandoned entirely. The printers' unions, united in the Northern Typographical Union, continued to grow, with 36 branches in 1834 and 44 in 1840. In 1836 the Scottish printers' unions joined in a loose federation, and the following year the Irish did the same. In the summer of 1837 all the skilled trades of Glasgow, except the painters and hand- and power-loom weavers, were on strike. And when the leaders of the Glasgow cotton-spinners' association were sentenced to transportation for conspiracy there was an immediate outcry from all parts of the country and the 'Dorchester committees' of trades' delegates revived to protest.

Even schemes of co-operative production were not abandoned. The Ropemakers of the Port of London, for example, organised a co-operative scheme in 1836, and in 1845 the Oldham Spinners' Union rented land 'in order to give employment to the hands who had been thrown out of work'.[35] These schemes had no communitarian goal, but were intended to provide employment.

Chartism was largely a protest of the London artisans and the distressed handworkers of the North and Midlands. Both groups were threatened – indeed doomed – by the advance of industrialisation. However, the number of those whose position was improving as a result of the new processes was increasing. Among the engineers and the iron-workers there was growth. Unlike the handworkers', their protest was not one of despair, but was becoming sophisticated. Protests against the disruption that industrialisation had brought to a traditional society were passing their peak and, increasingly, the inevitability of the process was being accepted. Workers were using their unions, not to overthrow the existing system, but to make the best of it.

The engineering unions had taken almost no part in the Owenite agitation and between 1833 and 1838 unionism expanded among engineers. New unions were formed and moves were made towards cutting down the number of separate societies. In 1838 the largest engineering unions of Yorkshire and Lancashire combined in the Journeymen Steam Engine and Machine Makers' Friendly Society. The Society then went on to centralise its organisation, and in 1843 appointed a full-time general secretary. The Society's aims were specific and limited – an end to 'systematic overtime' and to piece-work; the restriction of entry into the trade, admitting only those who served a full apprentice-ship. Similar reorganisation took place among the ironmoulders. The first efforts were made to centralise the government and the finances of the union. In all cases it was difficult to achieve effective control from the centre: branches continued to strike without consulting the central body. However, by the early 1840s the trend was obvious.

Change and growth in all unions were, however, limited by economic conditions. The widespread depression in industry between 1836 and 1842, accompanied by severe unemployment, was not conducive to trade union growth. The years after 1842 brought a revival in trade and in union activity. A new federation of Lancashire cotton-spinners was formed in 1842, and here too there were signs of a new spirit of accept-ance of change. The new body incorporated both the mule-spinners and the new minders of self-acting machines. It took some time before the 'aristocratic' mule-spinners were really willing to accept semi-skilled minders as their colleagues, but they gradually adapted to change. Rather than oppose the new machines, the spinners' union set out to ensure that they were controlled by their members.

Several national unions began to appear. A National Association of Printers was formed in 1844 and the potters formed the 'United Branches of the Operative Potters' Society'. Schemes for inter-union co-operation also revived. Early in 1843 a committee of Sheffield trades was formed under John Drury, secretary of the razor-grinders 'in order that such measures may be resorted to as shall tend to place us artisans in a better condition'. In the following year this committee summoned a national conference out of which arose a new 'National Association of United Trades for the Protection of Labour', established in 1845. In its aims and activities it reflected its origins in the largely unmechanised trades of Sheffield, with its small workshops and blurred dividing lines between master and journeyman. The solutions offered were the old ones of co-operative production and, the favourite Sheffield one, alliance between masters and men.

The National Association of United Trades looked back to the thirties and forward to the fifties. It was intended to bring about a 'general confederation or union of trades', but to achieve only 'a fair day's wage for a fair day's work', rather than a fundamental alteration in society. Aggressive industrial action was abandoned and the Association was 'to settle by arbitration and mediation all disputes arising between members and between members and their employers', through local courts of conciliation and arbitration. Co-operative production schemes were to be established 'to employ members . . . thrown out of employment in consequence of resisting reduction of wages, or other acts injurious to their interests'.[36] It appealed to the small handicraftsmen of the Midlands and Sheffield. The large and important unions took no part in it. Its energy and finances were used in legal actions, and its effective life was only two or three years, though it had a shadow existence for another twenty years.

Another section of workers among whom unionism revived was the miners. County unions appeared at the end of the 1830s in Northumberland, Durham, Lancashire and Yorkshire. In 1842[37] these united in a federation, the Miners' Association of Great Britain and Ireland, under the leadership of Martin Jude. Missionaries were sent to every coalfield in the country to organise the miners, and by 1844 a membership of 100,000 was claimed. The Association attacked many of the miners' grievances – over wages, hours, truck, methods of weighing coal, working conditions in the mines and the hiring system.[38] An effort was made to achieve some uniformity of wages throughout the country. Its best-known action was the appointment of W. P. Roberts, a Chartist solicitor, as 'the miners' advocate', to defend miners in the numerous prosecutions under the Master and Servant Acts and to ensure that what little protective mining legislation there was in existence was obeyed. While some minor concessions were granted, the strike activity of the Association was, on the whole, a failure. The defeat of the Northumberland and Durham men in their four-month strike of 1844 weakened the Association, and the depression in the coal trade in 1847–8 finally brought about its complete collapse.

The process of consolidation and centralisation continued among the engineering trades and, thanks largely to William Newton in London and William Allan in Lancashire, the bulk of the engineering unions were brought together in 1851 in the 'Amalgamated Society of Engineers, Machinists, Smiths, Millwrights and Pottermakers', with 11,000 members. There was centralisation of administration and of finances; regular weekly payments of 1s were levied on members and in return extensive benefits were paid during sickness or unemployment.

The question of whether or not the A.S.E. was a 'new model', as suggested by the Webbs, is outside the scope of this paper. But it is important to see the development of 1851 as the culmination of a process that had been going on at least from the 1820s. The aim of unions was to strengthen their bargaining power *vis-à-vis* the employers: hence the trend towards national unions, federations and general unions. The weakness of federations and general unions having been experienced during the preceding twenty years, the engineers were establishing a stable and effective national union.

The restriction of entry was not new. Other highly skilled trades which wished to protect their skill and retain their scarcity value had adopted the same methods. The compositors, for example, had high entry fees, strict apprenticeship and little militancy. What was new about the A.S.E. was its extent, its stability and its success. There was no sudden conversion of trade union leaders to the views of the classical economists on supply and demand, as is commonly asserted. They had always been conscious of the pressure of numbers. With the example of the handloom weavers after 1815 before them, no trade was going to allow an unrestricted inflow of new members if it could be prevented. If violence was rejected then the alternative was strong unionism, covering almost all the workers and recognised by the employers. The high benefits of the A.S.E. were principally intended to attract and to hold members.

By 1850 the British economy had passed from the stage of 'take-off' to the stage of 'maturity', to use Professor Rostow's terms. British trade unionism had gone through the same process. Between 1824 and 1850 there was turmoil and transition and an attempt by the workers to respond effectively to industrialisation. Some, such as the handloom weavers, could do nothing but protest and make futile efforts to halt or at least slow the process. But increasingly large sections were feeling the advantages of industrialisation, and their problem was a different one. They wished not to halt the process, but to get maximum advantage from it. They strove to ensure that their members retained control of the new machines and techniques.

This paper has dealt with the organisations of skilled and semi-skilled workers. The huge mass of unskilled labour was largely unaffected by unionism. Some organisation among the agricultural labourers was short-lived. The general labourers, the street-cleaners, the coal-porters, the carters and a host of others remained unorganised. It was the skilled craftsmen and a few groups of semi-skilled, such as spinners, who adapted the exclusive techniques of the craft societies, who were able to build up effective unions and strong bargaining positions between 1830 and 1850. It was this 'labour aristocracy' that was to dominate the trade unionism of the rest of the century.

BIBLIOGRAPHICAL NOTE

The best short introduction to the period is H. Pelling, *A History of British Trade Unionism* (Macmillan, Penguin, 1963), which contains a full bibliography. S. and B. Webb, *The History of Trade Unionism* (Longmans 1894, 1920, 1950; Frank Cass, 1968) remains indispensable. For a detailed study of general unionism and of Owenite influences, G. D. H. Cole's *Attempts at General Union* (Macmillan, 1953) should be used in conjunction with the work of W. H. Oliver, 'Robert Owen and the English Working Class Movement', *HT* viii (1958) and 'The Consolidated Trades Union of 1834', *EcHR* 2nd ser., xviii (1964). The best examination of Operative Builders' Union is in R. Postgate, *The Builders' History* (National Federation of Building Trade Operatives, 1923). Studies of the organisation of individual trades vary greatly in value, but the most useful are J. B. Jefferys, *Story of the Engineers* (Amalgamated Engineering Union, 1946), H. J. Fyrth and H. Collins, *The Foundry Workers* (Amalgamated Union of Foundry Workers, Manchester, 1959) and W. H. Warburton, *History of Trade Union Organisation in the North Staffordshire Potteries* (Allen & Unwin, 1931). H. A. Turner, *Trade Union Growth, Structure & Policy* (Allen & Unwin, 1962) is an important study of the cotton unions and contains illuminating comparisons with other unions. On mining unionism there is A. J. Taylor, 'The Miners Association of Great Britain and Ireland', *Economica,* xxii (1955).

Changes in unionism must, however, be seen against the background of changes in society and industry. Only E. P. Thompson's *Making of the English Working Class* (Gollancz, 1965; Penguin, 1968) tackles this successfully and it ends in the early 1830s. But N. J. Smelser's *Social Change in the Industrial Revolution* (Routledge, 1959) deals with the Lancashire cotton unions. A number of the chapters in E. J. Hobsbawm, *Labouring Men* (Weidenfeld & Nicolson, 1964) contain brilliant insights into trade union development.

Two volumes of documents cover this period and repay study: Max Morris, *From Cobbett to the Chartists* (Lawrence & Wishart, 1948) and G. D. H. Cole and A. W. Filson, *British Working Class Movements: Select Documents, 1789–1875* (Macmillan 1951, 1965).

There are few studies of local unionism, but S. Pollard's *History of Labour in Sheffield* (Liverpool U.P., 1959) is of value, though Sheffield is hardly representative. For Scotland there is W. H. Marwick, *A Short History of Labour in Scotland* (Chambers, Edinburgh, 1967).

NOTES

1. G. M. Young, *Portrait of an Age* (1960 ed.), p. 27.
2. R. Postgate, *The Builders' History* (1923), p. 181.
3. E. P. Thompson, *The Making of the English Working Class* (1965), esp. part ii; E. J. Hobsbawm, *The Age of Revolution* (1962), ch. 11.
4. The best description and analysis of the artisan's position is in Thompson, op. cit., ch. 8.
5. The rules of the two bodies are printed as appendices in G. D. H. Cole, *Attempts at General Union* (1953), pp. 161–71.
6. *Poor Man's Advocate,* 18 Feb 1832.
7. For the changing position of the 'tramp', see E. J. Hobsbawm, *Labouring Men* (1964), ch. 4.
8. S. and B. Webb, *The History of Trade Unionism* (1920 ed.), p. 115.
9. Quoted in H. L. Beales, *The Early English Socialists* (1933), p. 28.

10. [E. C. Tufnell], *Character, Objects and Effects of Trades' Unions, with some remarks on the Law concerning them* (1834), pp. 49 ff.

11. S. Pollard, 'Nineteenth Century Cooperation: From Community Building to Shopkeeping', in *Essays in Labour History*, ed. A. Briggs and J. Saville (1967), pp. 74–112; A. E. Musson, 'The Ideology of Early Cooperation in Lancashire and Cheshire', *TLCAS* lxviii (1958).

12. *Herald to the Trades Advocate*, 30 Oct 1830.

13. Musson, loc. cit.

14. W. Lovett, *Life and Struggle of William Lovett* (1967 reprint), p. 35.

15. R. H. Tawney, *The Radical Tradition*, ed. R. Hinden (1964), p. 39.

16. R. Postgate, *The Builders' History* (1923), p. 58; W. H. Warburton, *The History of Trade Union Organisation in the North Staffordshire Potteries* (1931), p. 65.

17. Quoted in Cole, op. cit., p. 85.

18. W. H. Oliver, 'Robert Owen and the English Working Class Movement', *HT* viii (1958).

19. N. R. Wood to R. Owen 14 June 1834 (Owen Coll., Holyoake House, Manchester, 703).

20. *Pioneer*, 3 May 1834.

21. *Crisis*, 18 Jan 1834.

22. Ibid., 29 Mar 1834.

23. *Pioneer*, 14 June 1834.

24. *Crisis*, 11 Jan 1834.

25. *Pioneer*, 28 June 1834.

26. Webbs, op. cit., p. 157; Lovett, op. cit., p. 71.

27. J. L. and B. Hammond, *The Bleak Age* (1947), p. 173; Webbs, op. cit., p. 135.

28. W. H. Oliver, 'The Consolidated Trades Union of 1834', *EcHR* 2nd ser., xvii (1964), 85–6.

29. Asa Briggs, 'The Language of "Class" in Early Nineteenth Century England', in Briggs and Saville, op. cit., p. 47.

30. *The United Trades' Cooperative Journal*, 6 Mar 1830.

31. Quoted in A. Briggs, *Age of Improvement* (1960), p. 286.

32. Thompson, op. cit., p. 738.

33. G. Wallas, *The Life of Francis Place* (1925), pp. 265–6.

34. A. Campbell to R. Owen, 26 Mar 1838 (Owen Coll, 1005).

35. S. J. Chapman, *The Lancashire Cotton Industry* (Manchester, 1904), p. 226.

36. Evidence of Thomas Winters to the Select Committee on Masters and Operatives (Equitable Councils of Conciliation), *PP* (1856), xiii, 1.

37. Webbs, op. cit., p. 181, wrongly give the date as 1841.

38. Under the hiring system the miners would contract for a long period, usually a year, and be compelled to work if required, but employment was not guaranteed. See R. Challinor and B. Ripley, *The Miners' Association: A Trade Union in the Age of the Chartists* (1968).

5. Chartism

ALEX WILSON

CHARTISM was the campaign for democratic rights which swept across most parts of Britain in 1838 and 1839, developing considerable strength. The Chartists maintained an impressive agitation until 1842 and succeeded in generating a loyalty among the working classes which held out the promise of eventual revival during the next decade, even while the remnants of Chartist organisation were withering away. It was an epoch-making stage in British political radicalism during which the working-class radicals took over the reins of leadership from the middle-class reformers and radicals and conducted a movement which left an indelible impression on both the governing and governed, raising the question of the condition of the people as the most important of public matters.

The basic aims of the Chartists had a strong moral philosophical and practical appeal. What they stood for were the rights of man and the regeneration of British society. They saw themselves following variously in the footsteps of William Tell, George Washington, Jean-Paul Marat and Thomas Paine in the pursuit of a freer and more equal society, in terms of legal, political and social rights. They would bring about the social and economic regeneration of an increasingly sick society by political action to secure benevolent legislation and administration, and by educational provision, voluntary action and self-help.

Their major demand was for parliamentary reform, which was based on the familiar radical demands of universal suffrage, annual parliaments and vote by ballot, plus the less frequently voiced demands for equal electoral districts, payment for M.P.s and the abolition of property qualifications for successful candidates. Coupled to this major demand for six points of 'The People's Charter' went a mixture of minor demands, which varied from area to area. These most often included taxation reform, amelioration of the New Poor Law system and, in the early days, repeal of the Corn Laws. Chartists also felt strongly about factory legislation and the Ten Hours Bill, about the persistence of truck, about temperance, education, disestablishment of the State Church and municipal and borough reform.

The achievement of these demands was seen to depend on a judicious combination of activities. There could be reasoned pressure on M.P.s through petitions, inquiries, submissions and invitations to public meetings. Outside Parliament there would be political action, largely on the basis of political unions agitating in the major towns and organising lecturing missions into the surrounding areas, with leadership drawn from respected middle-class radicals, journalists from radical publications, delegates of trade unions and other working men's organisations. In addition there would have to be large demonstrations and processions, indicative of the support for and latent physical strength of the movement. A significant minority of Chartists believed it necessary to overawe the Government and middle-classes, and that merely a token show of force would not suffice to put an end to intolerable oppression.

I

The rank and file of the movement was drawn almost entirely from the working classes, with its complexion varying considerably from one area to another, affected by the industrial pattern prevailing and by the underlying social and political traditions. The national and local leadership, however, was seldom concentrated in the hands of working-class men and included landowners, magistrates, doctors, parsons, merchants, small manufacturers, shopkeepers, school-teachers, editors, publishers and poets in addition to the numerous shoemakers, tailors, printers and trade union officials.

The most important of their activities were bound up with the establishment and maintenance of Chartist newspapers and local organisations, each of which depended heavily on the other and on steady financial support for effectiveness and survival. In addition to the *Northern Star*, which provided a remarkable national service throughout the Chartist period, a large number of local and regional newspapers and circulars were launched. These had often to meet the thinly disguised hostility as well as the mighty competition of the *Northern Star*. Many were short-lived, but several lasted for a number of years. The local associations often conducted an incredible number of committee and plenary meetings. Many sent delegates to city or large-town societies. Some formed female universal suffrage associations. Most rented halls, but a few purchased or even built their own premises. Numerous socials and soirées were held, as well as public meetings on their favourite themes and topical issues. Chartist premises were sometimes used during the week as schoolrooms for children and evening schools for adults and on Sundays as halls of worship for all, with the services conducted by the Chartist teacher/preacher.

Especially in Scotland, associations formed Christian Chartist congregations, while numerous Chartist temperance societies were formed throughout the country. In most localities there was a Chartist newsagent (and correspondent), and some of the local leaders opened temperance coffee-houses where committee meetings could take place rather than in pubs. A few of them went a stage further and ran boarding-houses which were especially useful to the itinerant lecturers and delegates. Arising out of 'exclusive dealing' measures designed to influence or punish unsympathetic shopkeepers, a considerable number of Chartist retail co-operative societies were founded. And in the latter years of the movement the outstanding Chartist plan was Feargus O'Connor's Co-operative Land Plan (and lottery). This attracted widespread support and hundreds of branches were formed to publicise the scheme and encourage Chartists to invest their savings in the shares.

In most of the cities and large towns of the kingdom there took place mammoth demonstrations and processions, which were modelled on those of 1831–2 and drew in the Chartist faithful from miles around. From the larger towns missions were sent out into the neighbouring villages and mining districts, and a number of county organisations were established to support regional agitation. Major conferences or con-ventions were held in London in 1839, 1842, 1845, 1848 and 1851; in Birmingham in 1839 and 1842; in Manchester in 1840, 1842 and 1845; in Leeds in 1841; and in Glasgow in 1839, 1840 and 1842.

National organisation was set up in Scotland under the Universal Suffrage Central Committee for Scotland in August 1839, and for England and Wales under the National Charter Association in July 1840 (with considerable support forthcoming from Scottish branches after 1842). Funds were raised for national and local purposes in the form of both regular subscriptions and contributions to appeals, and the contribution lists were carefully vetted. Chartist leaders, sometimes free-lance, sometimes under the auspices of the N.C.A. or the Land Company, perambulated the country, but seldom travelled in comfort, shivering on top of stagecoaches or in open third-class railway trucks.

In many parts of Britain there was open talk of armed rebellion, and in a few places there was serious plotting of revolution, coupled with the accumulation of pikes and muskets. There was a curious conspiracy to co-ordinate a series of simultaneous risings in the North, the West

Riding and South Wales, which broke down because of the problem of effecting reliable communication and because of belated realism or cold feet on the part of some of the leaders. The outcome was the armed rising or demonstration at Newport in November 1839, and a series of risings at Sheffield, Bradford and Dewsbury, in consequence of which hundreds of Chartists were to suffer imprisonment or transportation. A similar fate was shared by many of their colleagues after the industrial troubles in the Midlands, Lancashire, Yorkshire, Lanarkshire and Forfarshire in 1842, and again after the feverish alarms induced by continental revolutions and Irish unrest in 1848.

The basic beliefs of the Chartists were deceptively simple. The main one was that the vote was a fundamental human right, which should be shared by all men, and probably also by women. The next was that working-class misery arose from the landed and employing classes taking too much of the produce of labour, aided and abetted by class legislation. A third was that control of legislation was necessary for social justice to the working classes. From there on there were deep divisions which tended to get deeper for almost a decade.

The main division might be described as the credibility gulf which lay between the pessimistic school and the optimistic school over the possibility of worthwhile alliance between the middle and working classes. One school, led by Bronterre O'Brien and Julian Harney, were clear in their minds that such partnership was illusory, except perhaps for increasing the power of the middle classes. This merely spelled growing misery for the wage slaves. The employing classes wanted the New Poor Law, not so much to keep down Poor Rates as to drive down wages. Likewise, the resistance of the employing classes to the Ten Hours Bill was dictated by their refusal to spread work. And the employing classes wanted Corn Law Repeal, not to improve living standards but to enable them to push wages down still further. There was an irreconcilable conflict of interest between the middle and working classes. To this school belonged a relatively small proportion of the leaders of the movement, but a very substantial proportion of the rank and file.

William Lovett, John Collins and a multitude of the second-rank leaders belonged to the main stream of radical reform, with a faith in education, reason, enlightenment and persuasion as the basic tools of politics. They tended to be optimistic both about industrial development, in which they saw a common interest of masters and men in full employment and adequate credit provision, and about the feasibility of effective partnership between reformers of the middle and working classes to remove the lingering power of the aristocracy and Tories. Economic well-being, in their eyes, was being thwarted by the class legislation of the landed interests and the millocrats. They were concerned with the Corn Laws, taxes on necessities, excesses in Government spending, defence and corruption. Many were more disturbed by Government interference with the freedom of Press, religion and trade unions than by the New Poor Law.

Around this basic divergence of sincerely held beliefs revolved the two great issues which were to dog the progress of the movement. One was the question of how much show of potential physical power could be paraded before the authorities and Parliament without frightening away middle-class sympathisers in the country and Radical allies within Parliament. The other issue was whether the leader, or leaders, should be men whose reputation would be respected outside the ranks of the Chartists. On both these issues, the national leaders were never able to find stable agreement, while the local leaders were often pushed into actions and positions which both divided them and made wider alliance less possible. A serious complication in all this was that the problems of decision-making were aggravated by the still primitive systems of communication available to them, before the railway and electric telegraph networks were developed to any great extent, and by their frequent resort to double-talk, in case spies were present or their correspondence might be opened.

Especially for the few who were bent on violent revolution, the problem of communications proved a hopeless stumbling block, leading most of them to distrust each other. The only Chartist who effectively overcame this problem was Feargus O'Connor, who quietly exploited the opportunities which the mass circulation of his newspaper, the *Northern Star*, offered him to guide local decisions throughout Britain into the same mould. Through his nation-wide chain of agents, correspondents and spies, O'Connor was able to keep his finger on the pulse of each 'locality' of the movement, and perhaps even more than his personal charm, confidence, affability and oratorical ability, this was the key to his success in taking over the movement and his power to control its destiny between 1840 and 1850.

II

From R. G. Gammage in 1854 onwards, most of the historians of

Chartism who have based their analyses on original source material have recognised that the movement was a national federation of regions, each of which was focused on one or two large towns, and each of which played a somewhat distinctive role, largely determined by their political history and socio-economic background. In some regions support for the political platform of the Charter was the result of a deliberate and opportunist decision to pursue a stage further the familiar demands of the radical reformers. In other areas support for the Charter was much more the expression of working-class distress and desperation.

Nevertheless, some studies of the movement have created the impression that what happened in Chartist conventions determined the course of the movement, or that only what took place in London was really important, or that the Chartist agitation was the inevitable outcome of appalling economic distress and that its disappearance was equally inevitable once economic depression had receded. And somehow that extraordinary tag is often attached to 1848 – 'The Year of Chartism'.

The general tendency to emphasise, quite justifiably, the distinctiveness of Chartism from preceding radical movements has resulted in an excessive writing-down of the old force of political radicalism. Few have gone as far as Élie Halévy in asserting that Chartism was not a creed but the 'blind revolt of hunger'; but most students of Chartism have been somewhat bemused by the connection between trade depression and political excitement.[1] P. W. Slosson, for instance, argues that it 'was not so much that the exceptional prosperity of these years [after 1842] weakened the Chartist movement as that the exceptional misery of the preceding period had created the movement and was alone able to maintain it'.[2] The connection was neither as simple nor as mechanistic as this. But for such political events as the decision to make haste with the building of Poor Law 'bastilles' in the North, or the trial of the Glasgow cotton-spinners, or the willingness of the Birmingham Political Union and the London Working Men's Association to move in alliance, the agitation for the 'People's Charter' might have remained a small-scale, localised affair. Moreover, distress and unemployment could not merely provide political agitations with the strength of mass discontent, but they could also sap the strength of existing organisations, leaving movements disorganised and demoralised over dues and debts. This happened to many trade unions and co-operative societies of the period, and it largely destroyed the Scottish Chartist organisation in 1842.

Several of the most valuable studies of Chartism, such as those of

P. W. Slosson, F. F. Rosenblatt, Édouard Dolléans and G. D. H. Cole, have tended to give too much weight to new forces, such as the hostility to the New Poor Law, most of which operated over limited areas of the country, and some of which affected only small sections of the population.[3] Apart from the anti-Poor Law agitation, moreover, the importance to Chartism of such movements as Owenism, Trades Unionism or even Factory Reform lay not so much in providing masses of devoted supporters to the cause as in supplying it with an adequate number of capable working-class leaders. In some parts of the country the anti-Poor Law agitation was still a dead letter, while the strongest-held grievance was antagonism to the Corn Laws. Historians of Chartism have too readily assumed that the radicals who became Chartists did not play their part in the petitions and agitation against the Corn Laws before the formation of the Anti-Corn Law League.

The idea that 1839 or 1842 might well have seen the achievement of the British class war revolution and the overthrow of the bourgeoisie has stirred the imagination of a few writers who have fondly imagined far greater readiness for revolutionary action than even panicky magistrates were able to uncover. T. Rothstein laments the decision of the Convention in May 1839 to move to 'middle-class Birmingham', instead of 'Manchester, Leeds or Glasgow, where a revolutionary proletariat was alive and acting'.[4] That the proletariat of Glasgow or Leeds was more warlike than that of Birmingham would have been strongly contested by such a Chartist authority on revolution as Dr John Taylor, who declared that a better and safer centre for revolutionary purposes was not to be found than at Birmingham.[5]

Further evidence of revolutionary readiness is often adduced from the disturbances in 1842, caused by the nocturnal marauding activities on potato fields of Lanarkshire miners, and by strikers and unemployed industrial workers and miners in the Midlands, Lancashire and Yorkshire. Yet none of these took place by Chartist design, and readiness for violent action was more observable from the special constables and militia than from the largely leaderless bands of unemployed workers, engaged in the comparatively peaceful and undestructive actions of pulling potatoes and boiler-plugs.

Similarly it seems that some historians have been wonderfully excited by the alarmist accounts which appeared in the *Northern Star* and other London newspapers, in March 1848, of the 'Bread Riots' in Glasgow. These are taken to have a deep Chartist significance by Reg Groves, who quotes a long and lurid account of cavalry charges on mass gatherings on Glasgow Green and of all-night fighting and barricades, in order to prove that the Glasgow Chartists were ready to apply physical force.[6] Perhaps it should be added that the Glasgow Chartists were astonished by the London reports, and that the Glasgow newspapers painted quite a different picture.

Neither Rothstein, who is capable of finding that the minds of Lovett, Collins and Vincent had become 'unhinged' after their release from prison because they concentrated their energies on education, religion and temperance, nor Groves, with his remarkable emphasis on the power of the masses, their readiness for revolutionary action and their freedom from 'pedantic, self-righteous reformist activities and policies', seems to have understood the many-sided nature of the movement. In few areas was it true that the Chartist movement was 'a passionate readiness for revolutionary struggle'. Nor were the trade unions 'revolutionary in temper'. Nor did labour regard itself as being engaged in Chartism 'in a bitter and bloody fight for class power'. The demands of the Charter were not seen as the 'expression of the workers' will to political power as a class'. Neither is it possible to say with much justification that the Radicals were 'despised and hated', nor that 'from 1842 onwards the Chartist rank and file had opposed and fought the Radicals on every political issue'.[7]

Despite the somewhat slight treatment of Chartism in his *English Radicalism*, S. Maccoby succeeds in providing a well-balanced perspective to the movement. This is especially important in relation to the big cities, Glasgow, Birmingham, Manchester and Leeds, where political radicalism was strong before the days of Chartism, and where many of the Chartists saw themselves continuing the old radical tradition, with little intention of isolating themselves from the current events in municipal and national politics. By setting the movement against the background of contemporary Liberal opinion, Maccoby helps to explain the readiness of many Chartists to accept the leadership of Joseph Hume, or Joseph Sturge, or the parliamentary Radicals, and also the incapability of the parliamentary Radicals to provide such leadership.[8]

Because of this lingering strength of the older political traditions in several centres of Chartism, numerous conclusions which have been applied to the movement in general have only limited validity. The heterogeneous nature of Chartism was being only slightly exaggerated by John Duncan of Dundee when he wrote, during a controversy with Dr Peter Murray McDouall, that within their ranks they numbered

'Repealers and anti-Repealers, anti-Poor Law men and Malthusians, O'Connorites, O'Brienites, Cobbettites, Churchmen, Dissenters or no-Church-at-all-men, and others . . . differing in their views of political economy, morals and religion, wide as the poles asunder'. It was no exaggeration, however, to suggest that the strength of the Scottish movement had lain in the tolerance allowed to its members on most questions apart from the fundamental principles of the Charter on constitutional reform.[9]

Within this union of men of widely varying philosophies it also becomes dangerous to assert the existence of broad underlying ideological doctrines. The temptation to find more than a rudimentary socialist basis in Chartism has led several authors to draw untenable conclusions. Julius West, for instance, draws the distinction between the Free Traders and the Chartists that the 'Free Traders were conscious and deliberating adherents to the individualistic theory of *laissez-faire*. The Chartists, permeated with Socialist ideas, were virtually committed to the opposing theory of State interference.' Yet in some parts of the country the majority of the Chartists had been Free Traders, and many of them remained so. Few of them were ever socialists in the Owenite sense of the term, and even fewer were socialists in any Marxist, or even Fourier or Saint-Simonian sense. The 'Socialists' (i.e. Owenites) were generally regarded by the Chartists as sympathetic, but comparatively unimportant and often isolationist. Some Chartists were indignant at being occasionally labelled 'Socialists and Infidels'.[10]

H. U. Faulkner and Julius West are among the few historians to place emphasis on the fact that 'Chartism ought not to be considered entirely as a political movement' in view of the 'many elements which looked to the moral regeneration of the working classes'. To a very large extent Faulkner succeeds in giving proper expression to the moral fervour of the Chartists in Temperance Chartism and in the Christian Chartist Church movement.[11] West also notes the 'dominant influence' which some of these 'new projects', including Chartist co-operation, exercised over the movement, though he tends to credit too many of these projects as being the 'new idea' of Vincent, Collins and other leaders, even when they had already been practised for some time in various parts of the country before being popularised by Vincent, Collins and company.[12]

Perhaps more serious than enthusiastic attempts to read too much into the Chartist movement are the numerous half-truths and misleading sweeping statements perpetrated by Mark Hovell in his usually perceptive and valuable trail-blazing history of the movement. Hovell's starting-point – the assumption of the low calibre of the working-class leaders – is particularly ill-judged, and in most areas does not stand up to close examination. 'It is clear', writes Hovell, 'that the more prosperous intelligent organised workers kept aloof from it.' This point was also clear to Beatrice and Sidney Webb, but such a sweeping and unqualified statement is false in its implication, for the movement drew much of its remarkably capable local leadership from exactly this source. On this point, Max Beer arrived at a conclusion more in accordance with the position in many parts of the country than Hovell's analysis: 'The adherents of Chartism belonged, as a rule, to the better paid and mentally active sections of the working class.... [Chartism was] not a movement of the lowest strata of society, but of the best elements of the industrial population.'[13]

Hovell notes that Scotland was the seat of Christian Chartism. But he proves to be less perceptive than Feargus O'Connor was, when he concludes that 'it was but a protest' against oppression, which died away without seeming to have 'struck a deep root'. Fairly representative Scottish conferences meeting at Edinburgh to pledge the adherence of the Scottish Chartists 'only to peaceable and constitutional methods' are fated to be styled meetings of 'Edinburgh Chartists', or to take place a year early. Or again, despite the fact that the intentions of the convenors and members of the Scottish conference at Glasgow in August 1839 were primarily to support and strength – the national movement, this is deemed to have marked the complete withdrawal of the Scottish Chartists from (whatever Hovell may have meant by) 'the English movement'. Similarly, the tours of George Julian Harney in 1840 are deemed to have been made 'in the employ of the Scottish Chartists', yet Harney was unable to obtain any welcome or countenance from the only body which could speak for 'the Scottish Chartists'.

This process, by which Hovell leaps to a number of doubtful conclusions for which he produces little or inaccurate evidence, and then proceeds to a series of deductions which are often less than half-truths, reaches its climax in Hovell's remarkably credulous findings that 'martial preparations were carried on even in the remote districts of Scotland, as far as Aberdeen, though the little weaving towns, (like Kirriemuir) were the chief centres of excitement'. Yet the only evidence adduced to support such an important statement is a romance by J. M. Barrie.[14]

III

Whereas the role of socialism in the Chartist movement has been over-played, the role of trade unionism has been too heavily discounted. It is true that the Chartists constantly looked to the trade unions for support and were often disappointed with the rather slight help which was forthcoming from this source at the more normal periods of the agitation. It is far from true to say, however, that the trades as such kept aloof from the movement. Throughout much of this period the relation-ship between the trades and Chartist associations remained close, and there were numerous occasions on which members of the trades societies participated as organisations as well as individuals.

On this aspect, Slosson, Hovell and others have tended to follow the dicta of Sidney and Beatrice Webb. 'There is no reason to believe that the Trades Unions at any time became part and parcel of the Chartist movement', they wrote. 'It may be doubted whether in any case, a Trade Union itself as distinguished from particular members who happened to be delegates, made any formal profession of adherence to Chartism. . . . There must . . . have been something more than mere adherence to the rule [excluding politics and religion from union discussions] in the unwillingness of the trade societies to be mixed up with the Chartist agitation. The rule had not prevented the organised trades of 1831–2 from taking a prominent part in the Reform Bill Movement. The banners of the Edinburgh Trade clubs were con-spicuous in the public demonstration on the rejection of the Bill of 1831.'[15]

It seems incredible that the Webbs could have given vent to such a measured conclusion without checking this surprising revelation against contemporary reports of Chartist processions and demonstrations, at least. If they had done so their puzzlement would have disappeared, for they would have found the same trade society banners which had flown at the 1831–2 Reform demonstrations being carried again, along with some new ones, at most of the great Chartist demonstrations from May 1838 to 1843. Long before the Webbs wrote, R. G. Gammage had described the elaborate panoply of an Aberdeen Chartist demonstration in 1843 in honour of O'Connor and Duncombe, with all the gaudy insignia and expensive trappings of numerous trade societies.[16]

The very first of the great demonstrations which launched the Chartist movement, on Glasgow Green on 21 May 1838, was organised completely by the trades of Glasgow, and more than seventy trades societies were reported as having marched to it. There were few demonstrations in Scotland in which the union banners did not fly prominently. In September 1840, for instance, another Glasgow demonstration, in honour of Collins and McDouall, saw the Cabinet Makers, Upholsterers, Plasterers, Carvers, Gilders, Pianoforte Makers, Turners, Plumbers, Tailors, Boot and Shoemakers, Boilermakers, Dressers, Twisters, Dyers, Joiners, House Carpenters, Tobacco Spinners, Bricklayers, Masons and other trades societies marching in the procession. Or again, at Aberdeen a month later, when Harney, Duncan and O'Neill were the guests of honour, the procession was led by the Convenor of the Aberdeen Trades on horseback, followed by the Tailors, Machinemakers, Moulders, Flax-Dressers, Sawyers, Boiler-makers, Woolcombers, Slaters, Tanners, Curriers and Carpet Weavers.[17]

The Webbs also managed to turn a blind eye to trade union financial support for Chartism. 'We never find the trades societies contributing to Chartist funds, or even collecting money for Chartist victims', they declare. Yet in Glasgow contributions of National Rent were forth-coming from many unions, including the Operative Masons, Shoe-makers, Cabinetmakers, Carvers, Bakers and Confectioners, Turners, Gilders, Upholsterers, Coopers, Brushmakers, Plasterers, Potters, Ships Carpenters and Tenters. During the next two years several of these unions were again making contributions to funds for the Central Committee for Scotland and for the defence of John Frost.[18]

In Glasgow, when the Universal Suffrage Association was formed, its Council was composed chiefly of delegates from the trades, and in Edinburgh and Dundee some of the trades were organised into universal suffrage societies. In Dundee these societies then combined into the 'Dundee Trades Democratic Universal Suffrage Association'. Such efforts did not succeed in embracing all the trades societies, and did not last long, but the picture is not one of isolationism, but rather of fairly close collaboration.[19]

IV

Understandably, the ideas which were the stock-in-trade of the Chartist leaders have been given much more attention than the individuals who propounded them. Yet these individuals often modified, or even radically altered, their views in the course of time. It seems also fairly clear that their audiences formed their judgements at least as much on the personality and reputation of their leaders as on their theories. The difficulties of making studies in depth over an adequate period and of publishing biographies of largely forgotten men have resulted in a serious dearth of Chartist biographies. For many years the only major contributions in this field were David Williams's study of John Frost and G. D. H. Cole's excellent volume of *Chartist Portraits*. In recent years there have been a few serious efforts to provide a definitive picture of Feargus O'Connor and other leaders.

The Chartist tragedy needed above all else a balanced account of the character, actions and influence of O'Connor, in whom so many of the potentialities and dilemmas were personified. On the whole historians have correctly assessed the insidiously destructive effect on sound organisation and consistent policy which the braggadocio, domineering despotism and vacillation of this Irish demagogue spelt for the movement. But they have tended to underestimate the positive contribution engendered by the inspiration, hope and affection which his warm-hearted flamboyance aroused in the Chartist masses. The curious consistency of O'Connor's often unpredictable changes of face is well developed in the biography by Donald Read and Eric Glasgow. Although the treatment of O'Connor's relationship with other national and local leaders, and with organisations such as the N.C.A., is surprisingly slight, the picture of O'Connor which emerges is a convincing one, both critical and sympathetic in about the right proportions.[20]

O'Connor was dreadfully egocentric and wanted to be the unquestioned leader. Yet once the Charter was launched, a demagogue leader was needed. Lovett could not play the part, whereas O'Connor was excellently equipped to do so. Lovett, Place and others have complained that noisy demagogy deprived the movement of all chance of success. But their assumption that Parliament might concede the Charter to a quiet rational movement was probably no more tenable than Feargus O'Connor's hope of frightening it into concession. He tried bluster and intimidating tones in 1838–9, 1842 and in 1848. They failed completely on each occasion:[21]

Yet the attempt to stampede the authorities was worth making. Parliament and government had certainly been intimidated by threatening agitation during the Reform Bill crisis of 1831–32. The difference of course was that then the threats had come from the middle-classes with economic power behind them. They could threaten successfully: the working-classes could not. The failure of

O'Connor's bluff proved this. In contemporary social, economic and political circumstances the people could not achieve reform without the middle-classes beside them and without the assistance of an enlightened parliamentarian, such as Peel. . . . O'Connor slowly learnt all this from his own failures. In his last years, although personally discredited, he persisted in pointing out the right road for working-class agitation in the future.

This was rather a strange outcome for the ebullient demagogue whose thinly veiled threats of violence, judiciously mixed with protestations of peace, had made him the bogyman of the English middle-classes. Yet the eventual viewpoints of Julian Harney and Ernest Jones were similar.

The outstanding work in the biographical field, however, is that of A. R. Schoyen on George Julian Harney. In *The Chartist Challenge* is to be found the clearest picture of the intellectual ferment and moral enthusiasms which swept so many capable young men into the exuberant activities of 1837–40, and of the satisfactions, difficulties and tribulations which were to attend the efforts of a clear-minded but inexperienced revolutionary. The transformation in Harney's attitudes to organisations, colleagues and supporters, and the broadening and deepening of his personality in response to events, experience, illness, marriage, opportunities and study provide an invaluable insight into the mind and calculations of one of the chief pilots of the movement. The unfolding of the main stream of events during the whole course of the movement through the journeyings, speeches, writings, organising and publishing efforts of Julian Harney has a decidedly authentic ring which brings Chartism fascinatingly back to life.[22]

Schoyen's account of the closing years of the movement provides a valuable addition to the studies of this period, of which the most useful are those of John Saville and F. E. Gillespie.[23] Among the salient features of this section are the toll which emigration took of the younger generation of Chartists, the pull of the adventurous and liberty-loving United States and the element of disillusion felt by Harney and others with the social life and economic trends they found there, and the growing interest of the working classes in foreign affairs, especially continental Liberalism and Russian imperialism. An interesting point, too, is the extraordinarily inept efforts of Karl Marx and Friedrich Engels to influence British working-class organisations, despite much assistance from Julian Harney and Ernest Jones.

The advantages of reliance on primary and contemporary sources, and of providing a fairly wide coverage of regional and organisational studies emerge clearly from the volume of *Chartist Studies* edited by Asa Briggs. In it the course of the agitation, and the efforts at organisation in several cities and regions are described in some depth. These provide a solid corrective to some of the more imaginative histories of the movement.[24]

The chapter on Chartism in Wales does much to clear up the mystery of the Newport Rising, while other chapters indicate many of the obvious factors of the movement which are often never mentioned. The interdependence of town and hinterland, for instance, is really important: 'Without Bath the Chartists of Wiltshire would have been poorly led; without Wiltshire the Chartists of Bath would have lacked the exhilaration of a mission-field.' Much of the strength or militancy of a region might be less attributable to the Chartists in the principal town or city, such as Leeds or even Manchester, than to the Chartists in the surrounding towns. An inspiring individual such as Thomas Cooper or Henry Vincent could have a dramatic effect on the course of Chartism in Leicester or Bath and the West Country. The pervasive influence of the messianic O'Connor, which penetrated to every corner of the movement, proved almost everywhere to leave behind a legacy of rank-and-file loyalty to the great Feargus, and of leadership 'treachery', frustration, fury and dismay. These studies indicate also the desirability of having similar studies of Chartism in Birmingham, Nottingham, Newcastle and London to set alongside those of Leeds, Manchester, Leicester and Glasgow; and specialist essays on the National Charter Association and the Chartist Press to accompany those on the Chartist Land Plan, Government policy towards the Chartists, and relations between the Chartists and the Anti-Corn Law League.

Particularly useful is the chapter on Home Office and Government policy towards the Chartists, and their reaction to a miscellaneous flow of information from mayors, magistrates, sheriffs, lords-lieutenant, troop commanders and spies about Chartist plans, demonstrations, suspected plotting and arming, drilling and threats to the maintenance of public order.

The Whig and Tory governments in turn responded to these with rather more alacrity than to reports of chronic distress, but with far greater forbearance than has usually been recognised by the Chartists themselves or by the historians. The official attitude towards Chartist meetings was reasonable, and normally imposed considerable restraint on magistrates from provocative interference with meetings. Large public assemblages were considered illegal only when attended by 'such circumstances of terror as to excite alarm and to endanger the public peace'. Speeches and writings which were adjudged by the Home Office to be clearly illegal and seditious did not in most cases result in prosecution. Indeed, 'so determined was the Whig Home Secretary to avoid the charge of interfering with freedom of discussion that he was quite prepared to tolerate violent speeches and writings.' As for the thorough and systematic preparations by the Government, which Hovell indicates, against a general insurrection of the Chartists on 6 May 1839, the evidence shows that these did not exist. The Government, in fact, was slow to make any change in the law relating to arms, in order to suppress what it regarded as 'an abuse of the rights secured by the Bill of Rights'. As the Chartists maintained, there was nothing illegal in the mere possession of arms. Nor did the Government show any reasonable speed in reforming the police arrangements for the English counties, even after the report of the Royal Commission in May 1839.

The reader will search the Home Office Papers and the letters of Whig statesmen in vain for evidence of any systematic plan to crush the popular movement, as by arresting its leaders [concludes F. C. Mather]. Everything, in fact, seems to point to the conclusion that the Whigs were merely concerned to lop off the disorderly excrescences of Chartism, and that they only acted against the movement when they were convinced that the peace was seriously threatened. They held back until the very last moment before striking a blow, and seized the earliest opportunity to proclaim the emergency at an end.

In contrast, the Tory Government of 1842 was much quicker to show serious alarm, to discover 'a formal conspiracy lurking behind disturbances which historians have since adjudged spontaneous', and they were more ruthless in their determination to stamp out the imagined Chartist insurrection. At the same time, the social consciences of some Tory Ministers were more deeply affected by the distressed condition of their people than ever appeared to be the case with Whig Ministers.[25]

V

In contemporary eyes, the whole Chartist affair savoured a good deal of melodrama, and even farce. Respectable society enjoyed from time to time a laugh at the folly, discomfiture and disappointment of the

Chartists. The laughter tended to sound rather self-conscious and uncomfortable, and to indicate that the Chartists had succeeded in giving a severe shock to the established order. Among the Chartists and their leaders there lingered a deep sense of tragedy, a feeling that the time had been exactly ripe for a radical change in British society, but that by disunity, misguided counsels and lack of decisiveness the opportunity had been missed and might not recur for a generation or more.

This sense of setback and failure was widely shared by the heterogeneous elements who had built up the movement. It was felt most strongly by those who had seen Chartism as a short-term programme with immediately realisable goals, but also by those who had looked on it as a long-term propaganda campaign and part of the process of political education and social regeneration. It was felt strongly by those who had regarded the Charter as a minimum programme, providing the basis of political rights on which the social rights of the industrious classes would still have to be built, and to a lesser extent by those who had supported the Charter as a maximum programme, many of whom now felt that injudicious conduct of the agitation had reduced the scope for further radical campaigning. It was felt equally strongly by those who had regarded Chartism as a purely working-class movement, which could only be contaminated by middle-class participation and sympathy, and by those who had regarded it as a set of political rights which would be supported by right-thinking democrats of all classes.

Despite this sense of failure and disappointment, there was surprisingly little bitterness and regret shown in the aftermath of the movement, but rather nostalgic pleasure at having played some part in an honourable campaign which had probably not been fought in vain. This is not surprising if one considers what the Chartist movement had really meant to the working classes of the country. For the mass, it had meant primarily excitement, entertainment and a sense of participation in something important. Into lives which were all too drab and monotonous had crept an excuse for an occasional holiday, social gatherings, discussions and a sense of purpose. There was both a satisfaction in hearing and seeing that others cared about their condition, and a feeling that they themselves might be important after all and capable of affecting the world around them. Chartist meetings provided some of the fun of the fair, the excitement of a horse-race, the purgative righteousness of attendance at church. Besides that the hope and promise were being held out that the future would not be intolerably bleak. For many it meant a grounding in political affairs and an education in political and social action. For the few who were the activists, who sacrificed their time and energy and risked livelihood, personal security and family relationships, there was drama, play-acting, education and challenge – and often the enjoyable excitement of living dangerously in the public eye.

Chartism drew these leaders from the existing social and political movements. Chartist organisation and agitation provided educational opportunities and a career ladder for many working-class men with latent talent and aspirations. And after the tide of Chartism ebbed in 1842, or after 1851, these leaders were largely returned to their other movements – often with enhanced reputations, greater self-confidence and useful organisational experience and contacts.

How far the agitation was responsible for any improvement in the mental and physical welfare of the British people is beyond exact assessment. The movement provided a vehicle for the expression of their pent-up grievances, and was the means of training considerable numbers of working-class families to adopt a high sense of social obligation. The process of political education of the people was speeded up on a remarkably widespread scale by the Chartists, and it established a pattern of local democratic behaviour which is still with us.

The total picture of Chartism is one of sincere, deeply felt, honest endeavour on the part of a wide variety of human types who were typical of the most lively sections of society in the 1840s, who showed considerable determination and resourcefulness in meeting the problems of their society, and who would have been useful members of British society at any time between 1830 and the present.

BIBLIOGRAPHICAL NOTE

With one or two exceptions, the most important of the studies on Chartism have been mentioned in this chapter and are listed in the notes. The outstanding book for a reliable and fairly comprehensive picture of the movement is Asa Briggs (ed.), *Chartist Studies* (Macmillan, 1959). Despite its numerous weaknesses, Mark Hovell's *The Chartist Movement* (Manchester U.P., 1943 ed.) is still the best general history of Chartism and is essential reading for the serious student. It is well worth while to supplement this with R. G. Gammage's pioneering *History of the Chartist Movement* (Browne & Browne, Newcastle, 1894) and L. C. Wright's *Scottish Chartism* (Oliver & Boyd, Edinburgh, 1953) – which draws attention to the strong social reformist features of Chartist organisation in Scotland.

Of the studies of special aspects of the movement, the most important are the three Columbia University monographs – P. W. Slosson, *The Decline of the Chartist Movement* (Columbia U.P., New York, 1916; Cass, 1967), F. F. Rosenblatt, *The Chartist Movement in its Social and Economic Aspects* (Columbia U.P., New York, 1916; Cass, 1947) and H. U. Faulkner, *Chartism and the Churches* (Columbia U.P., New York, 1916) – and F. C. Mather's *Public Order in the Age of the Chartists* (Manchester U.P., 1959). Mr Mather here provides a more detailed analysis of the issues of law and order than in his chapter in *Chartist Studies*.

Finally, there are the biographical studies. Meriting the highest priority is A. R. Schoyen's *The Chartist Challenge* (Heinemann, 1958), but also important are G. D. H. Cole's *Chartist Portraits* (Macmillan, 1941), David Williams's *John Frost* (Wales U.P., Cardiff, 1939), Donald Read and Eric Glasgow's *Feargus O'Connor* (Arnold, 1961) and John Saville's *Ernest Jones: Chartist* (Lawrence & Wishart, 1952).

NOTES

1. É. Halévy, *Short History cf the English People (1830–41)* (1941), p. 330.
2. P. W. Slosson, *The Decline of the Chartist Movement* (New York, 1916), p. 188.
3. F. F. Rosenblatt, *The Chartist Movement in its Social and Economic Aspects* (New York, 1916); E. Dolléans, *Le Chartisme*, 2 vols (Paris, 1912–13); G. D. H. Cole, *Chartist Portraits* (1941).
4. T. Rothstein, *From Chartism to Labourism* (London, 1929), p. 59.
5. Add. Mss 27821, fo.125.
6. R. Groves, *But We Shall Rise Again* (1938), pp. 173–4, 179.
7. Rothstein, op. cit., p. 68; Groves, op. cit., pp. 10–12, 19, 213.
8. S. Maccoby, *English Radicalism, 1832–52* (1935).
9. *Northern Star*, 5 Feb 1842.
10. J. West, *History of the Chartist Movement* (1920), p. 176.
11. H. U. Faulkner, *Chartism and the Churches* (New York, 1916), p. 52.
12. West, op. cit., pp. 150, 153–4, 156.
13. M. Hovell, *The Chartist Movement* (Manchester, 1943 ed.), p. 27; M. Beer, *A History of British Socialism* (1948), pt iii, p. 4.
14. Hovell, op. cit., pp. 120, 138, 174, 187, 191, 193, 202–3.
15. S. and B. Webb, *History of Trade Unionism* (1902 ed.), pp. 158–9.
16. R. G. Gammage, *History of the Chartist Movement* (Newcastle, 1894), pp. 270–1.
17. *Scottish Patriot*, 26 Sept 1840; *Northern Star*, 17 Oct 1840.
18. Webbs, op. cit., p. 160; *Scottish Patriot*, 14 Dec 1839; *True Scotsman*, 20 Oct 1838, 2 Feb 1839.
19. *Scottish Patriot*, 10 Aug, 17 Aug, 14 Dec 1839.
20. D. Read and E. Glasgow, *Feargus O'Connor* (1961).
21. Ibid., p. 149.
22. A. R. Schoyen, *The Chartist Challenge* (1958).
23. F. E. Gillespie, *Labor and Politics in England, 1850–67* (Durham, N.C., 1927); J. Saville, *Ernest Jones, Chartist* (1952).
24. A. Briggs (ed.), *Chartist Studies* (1959).
25. Ibid., pp. 372–405.

6. The Agitation against the Corn Laws

W. H. CHALONER

CONTINUED interest in the struggle for repeal of the Corn Laws and the adoption of Free Trade by successive Whig, Liberal and Conservative Cabinets as the official policy of the British Government, a decision so important for world economic development between 1846 and 1931, has given rise to a considerable literature on the subject. It can now be seen that the publication of D. G. Barnes's *A History of the English Corn Laws from 1660–1846* in 1930 and C. R. Fay's somewhat neglected *The Corn Laws and Social England* in 1932, far from exhausting the possibilities for future research, opened a fruitful line of advance for the understanding of the relationship between early Victorian economics and politics. The repeal of the Corn Laws in 1846–9 and the subsequent espousal of Free Trade in the 1850s and 1860s form perhaps the most extraordinary example in history of the thorough-going application of a rational system of economics to the commercial and industrial life of a nation. That the policy of Free Trade survived almost unmodified until the troubled period of 1915–31 is a witness not only to the richness of Britain's natural resources and to the adaptability of her entrepreneurs, farmers and workers, but also to the tough theoretical basis of Free Trade economics and to the organisational skill of the directors of the Anti-Corn Law League. Modern interest in the politics of the pressure group has called for a fresh examination of the methods of the League and its successors.

Few scholars today would present the struggle against the Corn Laws between 1813 and 1846 as a wholly disinterested crusade for an end to the hated 'bread tax', a view of the controversy which revived in popularity after 1903 as a result of the Free Trade agitation against Joseph Chamberlain's Tariff Reform proposals. The leaders of the powerful agitation in the 1830s and 1840s freely and unashamedly admitted that repeal was in their own economic interests as producers and exporters, but also claimed that repeal would benefit the mass of lower-income consumers who had been, since the abolition of the wartime income tax in 1816, the victims of a highly regressive system of indirect taxation operating through customs and excise duties. From these positions it became easy to represent the Repeal of the Corn Laws as a national necessity.

In 1813, when the new Corn Bill was introduced into Parliament, the British public still retained vivid memories of the record high grain prices of 1811–12, which had been the main cause of the Luddite riots. The proposals in the Bill to allow foreign wheat into Britain on payment of duties only when the price was 90s 2d a quarter or higher aroused a widespread dissatisfaction, particularly since in June 1813, just before the new crop was harvested, the price of British wheat still hovered around 117s 10d a quarter. The Bill was withdrawn, however, just before the bumper harvest of 1813 sent prices plummeting to around 79s (May 1814). Two years later the notorious Corn Law of 1815 prohibited the entry of foreign wheat until the price of the British article had reached 80s a quarter, in spite of a noisy agitation in the Press and among the London populace against the measure. Corn-growing farmers and their landlords thereby laid themselves open to the imputation that they were deliberately trying to secure for themselves for ever a range of prices which had been temporarily produced by war, scarcity and inflation.

In the difficult years of post-war depression – the years of deflation and recurrent sharp spells of unemployment – the agitation for the repeal of the Corn Laws went hand in hand with the movement for the reform of Parliament. Naturally the agitation had its ups and downs, depending in large measure on the level of prices and the state of employment, and it was only in the years immediately after 1832 that the two agitations diverged to form the Chartist movement (1838) and the Anti-Corn Law League (1838–9). In the 1820s and 1830s the theoretical and practical arguments for throwing the ports of Britain open to the free import of foreign grains were elaborated. Cobden, Bright and their multifarious adherents found weapons ready-fashioned and sharpened to hand when they came, rather late, to the struggle. In 1820 the celebrated petition of the merchants of London, drafted by Thomas Tooke, statistician, economist and successful Russia merchant, was presented to the House of Commons, and laid down the following propositions:[1]

That foreign commerce is eminently conducive to the wealth and prosperity of a country, by enabling it to import the commodities for the production of which the soil, climate, capital and industry of other countries are best calculated, and to export in payment those articles for which its own situation is better adapted.

That freedom from restraint is calculated to give the utmost extension to foreign trade, and the best direction to the capital and industry of the country.

That the maxim of buying in the cheapest market and selling in the dearest, which regulates every merchant in his individual dealings, is strictly applicable as the best rule for the trade of the whole nation.

That a policy founded on these principles would render the commerce of the world an interchange of mutual advantages, and diffuse an increase of wealth and enjoyments among the inhabitants of each state.

In 1827 General T. Perronet Thompson published the first version of his popular *Catechism on the Corn Laws*, which aroused such interest among the hard-bitten compositors in the printing house that the author, 'when he called to correct the proofs, found the place ringing with shouts of laughter'.[2] Wellington's reception on his journey from Liverpool to Manchester on the occasion of the opening of the new railway uniting the two towns in 1830 is said to have been punctuated by cries for repeal of the Corn Laws, and it is important to remember, too, that Ebenezer Elliott published the first edition of his highly emotional *Corn Law Rhymes* as early as 1831.

It is becoming increasingly clear that the agitation was endemic in the chief manufacturing towns, lying dormant during periods of low wheat prices but flaring up vigorously in times of dearth and depression. For example, during the widespread economic distress which followed the collapse of the boom of 1824–5 Charles Sutton, of the Radical newspaper *The Nottingham Review*, kept up a constant campaign against the Corn Laws and in the issue for 21 April 1826 he declared, with some exaggeration, that these laws had been responsible for 'an unparalleled mass of wretchedness, distress, privation and consequent disease among the poor labouring classes of the community'. An Anti-Corn Law petition from 'The United Artisans and Mechanics of Nottingham' against the Corn Laws was presented to Parliament in January 1828, but for the next five years agitation in Nottingham on this question appears to have died out.[3]

This period of quiescence may be compared with Archibald Prentice's reference to the 'seven years' sleep' on the question in Manchester.[4] In fact an Anti-Corn Law Association existed from as early as 1833 at

Sneinton, a residential suburb of Nottingham, for the holding of monthly meetings to diffuse information on all aspects of the Corn Law question. Although this was a small body, and obviously not of the same crucial importance as the 1838 Association in Manchester, nevertheless it is interesting because it maintained a continuous existence until 1846,[5] and indicates the depth of active concern on the subject outside Lancashire.

In 1828 a new Corn Law reached the statute book in replacement of that of 1815, and by its terms a sliding scale of duties on foreign wheat was substituted for the more severe provisions of the Act of 1815. When British wheat reached 66s a quarter, foreign wheat could enter the country on payment of a heavy duty of 20s 8d a quarter. As the price of British wheat rose from 66s the amount of the duty fell very rapidly, so that when British wheat stood as 73s a quarter, foreign wheat could come in on a nominal payment of only 1s a quarter. This clumsy scale encouraged speculation buying of British wheat on the corn exchanges in order to force up the price, for as the price of British wheat rose by only 7s (from 66s to 73s) the duty fell by 19s 8d, thus giving a double profit to the lucky speculators who had bought wheat in the Netherlands for bonding in Britain, while they had at the same time forced British internal wheat prices up. The excessive fluctuations which marked the period 1829–42 appear to have been to some extent the result of the Act of 1828. There was also generally a superficial difference of about 30s a quarter between English wheat prices and the lower price of wheat in Prussia.

Evidence of the extent to which the polemical bases of the Anti-Corn Law agitation had been worked out long before Cobden and Bright took up the matter is to be found in a publication of 1835 by Mrs Jane Loudon, entitled *Philanthropy, the pursuit of happiness practically applied to the Social, Political and Commercial Relations of Great Britain*. It contained two chapters on 'The Bread Monopoly' and 'On the Corn Laws and Currency', in the course of which the author dealt very firmly with the allegation that industrialists advocated repeal of the Corn Laws only because cheap food would mean lower wages for their workers:[6]

> Cheap food, it is true, from whatever cause it proceeds, puts it in the labourer's power to accept lower wages, down, if he please, to the new starving point; but, will he do so, if the self same cause which gives cheap food, gives full employment to labour, and therefore

enables the labourer to demand, and obtain higher wages? Were food, therefore, made cheap by the abolition of corn laws and all other monopolies, the opening of trade, which would be the immediate consequence of such a measure, by doubling and trebling the demand for our manufactured goods, would give full employment at the same time with cheap food, so that labourers being no longer compelled to undercut each other, in an overstocked labour market, labour would at all times, obtain a fair proportion of the wealth it created. . . .

British public opinion by this time had become uneasily aware of the spread of the 'Industrial Revolution' to the continental countries and during the 1830s and 1840s the Free Traders frequently used the argument that European agriculturalists, when they found production for the British market hazardous, and therefore not particularly profitable, would eventually transfer their labour and capital either to industrial pursuits or to the production of raw materials for European industry, processes which would have disastrous repercussions on the British export trade in manufactured goods. In the words of Ebenezer Elliott, British manufacturers feared the competition of

> Saxon web, from Polish wool
> Grown where grew the wanted wheat
> Which we might not buy or eat.

The opening of British ports to the free entry of foreign grain, they argued, would discourage this alarming tendency in the national economies of the European countries.

A National Anti-Corn Law Association came into being in London at the end of 1836. Its nation-wide but strangely assorted membership included many Liberal and Radical M.P.s, Ebenezer Elliott, 'the Corn Law Rhymer', Archibald Prentice of Manchester, Alexander Galloway, the Radical master engineer of London, John Marshall, the linen magnate of Leeds, Francis Place, T. Slingsby Duncombe, M.P., the Chartist sympathiser, and William Howitt, the Quaker publicist of Nottingham. Prentice considered this Association unrepresentative; it lacked 'the support of a numerous constituency; and there was no arrangement for united action':[7]

> Little else, therefore, came of it than to keep notice directed to the subject of the Corn Law, which in two years more, with the sterner teacher in its train, was to force itself upon the attention of the

sufferers; and to bring new men, with better organisation, into the field of contest.

Prentice's 'sterner teacher' was the rapid rise in the price of wheat. By December 1835 the price of wheat had fallen as low as 35s 4d per quarter, as compared with 60s 4d at the time of the Reform Bill crisis in August 1832. From the spring of 1836 onwards, however, wheat prices soared, reaching a high point in mid-September 1839 at 73s, at which price the ports were to be opened, under provision of the Corn Law of 1828, to an eventual import of $1\frac{1}{4}$ million quarters of foreign corn at the nominal duty of 1s per quarter. Even this only arrested the rise temporarily. Although in the odd years of bumper harvest Britain still almost fed itself, such years were few. The difficulty arose in years of bad harvest, when 8 per cent to 10 per cent deficiencies in Britain's food grain requirements had to be made good. Imports from Canada were as yet unimportant owing to the high cost of transport over long distances in the small wooden-hulled vessels of the time, and such imports from North America therefore consisted largely of newly milled flour in barrels, which were less bulky than a grain cargo. Britain depended for the wheat imports she required mainly on the small surpluses available from the rather backward agriculture of Europe. These surpluses came chiefly from Denmark, Poland, Prussia and Russia, where the great landlords either grew wheat as a cash crop or drew their rents partly from the sale of surplus wheat by their peasants. France also was occasionally an important source of supply, as she had been from time to time during the later stages of the Napoleonic Wars, but French supplies of wheat could not always be depended on. For example, there had been acute shortages of grain over wide areas of France in 1818, when famine was not far away. Dr Susan Fairlie's researches have shown that after about 1836 north-western Europe 'became collectively deficient in the bread grains'[8] and European wheat surpluses became smaller and of less frequent occurrence. It was in Britain's interest to look for fresh sources of supply, and by the mid-1840s Peel, by now Prime Minister, knew from the reports of British consular agents that supplies of purchasable European wheat would dwindle in the future. New sources of supply were found after 1846 in the countries of the Mediterranean and particularly in Egypt. This expansion of the grain trade from the Mediterranean went hand in hand with a great increase in exports of Manchester goods to the same area, suggesting that the Free Traders' analysis of the situation, calling for what could be described in modern terms as a policy of 'full employment through Free Trade', was a correct one.[9] By 1855 the Ottoman Empire imported far more Manchester piece-goods than all the European countries put together, and in 1856 the chairman of the Manchester Chamber of Commerce could say:[10]

> As to cottons in Alexandria, we have no rivals and mainly by reason of the increase of our grain trade . . . there has been a large increase in our exports of cotton to that place. In 1843 we exported to the value of £141,000: in 1851 £519,000: in 1854 £1,000,000.

The story of the creation of the Anti-Corn Law League in 1839, and of its predecessor the Manchester Anti-Corn Law Association, has often been told. Charles Pelham Villiers (1802–98), the Radical scion of an aristocratic family and M.P. for Wolverhampton from 1836 until his death, formed the link between the small group of parliamentary advocates of Free Trade and the growing body of Free Trade opinion in the North of England. Villiers's annual motions for a parliamentary inquiry into the working of the Act of 1828 helped to keep interest alive in London while Bright, Cobden and their allies were agitating the provinces and eventually deflecting public attention from Westminster to the textile areas of the North and Midlands. On the League machinery, Dr Norman McCord's *The Anti-Corn Law League, 1838–1846* (1958) is now the most modern source, based as it is on the George Wilson and Cobden papers.

It should be noted that although a good deal is known about the part which Manchester played in the agitation, thanks to Archibald Prentice's history, the bound files of the League press, the accounts of Alexander Somerville and J. G. Kohl and the survival of substantial portions of the Cobden and Wilson papers, less is known about Anti-Corn Law Associations in other cities and towns. Studies of the local associations in Birmingham and Nottingham have recently been made by Mr Derek Fraser and go some way to remedy this gap in our knowledge.[11] This is in strange contrast to the microscopic research which has been undertaken, often with a strong Marxist motivation, into the history of Chartism 'in the localities'.

The success of the League's efforts at organising the 'intelligent artisans' in support of Corn Law repeal has been unduly discounted, particularly by historians of Chartism. It will be recalled that in the immediate post-war years parliamentary reform and Corn Law repeal were linked issues which parted company only during the great depression which began in 1836–7. In Sheffield, for example, a Mechanics' Anti-Corn Law Association had been formed before 1832 and apparently survived into the early 1840s. On 15 January 1839 a Free Trade meeting at Leeds was thrown into confusion by Feargus O'Connor and his supporters, while a meeting of the Manchester Anti-Corn Law Association was ignominiously disrupted by a body of Chartist rowdies on the following 28 February.[12] One of the Chartists

> ... proposed to place in the chair one whom he called 'honest Pat Murphy' a potato-wheeler in Shudehill, who, whatever his honesty might be, was not very cleanly, and very far from being sober. The scene that followed was unexampled in Manchester, and almost baffled description. Upon the proposer calling out, 'will you take the chair, Pat Murphy?' one drunken and very dirty fellow mounted the table, his clogs making deep indentations on its surface, and bruising the reporters hands which were in his way, began to insult every body who asked him to get off, and replied to one who asked him to desist: 'D – n thy e'en, if theau spakes to me aw'll put me clogs i' thy chops.' The proposer then moved that Pat Murphy take the chair, and cried 'Come on Pat.' The man was then pushed or dragged over the heads of the people, amidst great noise and confusion and took his place before Mr Thomas Harbottle, the chairman.

The conclusion of the scene is thus reported:

> Proposer: 'Gentlemen, three cheers for Stephens' – the cheers were given. 'Three groans for Archibald Prentice' – and the groans were given. Mr Prentice expressed his thanks for the compliment. 'Gentlemen, three cheers for the National Convention.' (Cheers.) 'Three cheers for Oastler.' (Cheers.) 'Hand up the chair for Pat Murphy.' Some fellows here siezed chairs which were in various parts of the room, and threw them at the heads of the persons who stood on the stage. The consequence was that a scene of riot and confusion ensued, several gentlemen being severely hurt by the ruffians, who smashed the forms and glasses of the lamps. The respectable persons of the meeting, with the chairman, then quitted the room, and left it in the possession of the ringleader, who congratulated the meeting upon having done his bidding, and his party, who, we are informed, passed a vote of thanks to the delegates to the National Convention by way of amendment to the original motion.

As a result of this incident numerous trade unions in the Manchester area joined the Anti-Corn Law Association and in March 1839, with his shrewd instinct for spotting organising talent, Cobden invited the young Edward Watkin[13] to form the Operative Anti-Corn Law Association. By April the association had its own offices and headquarters and was meeting regularly on two evenings a week at a Manchester tavern. On 15 May these working-class Free Traders held their first big rally and Sir Charles Shaw, the Government Commissioner appointed to reorganise the Manchester police force, reported:[14]

... I am this moment arrived from the Anti-Corn Law meeting where there were at least 4000 operatives present. It is impossible to describe the quiet and regularity of this meeting and in my opinion it has been a complete proof of the inaccuracy of all the reports which have been brought here for some days. ...

Similar associations came into being, for example, at Carlisle, Huddersfield and Leicester, and in Dr McCord's opinion they did possess some independent life: 'The operative associations were not the mere creatures of the middle-class associations.'[15] When, for example, the revival of the League became a possibility in 1852, the members of the former Huddersfield Working Men's Anti-Corn Law Association renewed their organisation on their own initiative.

The operative associations had the additional purpose of providing the Anti-Corn Law movement with a vigorous proletarian bodyguard which could be used with effect against Chartists intent upon wrecking or taking over public meetings and demonstrations. During 1840 and the early months of 1841 Watkin busied himself with dividing Manchester into numbered sections, in each of which the operative branch association had its own officers, banners and all the other trimmings of political organisations. Cobden reinforced the power of these operative associations by forming an alliance with Daniel O'Connell, M.P., the Liberator, who at this time supported the aims of the League, although after his death in 1847 the Irish Repealers were to move over to friendship with the Chartists. Even before the Famine the Manchester area had a considerable Irish-born population, variously estimated at between 35,000 and 60,000, a large proportion of whom were supporters of O'Connell. The leader of the Manchester O'Connellites, Duggan, brought his 'strong-arm men' to the support of the Free Traders against the O'Connorite Chartists and a decisive trial of strength took place on 8 June 1841, when the Free Traders held an open-air meeting in the trade unionist forum of Stevenson Square, Manchester. Chartist attempts to infiltrate this meeting failed ignominiously in the face of Duggan's Irish Anti-Corn Law police. The question of possible collaboration with the Chartists still remained in Cobden's mind, particularly as Peel's new Corn Law of 1842 threatened to take the wind out of the Repealers' sails, for he wrote to Watkin on 19 January 1842:

> As regards your suggestion of fraternising with the O'Connorites, I don't think that party could be trusted, nor do I think they have much power now even for mischief. I should very much prefer to draw out 'the trades' of Manchester if this could be done, and to keep the agitation separate from any other. Still I think it very desirable to try to conciliate the Chartist leaders. The point to be aimed at with them should be to agree not to interrupt each other's proceedings.

Early in March 1842, however, the Free Traders demonstrated that they now had the upper hand by wrecking a Chartist meeting in Manchester, at which not even the great 'lion' Feargus O'Connor himself could secure a hearing. In the fighting which marked the collapse of the rally Feargus and many of his principal supporters received severe drubbings.[16]

Events now moved towards the Plug Riots of July and August 1842, when a spontaneous outbreak of strikes over a wide area of the Northern manufacturing districts caused large-scale public disorders and brought in its train a temporary revival of Chartism. Like Dr G. Kitson Clark, Dr McCord stresses the extent to which some of the League leaders, and in particular that bellicose Quaker John Bright, strayed from the paths of constitutional propriety, even though temporarily, when they advocated both a tax-strike and the closing down of cotton-mills by the masters as a means of bringing pressure to bear on the Government to repeal the Corn Laws.[17] For example, at meetings in the spring of 1842 at Ashton, Manchester and Lees, near Oldham, a campaign was begun by the League to 'stop the supplies until grievances were settled and the corn laws repealed'.[18]

There existed, of course, good precedents for the plan of a refusal to pay particular taxes – a commonplace of Radical agitation since well before Peterloo, and indeed since before the American Declaration of Independence (no taxation without representation), but the plan of a general industrial lock-out was novel and may be considered as the manufacturers' version of working-class proposals for the general strike or the Grand National Holiday, so beloved of such dissimilar groups as the Owenites and the Chartists. It is to Cobden's credit as a statesman that he eventually drew back after peering into the yawning gulf of civil disobedience and violence, over which the Chartists plunged to disaster and impotence, and helped to persuade the Council of the League not to adopt such a dangerous measure.

Attempts have been made to lay part of the responsibility for the Plug Riots in Lancashire and Cheshire at the League's door. The riots of 1842 in these two counties were in fact sparked off by the action of a firm of Tory cotton manufacturers, Jeremiah and John Lees of Stalybridge, in giving notice of wage reductions to their weavers (9 July 1842), an example followed by a second Tory cotton firm and two firms the members of which were supporters of the League, George Cheetham and Sons and Joseph Buckley Reyner and Co. of Ashton-under-Lyne,[18] so that honours seem about even in this respect.

It would appear that the League was the first British political organisation to harness the enthusiasm of youth in a regular fashion to the pursuit of its economic and social ideals, although no detailed research has been carried out on this aspect of its activities. For example, it is known that the Reverend J. R. Beard (1800–76),[19] Unitarian minister and schoolmaster of Salford, and the pioneer of the Unitarian home missionary movement, printed his sermon entitled *Diffusion, not Restriction, the Order of Providence* (1841) in pamphlet form at the request of the Young Men's Anti-Monopoly Association of Salford.[20]

One curious feature of the movement is provided by the sluggish nature of the reaction to the Anti-Corn Law League by the Protectionists among the agricultural interest. During 1843 the League had initiated an intensive campaign throughout the agricultural counties – tenant farmers were to be enlightened as to the true character of their Tory landlords, and the agricultural labourers were to be subjected to propaganda against the Corn Laws. In December 1843 these activities and Cobden and Bright's attacks on the Tory landed interest brought a belated riposte from a number of landowners and farmers who met in London under the chairmanship of the duke of Richmond on the occasion of the Smithfield Show. A network of agricultural protection societies came into existence, the first being the Essex Society for the Protection of Agriculture. The loose association of these bodies became known as the Central Agricultural Protection Association, or more popularly, 'the Anti-League'. Recent research[21] has shown that the 'Anti-League' did not depend so heavily on tenant farmer activists, held back by landed proprietors reluctant to imitate the radical political tactics of the Anti-Corn Law League, as was once believed: 'Though the Anti-League was always referred to as a farmers' movement, it was in reality a combination of country gentlemen, clergymen and the more important farmers.'[22] It failed to make an impression on British agricultural policy because Conservative politicians were reluctant to speak or vote against Sir Robert Peel until 1846, and it cannot be said that its literary contribution to the controversy was as solid or as logical as that of the Free Traders.

Peel's fiscal reforms of 1842–5 and the economic recovery of the mid-1840s associated with the railway boom meant that the League had a hard job to keep up its early momentum in this period. Nevertheless the capable businessmen who directed its fund-raising activities and propaganda raised larger and larger amounts every year – between £7000 and £8000 in 1840, £50,000 in 1843 and about £90,000 in 1844. On the dissolution of the League in 1846 Cobden received a gift of £75,000 to compensate him for the losses which he had suffered in his private business as a calico-printer owing to his absorption in the affairs of the League.

What is perhaps more important, the success of Peel's reforms and his close scrutiny of both the wheat supply position and the ceaseless arguments of the Free Traders converted the Prime Minister himself, and Peel became convinced that even his improved Corn Law of 1842 was indefensible. It is now known that Peel's decision to make provision for the eventual repeal of the Corn Laws had been taken before he knew of the failure of the Irish potato crop in the autmn of 1845. He had intended to bring the matter before the Cabinet in his own time, but the Famine forced his hand. The two Irish potato crop failures of 1845 and 1846 were thus the occasion and not the cause of the repeal of the Corn Laws.

When the final crisis of the Corn Laws came in 1845–6 it became clear that the agricultural interest was divided on the question. Great landowners often drew a large proportion of their rents from town properties, mines or ironworks, thus giving them a stake in urban and industrial prosperity, and although only relatively few of the great landed proprietors in the South, the Midlands or the North came out as ardent supporters of the League, nevertheless when it came to votes in the House of Commons, Peel was able to muster in favour of repeal a large majority composed of M.P.s with interests in the land. The latest analysis of the voting in Parliament is that undertaken by Professor

W. O. Aydelotte, which forms the basis of his article 'The country gentlemen and the repeal of the Corn Laws'.[23] Aydelotte shows that J. A. Thomas's contention that 'the movement for the repeal of the Corn Laws derived its main support from the solid backing of the industrial and commercial classes'[24] is incorrect. Aydelotte considers that 'the political leaders of the old governing class' were wise enough to sacrifice the Corn Laws in the face of a campaign marked by fierce criticism of the landed gentry: '. . . the Corn Laws question provided a focus for a great deal of the pent-up resentment against the old order of things, against the aristocratic domination of the country.' He sums up as follows:[25]

> As to votes in parliament, it is clear that a large proportion of those related to the aristocracy and gentry must have voted for repeal since these men constituted the great majority of the house of commons, about 80 per cent by my reckoning, and without the support of a substantial contingent of them the bill could not have passed.

It has often been pointed out that the short-term results of Repeal did not include an immediate fall in the prices of wheat and bread. Wheat prices remained reasonably steady in the 1850s and 1860s at around 52s a quarter, which provided a significant contrast with the experiences of the 1830s and 1840s, and justified the Free Traders' belief that once protection was abolished there should be no essential conflict of interest between the industrial and agricultural classes. Indeed, from about 1850 to 1879 British arable agriculture enjoyed what was later to be looked upon as its golden age, with prices which afforded adequate profits to the farmer and buoyant rents to the landlord, an era marked by considerable capital investment, heavy expenditure on manures and rising yields per acre. Only during the 1870s did North American wheat begin to bring world wheat prices tumbling down to reach their nadir at 22s 10d a quarter in 1894, as the result of heavy investment in prairie railroads and metal-hulled ocean-going shipping, which had both been in their infancy in the 1840s. Although Cobden in the 1830s and 1840s had spoken and written about the agricultural possibilities of the Middle West, no responsible statesman or economist of the 1840s could be expected to foresee, and cannot be blamed for not foreseeing, a situation like that of 1914 when Britain was dependent to the extent of over 80 per cent on overseas sources for her wheat supplies.

Although the Anti-Corn Law League was formally wound up in 1846, it would have been possible for it to be resuscitated at any time up to the outbreak of the Crimean War in the event of a real threat to reintroduce protection, as in 1852. The League produced two most interesting offshoots: the first was the Liverpool Financial Reform Association, founded in 1848 to advocate the drastic and systematic retrenchment of Government expenditure.[26] This body was still maintaining a fairly vigorous existence in the rather discouraging atmosphere provided by the Liberal Governments of 1905–15. It had a shorter-lived counterpart in London, the National Parliamentary and Financial Reform Association, which does not seem to have survived the 1850s. More significant was the second offshoot, the Lancashire Public School Association, founded mainly by former members of the Anti-Corn Law League in Manchester in 1847. They drew up a plan of secular education which they hoped would satisfy all parties, in the hope of overcoming the religious obstacles – thrown up by Anglicans, Roman Catholics and Nonconformists – which were hindering the development of the national educational system of England and Wales. Using the Massachusetts 'common school' system as a guide, they attempted to introduce a bill into Parliament which would establish a system of free, rate-supported and locally controlled public education. The movement spread rapidly outside Lancashire and in 1850 the Association was renamed the National Public School Association. The Association made extensive use of posters, pamphlets, public lectures and meetings to bring its aims to the notice of the public, while such prominent ex-members of the Anti-Corn Law League as T. Milner Gibson, W. J. Fox and Richard Cobden furthered the aims of the Association by virtue of their position as M.P.s. Although the National Public School Association was dissolved in 1862, its compromise scheme worked out in 1857 fore-shadowed Forster's Elementary Education Act of 1870.[27] It is therefore wrong to think of the Anti-Corn Law League's influence as being either confined solely to the tariff problem or as being limited to economic matters. After all, the outlook of the Free Traders was not a blinkered one and embraced such questions as the influence of the various social classes on national policy, the possibility of creating international peace by expanding trade relations, and the desirability of reducing the armaments which both created a vested interest in war and reduced the standard of life of those whom they were supposed to protect.[28]

BIBLIOGRAPHICAL NOTE

Norman McCord's *The Anti-Corn Law League, 1838–1846* (Allen & Unwin, 1958) is an important modern study, based largely on the private papers of George Wilson and Richard Cobden. It deals with many aspects of the struggle only briefly referred to in Archibald Prentice, *History of the Anti-Corn Law League* (2 vols, 1853; with bibliographical introduction by W. H. Chaloner, Cass, 1968), which is, however, still indispensable for the wealth of contemporary material which it contains, for instance, reports of meetings, lists of participants and parliamentary division lists. The standard work, D. G. Barnes, *History of the English Corn Laws from 1660–1846* (Routledge, 1930), contains an excellent account of the League and an extensive bibliography of the pamphlet literature. C. R. Fay's somewhat neglected book *The Corn Laws and Social England* (Cambridge U.P., 1932) is a store of exact information on the technical aspects of the operation of the laws.

J. D. Chambers and G. E. Mingay, *The Agricultural Revolution, 1750–1880* (Batsford, 1966) is essential for the latest research on agriculture during this period. The agricultural and fiscal background may also be examined in W. F. Galpin, *The Grain Supply of England during the Napoleonic Period* (Michigan U.P., New York, 1925); Sir Derek Walker-Smith, *The Protectionist Case in the 1840s* (Blackwell, Oxford, 1933); Lucy Brown, *The Board of Trade and the Free-Trade Movement, 1830–42* (Clarendon Press, Oxford, 1958); A. Redford *et al.*, *Manchester Merchants and Foreign Trade, 1794–1858* (Manchester U.P., 1934): R. L. Schuyler, *The Fall of the Old Colonial System: a study in British Free Trade, 1770–1870* (O.U.P., New York, 1945) and W. D. Grampp, *The Manchester School of Economics* (Stanford U.P., O.U.P., 1960) – which is not a very satisfactory study but contains a useful bibliography.

The following papers are also relevant to the same theme: Susan S. Fairlie, 'The nineteenth-century Corn Law reconsidered', and D.C. Moore, 'The Corn Laws and High Farming', *EcHR* 2nd ser., xviii (1965); G. L. Mosse, 'The Anti-League, 1844–46', ibid., xvii (1947); David Spring, 'Earl Fitzwilliam and the Repeal of the Corn Laws', *AHR* lix (1954); Mary Lawson-Tancred, 'The Anti-League and the Corn Law crisis of 1846', *HJ* iii (1960), which criticises Mosse's views; C. R. Fay, 'The movement towards Free Trade, 1820–1853', *Cambridge History of the British Empire* (Cambridge U.P., 1940), ii, ch. 11, and Sir John Clapham, 'Corn Laws Repeal, Free Trade and History', *Trans. Manchester Statistical Soc.* (1945). Since this paper was completed, Dr Susan Fairlie has published 'The Corn Laws and British Wheat Production, 1829–76', *EcHR* 2nd ser., xxii (1969).

The principal biographies are G. M. Trevelyan, *The Life of John Bright* (Constable, 1913); Lord Morley, *The Life of Richard Cobden* (2 vols, Chapman & Hall, 1881) – the official life, but a more modern study is much to be desired; Donald Read, *Cobden and Bright* (Arnold, 1967); Sir Edward W. Watkin, *Alderman Cobden of Manchester* (Ward & Lock, 1891); W. O. Henderson, 'Charles Pelham Villiers', *History*, xxxvii (1952); L. G. Johnson, *General T. Perronet Thompson, 1783–1869* (Allen & Unwin, 1957).

Various aspects of the League are examined in Donald Read, *The English Provinces, c. 1760–1960* (Arnold, 1964); W. H. Chaloner, *The Hungry Forties* (Historical Association pamphlet, 1967 ed.); Betty Kemp, 'Reflections on the Repeal of the Corn Laws', *VS* v (1962); J. A. Thomas, 'The Repeal of the Corn Laws, 1846', *Economica*, ix (1929) and *The House of Commons, 1832–1901* (Wales U.P., Cardiff 1939); W. O. Aydelotte, 'The business interests of the gentry in the Parliament of 1841–1847', in G. S. R. Kitson Clark, *The Making of Victorian England* (Methuen, 1962), pp. 290–305 and 'The Country Gentlemen and the Repeal of the Corn Laws', *EHR* lxxxii (1967) – which criticises the findings of J. A. Thomas; J. T. Ward, 'West Riding landowners and the Corn Laws', *EHR* lxxxi (1966); and G. S. R. Kitson Clark, 'The Repeal of the Corn Laws and the Politics of the Forties', *EcHR* 2nd ser., iv (1951) and 'The Electorate and the Repeal of the Corn Laws', *TRHS* 5th ser., i (1951).

Two recent studies provide a refreshing change from the overemphasis on the part played by Manchester in the agitation: Derek Fraser, 'Nottingham and the Corn Laws', *Trans. Thoroton Soc. of Nottinghamshire*, lxx (1966) and 'Birmingham and the Corn Laws', *Trans. Birmingham Arch. Soc.*, lxxxii (1967).

NOTES

1. The whole document is most conveniently printed in W. Smart, *Economic Annals of the Nineteenth Century, 1801–20* (1911), i, 744–7.

2. L. G. Johnson, *General T. Perronet Thompson* (1957), p. 129.

3. D. Fraser, 'Nottingham and the Corn Laws', *Trans. Thoroton Society of Nottinghamshire*, lxx (1966).

4. Archibald Prentice, *History of the Anti-Corn Law League* (1853), i, 88.

5. Fraser, loc. cit.

6. Jane Loudon, *Philanthropy* . . . (1835), pp. 107–8. Although some Leaguers may have held the opinions which Mrs Loudon refuted, Cobden denied that he had ever used such arguments.

7. Prentice, op. cit., i, 49–50.

8. Susan Fairlie, 'The Nineteenth-Century Corn Law Reconsidered', *EcHR* 2nd ser., xvii (1965).

9. The phrase 'full employment' first became current about this time. See the extract from Mrs Jane Loudon's book of 1835 quoted above and its use in a Whig–Liberal election broadside of 1841 (reproduced in F. von Raumer, *England in 1841* (1842), ii, 259–62).

10. C. R. Fay, *The Corn Laws and Social England* (1932), p. 120.

11. D. Fraser, 'Birmingham and the Corn Laws', *Trans. Birmingham Arch. Soc.*, lxxxii (1967) and 'Nottingham and the Corn Laws', loc. cit. An examination of the Anti-Corn Law agitation in Carlisle, for example, where Mr Carr, the baker and biscuit manufacturer, played a prominent part, would prove particularly interesting.

12. Prentice, op. cit., i, 117–18. For the whole question, see Lucy Brown, 'The Chartists and the Anti-Corn Law League', in Asa Briggs (ed.), *Chartist Studies* (1959).

13. For Sir Edward William Watkin, Bt (1819–1901), the railway magnate, see *DNB, 1901–11 Supplement* and A. E. Watkin (ed.), *Absalom Watkin: Extracts from his Journal, 1814–1856* (1920).

14. Quoted in Norman McCord, *The Anti-Corn Law League, 1838–1846* (1958), p. 97.

15. Ibid., p. 98. See also Joseph Livesey (of Preston) to Cobden, 14 Feb 1842. Livesey was publishing a halfpenny paper, *The Struggle*, which he claimed was 'exerting an influence among the working men far exceeding any other publication' (McCord, op. cit., p. 119).

16. Ibid., pp. 98–103; E. W. Watkin, *Alderman Cobden of Manchester* (1891), pp. 89–90. The political activities of the League in promoting the return of

M.P.s favourable to Repeal are well treated by Dr McCord, op. cit., pp. 78–120.

17. McCord, op. cit., pp. 121–31; G. S. R. Kitson Clark, 'Hunger and Politics in 1842', *JMH* xxv (1953).

18. A. G. Rose, 'The Plug Riots of 1842 in Lancashire and Cheshire', *TLCAS* lxvii (1957).

19. For Beard, see *DNB* and F. Boase, *Modern English Biography* (Truro, 1892), i, col. 208.

20. Cf. the foundation of the Young Men's Christian Association in 1844.

21. Mary Lawson-Tancred, 'The Anti-League and the Crisis of 1846', *HJ* iii (1960).

22. Ibid. Mr G. L. Mosse's views ('The Anti-League, 1844–1846', *EcHR* xvii (1947)) are considered to be inaccurate by Miss Lawson-Tancred. See also D. C. Moore, 'The Corn Laws and High Farming', *EcHR* 2nd ser., xviii (1965).

23. W. O. Aydelotte, 'The Country Gentlemen and the Repeal of the Corn Laws', *EHR* lxxxii (1967). See also W. O. Aydelotte, 'The Business Interests of the Gentry in the Parliament of 1841–47', in G. S. R. Kitson Clark, *The Making of Victorian England* (1960), pp. 290–305.

24. See J. A. Thomas, 'The Repeal of the Corn Laws, 1846', *Economica*, ix (1929) and *The House of Commons, 1832–1901* (1939).

25. Aydelotte, 'The Country Gentlemen', loc. cit.

26. W. N. Calkins, 'A Victorian Free Trade Lobby', *EcHR* 2nd ser., xiii (1960).

27. For details about the Lancashire Public School Association, I am indebted to Mr D. K. Jones.

28. Donald Read, *Cobden and Bright* (1967), pp. 230–49.

7. The Irish Agitation

J. H. TREBLE

THE Act of Union between Great Britain and Ireland which came into operation on New Year's Day, 1801, was designed in the eyes of its chief architect, William Pitt, to achieve two things. First it would in the short term ensure that the growth of republican–separatist sentiment, overtly and violently expressed by the 1798 United Irishmen's rebellion and Wolfe Tone, would be halted by integrating Ireland firmly into the structure of the imperial system of government. In the long term, however, Ireland could only be finally reconciled to the connection with Britain if it brought her people increased prosperity and the enjoyment of civil and religious liberty. This second theme was to form the basis of much of Pitt's thinking on the 'Irish Question' in the pre- and immediately post-Union period. He was to argue forcibly that if the Union were to be a source of strength and pride to both countries, it would necessarily have to be accompanied by a series of reforms which would have, as their ultimate goal, the economic, social and religious regeneration of the population of Ireland. Economic developments, it was hoped, might be left to the operation of market forces; for it was widely held by British politicians that capital would flow out from Britain, once the Union had been concluded, to broaden the small industrial sector of the Irish economy. But this doctrine of *laissez-faire* could not be applied to the more delicate sphere of human rights. Westminster alone could complete the process, begun by the Irish legislature in 1793, of granting Ireland's predominantly Roman Catholic population full citizenship. In concrete terms this meant, above all else, Catholic Emancipation – that is, the right of Roman Catholics to hold high political and legal office and to sit in the imperial parliament. It was this part of Pitt's programme which initially won over a powerful section of Irish Catholic opinion, including Archbishop Troy of Dublin, to support the idea of a 'Union of hearts', and which was most rapidly abandoned, in deference to the unbending hostility of George III, after the Union had become accomplished fact. Pitt's subsequent resignation on this issue did little to assuage the sense of injustice of those Irish critics of the 1800 measure, Daniel O'Connell among them, who had predicted that Ireland would lose everything and gain nothing by abandoning the hard-won concessions of 1782.

In their view the whole story of the struggle for Catholic Emancipation was to be a vindication of this thesis. For when that long overdue reform was finally placed on the Statute Book in 1829, it had been largely wrung from a hostile administration through the efforts of the Irish people themselves. The result of the Clare by-election of June 1828 in which the Catholic candidate, Daniel O'Connell, defeated Vesey Fitzgerald, at that time President of the Board of Trade, was the culmination of five years' hard work by the Dublin-based Catholic Association, an organisation dedicated to securing equality of opportunity for the despised 'Papists' through peaceful agitation. Faced by this unequivocal verdict of the Catholic forty-shilling freeholders Wellington and Peel decided that further resistance to Catholic claims was useless, since the pattern of voting in County Clare could be reproduced over whole tracts of the south of Ireland. In the end Emancipation was reluctantly conceded in 1829 because to have withheld it would both have jeopardised the Union and perhaps have handed the leadership of Ireland's Catholic masses to more extreme and less pacific elements in Irish society than the rigidly constitutionalist O'Connell.

Pitt's vision, however, of the tangible benefits which should accrue to Ireland as a result of the Union was not merely blighted by Britain's attitude to the specific question of Emancipation. Over the whole spectrum of Irish social and economic life the Union failed to alleviate hardship or the frightening dependence of the Irish peasantry on the land. Indeed, it could be argued that one of the indirect consequences of the Union was to increase that dependence by virtually destroying in the mid-1820s whole sectors of the Irish textile industry. The process of disintegration can be traced to the decisions, taken in the 1820s, to dismantle the remnants of the Irish tariff system. In 1821 the 10 per cent duty on English cotton goods was removed; in 1823 the levy upon English woollens met with a similar fate; in 1824 the silk tariff disappeared. Once the Irish market had been thrown open in this fashion to English competition the final blow could not be long delayed. It duly fell during the financial crisis of 1825–6 when Ireland was inundated with the products of English mills and looms. Faced with what amounted to dumping on a massive scale, and lacking the capital and perhaps the market to introduce the technological and organisational changes needed to fight off this severe challenge, the Irish textile industry outside Ulster crumbled. The history of the Dublin silk trade illustrated in microcosmic form the rapidity of this process. In 1824 there had been 1200 broad silk looms and 996 machines at work in the city; by 1831–2 there were only 150 looms 'of every description' still in use.[1] Thus Adam Smith's 'invisible hand', far from bringing about, as Pitt had hoped, a substantial expansion of Ireland's slender industrial base, had merely helped to extinguish incipient growth points in the economy. As a result the struggle for land could only become more acute as population continued to grow at what appeared to contemporaries to be a frightening rate and as the practice of subdivision, stimulated by reliance on the potato, continued relatively unimpeded either by the disfranchisement of the forty-shilling freeholders in 1829 or the Subletting Act of 1826.

In essence, therefore, the critics of the 1800 settlement were correct in asserting that the ties between Britain and Ireland had produced no diversification in the Irish economy and had done little to reform, or rationalise, the system of land tenure in the interests of the tenant and cottier. The tithe still remained both as an oppressive exaction in money terms and a seemingly perpetual reminder to Catholic Ireland of the power of the established Church. Security of tenure, fair rents and compensation by the landlord for the improvements made by the tenant, which together comprised the system known as 'Ulster tenant right', were almost unknown outside the province of Ulster. Elsewhere the operation of the conacre system, short leases, land rents inflated by the lack of alternative means of obtaining a subsistence level of existence, and discontinuity in employment, all adversely affected the peasant's hopes of achieving permanent improvement in his lot.

Last, but not least, there remained the growing problem of land-owners' absenteeism – a problem which reached serious proportions in the post-Union period. For absenteeism meant not merely the lack of close and intimate ties between landlord and tenant which might have done something to mitigate the evils of 'rack-renting' and arbitrary eviction: it also produced a serious drain of capital from Ireland itself. Whereas, for example, in the 1780s between £2 million and £3 million per annum were being transferred from Ireland to absentee landlords living in England, these figures, mainly the product of rent-rolls, had more than doubled to between £6 million and £7 million annually by the early 1840s. Beside these difficulties the complaints of middle-class Catholics in the first thirty years after the Union about the use of patronage by Dublin Castle in the 'Tory–Orange' interest and of discrimination against Catholics in the law courts paled into insignifi-

cance, although these issues, it is true, were to be used to attract
disgruntled Catholics to the Repeal banner when it was unfurled by
O'Connell for the first time in the closing months of 1829.

I

O'Connell, embittered by what he regarded as the House of Commons'
ungenerous reaction to the Clare triumph and furious at the raising in
Ireland of the freeholders' franchise from a 40s to a £10 limit, at last
focused the attention of his countrymen on the Union and the miseries,
as he saw them, that followed in its wake. The remedy for Ireland's
woes, he declared at Youghal in November 1829, was drastic but simple
– namely 'a repeal of that odious Union – that blot upon our national
character'. By this he meant not that Ireland should become the type
of autonomous republic which Wolfe Tone had envisaged in the 1790s,
but that she should seek 'a repeal of that cursed measure which deprived
Ireland of her senate, and thereby made her a dependant upon British
aristocracy, and British intrigue, and British interests'. In short, while
Ireland should continue to be 'bound to England by the golden link of
the Crown',[2] she should none the less insist on the restoration of the
1782 Constitution. By January 1830 O'Connell had associated this
demand for a domestic legislature in Dublin with a comprehensive list
of social and political reforms. Among other things he asked his compatriots to press for the abolition of tithes, taxation of absentee landowners in order to reduce that particular evil to insignificant proportions,
the ballot, an overhaul of the structure of Irish municipal corporations
and universal male suffrage. But it was not sufficient merely to formulate
demands in this fashion and to expect the government of the day to cede
them; they had to be presented in such a way that Wellington and Peel
would have little alternative but to repeat the concession they had made
to the Catholic Association in 1829. To achieve this goal O'Connell
founded the first of his Repeal Associations early in 1830. As with the
Catholic Association before it, he anticipated using this body as a
propaganda instrument to rouse the peasantry from their apathy and to
seek redress of their many grievances by persuading them to combine in
a mass 'moral force' agitation for the repeal of the Act of Union.

These initial manoeuvres, however, achieved little, for Wellington's
Tory ministry, alarmed at the implications of Repeal, took prompt legal
action to suppress this new organisation. By the time the Tories had lost
their hold on political power in November 1830, they had openly

demonstrated their determination to maintain the Union by dissolving no fewer than three successive anti-Union societies within the brief space of seven months. For Wellington in 1830 as for Peel in the early 1840s, the settlement of 1800 was designed to be a permanent feature of the political landscape of the United Kingdom. It followed therefore, in Tory eyes, that any attempt to tamper with the work of Pitt was tantamount to a betrayal of the constitution. The whole of Tory policy towards Ireland since the creation of the Union is only intelligible when viewed in this light. Successive shifts in the outlook and policies of Tory Cabinets and of Tory Lord-Lieutenants of Ireland between 1801 and 1830 reflected the Tories' interpretation of their best hope, at a particular point in time, of keeping Ireland tied to the British connection. Thus in the early years of the nineteenth century the Tory party on the whole favoured cultivating those sections of Irish society which might loosely be described as the forces of the 'Protestant Ascendancy' simply because they were overwhelmingly committed to the preservation of the Union. Later, as more moderate voices – Canning for example – sought to persuade the Tory leadership that the surest way of reconciling Ireland to the Union lay in abandoning discriminatory practices against Roman Catholics, their Irish policy entered a period of flux. The net outcome of this protracted internal debate was that Wellington and Peel, despite loud protests from the party's ultra-Protestant wing, abandoned, after the Clare by-election, their former antipathy to Catholic Emancipation and tried to present it to their rank and file as a social and political cement, calculated to make the Union more palatable to Ireland's rising Catholic middle class. Last, but not least, Peel's post-1843 Irish programme – the Charitable Bequests Act, the attempt to reform Irish university education, and the increase in the Maynooth grant – was largely concerned with killing Repeal with kindness. Given this general philosophy, O'Connell could scarcely have been surprised by Tory reaction in 1830 to his proposal to separate Ireland from the rest of the United Kingdom.

Nor could he have had any grounds for expecting better treatment from the Whigs when they returned to office under Grey after their long spell in the political wilderness. Although during the Reform Bill crisis itself O'Connell gave them valuable external support, they displayed little inclination to trust a man who was not only the antithesis of the image of a Whig aristocrat, but also dedicated to the 'dismemberment of the Empire'. Stanley, the new Whig Irish Secretary in 1830, disliked O'Connell as intensely as any ultra-Tory, distrusting both his demagogic

approach to politics and his anti-Union outlook. Convincing proof of
this hostility was quickly given when in January 1831 O'Connell and
several of his leading sympathisers were charged with conspiracy and the
publication of 'seditious libel'. Closely in the wake of these events came
a Whig-inspired onslaught on the Repeal press. Although the prosecution of 'the conspirators' was subsequently abandoned, it was no
surprise to thinking Irishmen when O'Connell made Repeal the central
issue of the 1832 General Election in Ireland.

Thereafter, strengthened by the return of a solid phalanx of Repeal
M.P.s, O'Connell continued his struggle for Ireland from the floor of
the House of Commons. In 1833, to the intense annoyance of Grey and
Stanley, he both secured major modifications of the Government's
Coercion Bill and took the administration to task for not going further
in reforming the Church of Ireland than the Irish Church Temporalities
Act of that year. The crowning moment of this particular phase of his
parliamentary career came in the following session when he secured the
first debate on the Repeal question since the enactment of the Union.

By this time, however – April 1834 – fortified by Lord John Russell's
views on lay appropriation of the surplus revenues of the Church of
Ireland, he was already drifting closer to a *rapprochement* with the liberal
section of Grey's Cabinet. Before another year had elapsed a Whig-
O'Connell alliance had ceased to be a matter of political speculation; and
it had become a new imponderable in the struggle for high office at
Westminster. Two factors contributed largely to this 'political revolution'. In the first place Stanley, Graham and Grey all left the Whig
Cabinet in May–June 1834 largely because they were opposed both to a
softening in Whig policy towards Ireland and to the Whigs conducting
any form of negotiations with O'Connell. Secondly O'Connell had been
perturbed by the return to power of a minority Tory administration in
November 1834.

The emergence of Peel as Prime Minister had made O'Connell think
hard and deeply about his role as an Irish politician in an imperial
context. While he accepted that neither of the major parties would grant
him Repeal in the immediate or even distant future, he was convinced
that Ireland might be able to obtain real concessions from such Whig
leaders as Russell, especially now that Stanley had broken with his
former colleagues. Conversely, he entertained little hope that the Tories
would depart very far from their traditional method of ruling Ireland –
that is, by a mixture of coercion and patronage exercised in the interests of a Protestant minority. These fears were reinforced when he

remembered the long history of antipathy between himself and Peel, dating back to the years 1812–18 when the latter had been Irish Secretary in Lord Liverpool's administration. The sequel therefore to the sudden change of government in November 1834 was a fundamental reappraisal by O'Connell of his whole political strategy. Instead of persevering with the Repeal campaign, he concluded in February 1835 the Lichfield House Compact with the Whig opposition – an alliance which in the short run was forged to dismiss the Tories from office but whose long-term aim was to develop an understanding between Whigs and Irish Repealers 'based on an exchange of political advantages'.[3] In practice O'Connell was agreeing to lend his support to a Melbourne-led administration and to drop the Repeal question entirely in return for a promise that Ireland would be governed in an equitable manner. The first part of the Repeal agitation was thus brought to an abrupt end with few positive achievements to its credit. Irish political life for the next six years was to be dominated by the attempt to translate the doctrine of good intent, embodied in the Lichfield House Compact, into a practical programme of co-operation.

II

There can be little doubt that from 1835 to 1841 O'Connell strove strenuously to honour his side of his bargain. Shortly after the formation of Melbourne's ministry in the spring of 1835, O'Connell, believing that 'the [Tory] party are down . . . for ever',[4] explained his reasons for his seeming volte-face in a *Manifesto to the Irish People*. Arguing that the Tories 'must be excluded rigidly in Ireland, or nothing *is* done', he went on to announce that Repeal had been placed in abeyance in order to test 'honestly and sincerely . . . the Union in the hands of a friendly Administration'. The Whigs, he asserted, should be given 'a clear stage and all possible favour, to work the Union machinery for the benefit of old Ireland'. Irishmen should thus 'rally round a Ministry which promises a new era, an era of justice and conciliation to the Irish people'.[5]

And certainly during the mid-1830s there seemed to be every indication that the Whigs were doing their best to remove many of the worst blemishes from Irish social and religious life. For one thing Thomas Drummond, Permanent Under-Secretary at Dublin Castle, strove, until his career was cut short by his premature death, to terminate the hitherto almost unbroken monopoly of the 'Protestant interest' in the sphere of public appointments. Another sign of change was that 'jury-packing' became less marked, while the Tithe Commutation Act of 1838 was a small but none the less significant step towards lightening one of the most deeply resented burdens of a largely Catholic population. O'Connell, impressed by these signs of Whig willingness to remedy long-standing abuses, told a group of Government supporters in Liverpool in 1836: 'They [the Whigs] have not coalesced with me, but I am ready to coalesce with them, because they are doing justice to Ireland.'[6] In September 1837 he reaffirmed his resolution to adhere to this alliance in a *Letter to the People of Ireland*: 'The Queen's Ministers are determined, if they can, to do justice to Ireland. Let us, then, work out our great experiment honestly – by honestly and cordially supporting that Ministry who are thus endeavouring to persuade us by acts and not by words that Repeal is needless.'[7]

None the less, with the passage of time it became less easy to gloss over the obvious failure of the government in one important field. The Tory-dominated House of Lords had thrown out or radically altered every Irish Corporation Reform Bill which the lower house had submitted to it during the course of the 1830s. O'Connell had asked English supporters of the Ministry in January 1836, 'Shall Ireland remain, nay, will you suffer Ireland to remain bearing the burthens of Corporations infinitely more odious and oppressive than either Scotland or England were ever afflicted with?'[8] That question was still unanswered in 1838–9. The result of Whig prevarication and weakness on this issue was that in August 1838 O'Connell founded the Precursor Society, an organisation pledged to press for the abolition of tithes, corporation reform, and increased parliamentary representation for Ireland. If, O'Connell concluded, the Whigs implemented this programme in full during the next year then he would become one of the foremost champions of the Act of Union. If on the other hand these legitimate requests were studiously ignored or frustrated by the obstructionist tactics of the Tory majority in the House of Lords, then he would have little alternative but to merge this society into a nation-wide movement for Repeal.

Although out of loyalty to his Whig allies he subsequently dropped all mention of Repeal from the Precursor Society's programme, he was increasingly coming round to realise that he would have to opt for this latter course. In a letter to P. V. Fitzpatrick, written in February 1839, he assessed in pessimistic terms the prospects for the forthcoming parliamentary session. 'With respect to Ireland, there is thorough indifference in both parties. In the Whigs coldness and apathy; in the

Tories, suspended hostility. They equally desire to keep Ireland out of sight, and to let her people continue in, I may call it, hopeless servitude.'[9] The passage through Parliament of an Irish Corporation Act in 1840 did little to impare the essential correctness of his analysis; for the final shape of that proposal was primarily determined by the House of Lords' unwillingness to cede to Ireland as broad a measure of municipal reform as England had enjoyed since 1835. It was against this sombre background of a tottering Whig ministry, controlled by rather than controlling the pattern of events, that O'Connell made his first move towards resuscitating the Repeal question in Ireland.

In April 1840 O'Connell founded the 'National Association for full and prompt justice or repeal'. Three months later he exchanged this cumbrous title, with its overtones of compromise, for the much shorter designation of the Loyal National Repeal Association. None the less, in spite of the early accession to the Repealers' ranks of the influential Archbishop John MacHale, the 'Lion of Tuam', O'Connell made singularly little effort to take the Repeal message to the Irish people until the Tories once more controlled the reins of power at Westminster. Although he complained to MacHale in the summer of 1840 that 'it is vain to expect any relief from England. All parties there concur in hatred to Ireland and Catholicity' [10] he at the same time studiously refrained from violating the terms of his 1835 understanding with the Melbourne ministry as long as it preserved even the most tenuous hold on office. It was entirely consistent with this position that as late as August 1840 he could advise a provisional committee of Liverpool Repealers not to press for Repeal, but to 'unite yourselves to the party which Mr Rathbone and Sir Joshua Walmsley lead' – that is, to the Liverpool Liberals – in order to secure the return of two Liberal members for the town at the next general election.[11]

That election, when it was finally held in July 1841, represented a devastating setback to O'Connell's political fortunes. In the first place it produced the first Tory administration – under Peel's guiding hand – with a majority in the House of Commons since 1830. O'Connell could therefore anticipate at best only limited opportunities of influencing, through parliamentary channels, the Irish policy of a party he had so consistently reviled. This factor alone must have made him seriously consider reviving the tactics so successfully employed by the Catholic Association on behalf of Repeal. His own natural inclination in favour of such a course of action was reinforced by the pattern of voting in Ireland during the election, since the main sufferers in the Irish constituencies had been not the Whigs but the group of Repeal M.P.s which gathered round O'Connell. This group had been 39 strong when it had initially emerged as an independent political force after the 1832 election. During the next decade, however, its strength had been slowly but surely eroded at successive appeals to the electorate, until after the 1841 campaign its numbers were reduced to a mere 18. Paradoxically enough, this low point in its fortunes was less the product of a massive revulsion of feeling among the Irish voters against the Repeal cause than a crushing indictment of O'Connell's own more recent policy. For his alliance with the outgoing government had so blurred any meaningful distinction between Whig and Repealer that the Irish electorate in 1841 had treated the two labels as virtually synonymous terms. The net outcome had been that Irish Whigs fared considerably better at the polls than O'Connell's severely tried band of Repealers. One consequence of the Lichfield House Compact, therefore, was to reduce O'Connell's following in the Commons to a handful and to compel him to carry on the struggle for Repeal on an extra-parliamentary basis.

III

As in the early 1830s, in 1841–2 O'Connell regarded Repeal as an indispensable precondition for the creation of a prosperous Ireland. Only a native parliament, he again argued, could completely restore to Ireland the sense of purpose which she so fully possessed in the years 1782–1800. More important, only such a domestic legislature would have sufficient drive to remedy those defects which continued to hamper the growth of religious harmony and the development of a more stable and more diversified economy. Repeal, among other things, would lead to protection of home industry from British 'dumping', the abolition of the tithe rent-charge imposed under the Tithes Commutation Act of 1838, and some degree of security for the tenant farmer. Precisely what was intended under this last heading was something of a mystery, for O'Connell's social conservatism prevented him from defining his attitude towards the land question with any degree of precision until Ireland was devastatingly hit by the widespread failure of the potato crop in 1845–6. Repeal, however, was not designed to benefit exclusively the Irish people. It was also to be an indirect means of raising the money wages of whole sections of the British working classes. According to a leading Repeal spokesman, W. O'Neill Daunt, the Union had throughout its history exercised a deleterious effect on the British operatives' standard of living: 'The plunder of Ireland by the Union drove her pauperised sons in crowds to England to pull down the wages of labour in the British markets.' The 'oppression of Ireland' had thus produced a situation in which 'the Irish operatives were literally taking the wages out of your pockets, and the bread out of your mouths.'[12] This thesis, which was an amalgam of the wage-fund theory and contemporary comment upon the role of the Irish immigrant in the labour market, was calculated to persuade the English working man to advance his own interests by lending his support to the Repeal cause. For once Repeal was secured, so this argument ran, Irishmen would return to their homeland, thereby removing the depressing effect which they had hitherto exercised on existing wage levels.

To ensure that this message on the merits of Repeal would reach as wide an audience as possible, O'Connell spent much of 1841–2 building up the organisational pattern of the Loyal National Repeal Association at the grass-roots level. His first need – for reliable local leaders – was quickly met by the overwhelming response of the Roman Catholic clergy to the Repeal call. Backed in many, but not in all cases, by their bishops, Catholic priests throughout the early and mid-1840s were to the fore in seeking the restoration of that domestic legislature 'which England so wickedly and unjustly robbed from Ireland'.[13] This was not merely true of Ireland; an identical pattern of behaviour was discernible in the areas of heavy immigrant settlement in England and Scotland. Even if his figures were wrong, it was not without some justification that the Reverend P. Levy of St Anne's, Leeds, could publicly proclaim O'Connell 'monarch of the affections of one million Irishmen in England'.[14] By working, therefore, through and with the priesthood in this way, O'Connell was able to ensure not only that his movement would keep broadly to the constitutional path of peaceful agitation, but also that the process of enrolling 'Associates' – all those who undertook to pay 1s per annum to the Repeal coffers – would proceed with the minimum of delay. The result of this co-operation was most tangibly expressed by the growth of local Repeal societies, affiliated to the parent body in Dublin. These societies in their turn had begun, before the end of 1842, to advance the 'good cause' in their own districts.

The work was carried on in three main ways. First, societies tried to disseminate knowledge of the basic principles which underlay the Repeal slogan by arranging a series of weekly or fortnightly meetings. At these functions it was customary for a prominent local Repealer, perhaps a Catholic priest, to deliver an address on the current state of the agitation or to read out extracts from O'Connell's latest speech. Second, Repeal Reading Rooms were established in many localities where Irishmen could read at their leisure the two principal Repeal newspapers, the *Freeman's Journal* and, after October 1842, the *Nation*. Last, but by no means least, the associate's interest in the Repeal question was constantly kept alive by frequent visits from the collectors of the Repeal Rent. None the less, for the spectacular breakthrough which O'Connell envisaged – to rally Ireland as the Catholic Association had rallied it in the 1820s – it was essential for the Repeal leadership at the national level to invigorate the movement they had created.

The necessary stimulus was to be provided by O'Connell's skilful manipulation of public opinion during the course of 1843. Already gratified by the infusion of new and youthful talent into the ranks of the Association – an infusion marked by the emergence of the *Nation* under Charles Gavan Duffy and Thomas Davis late in 1842 – he finally succeeded in rousing Irish public opinion to consider the future fate of the Union by his powerful and widely reported speech during Dublin Corporation's five days' debate on Repeal. This event, which took place in February 1843, constituted a watershed in the short history of the Loyal National Repeal Association. Thereafter, to the increasing consternation of Dublin Castle, it rapidly grew in strength: O'Connell had made the decisive impact on Irish society which had hitherto eluded him. After his triumph in Dublin Council chamber his main concern was to ensure that the gains which were won on that occasion were not speedily dissipated.

To this end, in the spring of 1843 he conceived the idea of holding a number of 'monster meetings' at sites closely identified with significant events in Ireland's struggle to preserve her national identity. These meetings, he hoped, would achieve two things. First, they would enable the Irish people to express their corporate will on the Repeal issue in the same way as they had shown their approval of the aims of the Catholic Association some fifteen years earlier. Second, they would demonstrate to Peel's ministry the folly of refusing to yield to the legitimate demands of a peaceful movement. O'Connell, however, in making this last assumption, was not merely basically misinterpreting the character of British Toryism but almost all shades of informed and influential political opinion in Britain in the 1840s. For the preservation of the Union still remained as much the policy of the Whigs as it was of the Tories. Russell might criticise individual aspects of Peel's management of Irish affairs between 1841 and 1846, but he was at one with the

Tory Minister in refusing even to consider Repeal as coming within the realm of practical politics. Few Radicals advanced very much beyond this position. Thus although O'Connell gave his blessing in the early 1840s to the Complete Suffrage Association's campaign for an extension of the franchise, he in his turn received less than whole-hearted support from that movement's leader, Joseph Sturge, the radical Quaker from Birmingham. Sturge might attack in November 1843 'the recent despotic proceedings of the government in Ireland', but he went on to argue that few Englishmen would sanction any move which would totally separate Ireland from the rest of the United Kingdom. Even so, he advanced a good deal further than most British politicians when he gave a cautious endorsement to the idea of a devolution of power along federal lines.[15] During the late 1830s and early 1840s only one important moulder of British opinion in fact ventured to go beyond a federalist solution to Ireland's difficulties; and that was the English Chartists under the aegis of Feargus O'Connor. The Chartist leaders were in favour of outright Repeal, although their support evoked little enthusiasm from O'Connell. Partly because of personal animosities between the two men, partly because O'Connell entertained a genuine dislike of the 'physical force' oratory of Chartist leaders in the years 1838–9, O'Connor's overtures to the Irish Repealers for a formal alliance between the National Charter Association and the Loyal Nation Repeal Association had no chance of success as long as O'Connell lived.

It is against this climate of opinion that the Government's reaction to the monster meetings campaign has to be set. By May–June 1843 Peel and his ministerial colleagues had begun to take the offensive against those who demanded the severance, in their existing form, of the ties between Britain and Ireland. On 9 May Peel had stressed, in the most solemn terms, the duty which the Queen's Ministers had of maintaining intact the Act of Union. The fearsome calamity of civil war was, he argued, preferable to the 'dismemberment of the Empire'. More impetuous spirits than Peel wanted to underline this commitment by taking firm action against those Irish magistrates who had been openly sympathetic to the Repeal cause. Among those who thought thus was Sugden, the Irish Chancellor, who at the end of the same month removed 24 J.P.s from the magistrates' roll because of their links with Repeal. Yet although Peel was to reprimand Sugden for the manner in which he had handled this particular affair, and although he managed to play down demands from De Grey, the Lord-Lieutenant of Ireland, for more extreme measures, he too believed in 'strong government' for

Ireland. It was Peel, for instance, who was to be responsible, before May had elapsed, for introducing an Arms Bill into the Commons designed to exercise effective control over the distribution of arms in Ireland. Initially O'Connell remained outwardly unperturbed by these developments. Continuing to adhere to the schedule of mass meetings he had promised to address in the early months of the year, he strove to present the Government's reaction to Repeal as the fumbling of men who were unsure of the future and unable to comprehend the trends of the present. Peel might for instance issue military threats, but even these could be answered in kind. Thus at Mallow, County Cork, in June 1843 O'Connell warned the Prime Minister of what might be the ultimate consequence of a policy of repression in Ireland. In his famous 'Mallow Defiance' – the one occasion when he seems to have departed from the constitutional path he had set for the Association – he informed his audience that 'you may soon have the alternative to live as slaves or die as freemen.'[16] If this were the choice they were confronted with, O'Connell had already decided on his course of action: 'They may trample me, but it will be my dead body they trample on, not the living man.'[17] But O'Connell's immediate concern lay only marginally in trying to persuade the Government into making a wrong move. His main aim was to keep the Repeal issue before the Irish peasantry and to persuade them that the struggle for an Irish Parliament could be, and indeed was being won. His proposal for the election of a Council of Three Hundred was calculated to serve this end. Briefly, he envisaged a collection of three hundred leading Repealers, who had received prior endorsements from the Repeal districts in Ireland, coming together in Dublin to draft a Repeal bill. Precisely how this quasi-legislature would operate and precisely how it would be regarded by Westminster were, however, two of the many vital questions left unanswered.

Nevertheless, in spite of the omission of such important points of detail, O'Connell could afford to feel well satisfied with his performance during the summer months of 1843. In terms both of the number of new associates enrolled and of the level of the 'Repeal Rent', 1843 had thus far surpassed his most sanguine expectation. By March the Rent was bringing in roughly £250 per week. By May the weekly average had risen to £1000, and by July to the staggering figure of £1900. Whereas the total income from this source in 1842 had been £5705, the corresponding result for 1843 was to be £48,706. Although it might be argued that some of this difference was produced by the current state of trade – 1842 was a notoriously 'black' year while 1843 was marked by a gentle upswing in the trade cycle – the overall differential was too wide to allow too much emphasis to be placed on this explanation. The Repeal Rent in 1843, in other words, can be regarded as a fairly sensitive indicator of a massive upsurge of support for Repeal among the Irish people. Many had come to believe, priests among them, that the government was about to accede to their wishes. As the Reverend Mr Synott put it when speaking at Enniscorthy in July 1843, 'The priests of Ireland have sounded the trumpets for the peaceful struggle – the people shouted . . . and down will fall the walls of Saxon Jericho.'[18]

By September 1843, however, O'Connell was painfully aware that 'Saxon Jericho' had not departed one inch from the rigid, unyielding policy which Peel had enunciated some three or four months earlier. As, therefore, he made arrangements for the last monster meeting of the year – to be held at Clontarf on 8 October – he must have been desperately worried about both how to maintain the momentum of the Repeal campaign and how to extract significant concessions from the Government. In particular, having virtually exhausted the complete repertoire of the forms of constitutional protest, he must have wondered precisely what tactical ploys within his self-imposed framework of 'moral force' methods remained open to him.

In the short run he was saved from having to find an answer to this problem by the Government. For it was roughly at this same point in time that Peel and Graham were considering a new approach to the Irish question, calculated to detach a portion of Irish Catholic society from their allegiance to O'Connell and Repeal. An essential precondition, however, for the introduction of their programme of reform was the reduction of the political temperature in Ireland itself. It was this consideration which above everything else turned the attention of the Government's legal advisers towards the pattern of the Repeal agitation in the autumn of 1843. It only needed a reference to 'repeal cavalry' in a public notice announcing the Clontarf meeting to produce a prompt reaction from Dublin Castle and Westminster. Within a very short space of time the Irish Executive had 'proclaimed' the rally scheduled to take place at Clontarf. This act had been followed up by an equally decisive move against the Repeal leadership, when O'Connell and his principal colleagues were arrested on charges of seditious conspiracy. During the following twelve months the attention of Irish Repealers was diverted away from Repeal as such and towards the course of, and sequel to, the State trials which were held in Dublin.

IV

Of all the aspects of Peel's Irish policy none was so counter-productive as the decision to prosecute the Repeal leaders in the courts of law. In the first place, the removal of all Roman Catholics from the jury lists by the Crown prosecutors was a tactical error of the first magnitude which Peel privately deplored, for it enabled the Whigs to charge the Conservatives with scant concern for the basic principles of justice. In the second place, the events of October–November 1843 convinced William Smith O'Brien, the Liberal M.P. for county Limerick and prominent Protestant landowner, that Ireland could only be governed well if she reverted to something akin to her 1782 Constitution. Thus one consequence of the legal attack on O'Connell was to drive Smith O'Brien into the ranks of the Repeal Association and thereby to give the Repealers their first Protestant convert of major public standing. O'Connell, overjoyed at this unexpected bonus, significantly appointed Smith O'Brien to overall charge of the Association's affairs when he and his fellow-conspirators began their prison sentences, in relatively pleasant surroundings, in May 1844. In the third place, the Crown's conduct of the State trials, above all the suspicion that the jury had been 'packed' with Protestants favourably disposed towards the Union, aroused Repealers in Ireland to a frenzy of protest against the Conservatives' conduct of Irish affairs. Largely as a result of the trials, money continued to flow into the Repeal treasury on almost the scale of the previous year. By the end of 1844 £43,884 had been raised throughout Ireland and among the immigrant communities in Britain for the 'Repeal Rent'. Not surprisingly, therefore, when viewed against these trends, a spirit of genuine optimism about future developments had, by the summer of 1844, returned to the Association's deliberations. Blackburn Repealers succinctly expressed this groundswell of opinion that better days lay ahead when, in a letter to Smith O'Brien, they asserted that 'tyranny may, indeed, imprison the Advocate [O'Connell], but can never chain up the *spirit* of liberty.' While 'the temporary supremacy of Ireland's foes' was to be deplored, 'we look forward with confident expectation, to their speedy downfall – whereafter no faction shall exult in the miseries of that suffering people.'[19] Smith O'Brien for his part promised to 'shrink from none of the labour and duties which can aid the Emancipation of my Country' as long as 'the Supporters of a Repeal of the Union adhere to their present maxim of peaceful perseverance'.[20]

When in September 1844 the House of Lords, acting in its judicial capacity as the court of final appeal, reversed the verdict of the State trials and released O'Connell and his fellow 'martyrs' from prison, these hopes seemed to be not without some justification. Yet amidst all the rejoicing which followed in the wake of this decision, two considerations which were to have an important adverse bearing on the outcome of the Repeal campaign were overlooked by the majority of Irishmen. First, it was logical to conclude that the old and trusted 'moral force' methods of the 1820s, which had won Catholic Emancipation and which O'Connell had pledged Repealers to use, would continue to make little impression on Peel's Conservative ministry. Second, O'Connell, when he eventually resumed his place in the political firmament, had lost much of his former sureness of judgement. Whether or not he was already suffering from the malady – softening of the brain tissues – which was ultimately to kill him, he alarmed the younger element in the Association, especially the group associated with Thomas Davis and Gavan Duffy at the *Nation*'s offices, by his flirtation in October 1844 with federalist notions.

v

The Irish federalists under the aegis of Sharman Crawford, the powerful advocate of tenant right, had tried to present to the Irish people a solution to current difficulties which fell a long way short of outright Repeal. Stripped to its essentials, their scheme envisaged the setting up of four local parliaments for Ireland, Wales, Scotland and England which should have charge of purely local affairs. In an Irish context this meant that the local legislature would 'make all the laws necessary for Ireland' and possess the right 'to impose and apply, with the consent of the Crown, all taxation necessary for the purposes of Ireland'.[21] But the imperial parliament would still continue in being at Westminster, drawing its members from the four constituent countries of the United Kingdom and controlling all facets of foreign and colonial policy. It was a proposal, therefore, of this nature that O'Connell was endorsing when he proclaimed his 'preference for the federative plan'. In the end, however, this manoeuvre only succeeded in antagonising all the interested parties.

Sharman Crawford, who had already in the mid- and late 1830s accused O'Connell of subordinating Ireland's true interests to the maintenance of the Whig alliance, scorned these overtures. 'With regard to O'Connell', he wrote to Smith O'Brien, he was 'humbugging both repealers and Federalists – trying to make the repealers believe they are Federalists – and the Federalists that they are Repealers – and keeping up a delusive joint agitation – knowing right well that whenever particulars came to be discussed they would split like a rope of sand'. The constitution of 1782 and a federal structure of government were, he concluded, 'so essentially different that it is impossible for the supporters of each to work together, unless one gave way to the other'.[22] The accuracy of these observations had in fact been vindicated by the reaction of the *Nation* to the proposal. Spurning all hint of compromise, it reminded O'Connell that the Association derived its *raison d'être* from its commitment to the repeal of the Act of Union. Federalism could thus by very definition play no part in its deliberations. After these rebuffs by both sides, above all after the magisterial rebuke from the *Nation*, O'Connell quietly abandoned all hope of integrating the Irish Federalists into a national movement for a limited form of devolution. On 26 November 1844 he marked his rededication to outright Repeal by publicly attacking those whose support he had been soliciting barely a month earlier: 'Federalists, I am told, are still talking and meeting – much good may it do them . . . but they are none of my children.'[23]

To most of his colleagues, including Gavan Duffy and Thomas Davis, this speech seemed to bring O'Connell's brief departure from the mainstream of Repeal thought to an end. In one sense this was true, for after this date O'Connell never again made any attempt to bridge the deep gulf which separated Repealers from Federalists. But in another sense the whole episode marked the beginning of a more perturbing development in the internal affairs of the Repeal Association – that is, the debate between O'Connell and the 'Young Ireland' group linked with the *Nation* about the meaning of Irish nationalism and its response to specific problems.

O'Connell, who had risen to eminence as the spokesman for the underprivileged Catholic majority in Ireland, never really succeeded in persuading his Protestant fellow-countrymen that Catholicism and Irish nationalism were not in his vocabulary synonymous terms. Although this assessment was less than fair – O'Connell throughout his political career was a persistent advocate of religious tolerance and equality – it did derive strong support from the manner in which he had chosen to conduct his Repeal agitation. In particular the close relationship which existed between O'Connell and the Catholic priesthood, and O'Connell's exhortation to his followers to attempt 'nothing without the co-operation of the clergy', conveyed the impression to many liberal Protestants that at the local level the Repeal Association was conterminous with the boundaries of the Catholic parish. It was thus scarcely surprising that relatively few of Ulster's substantial Protestant population had even contemplated joining a movement which had such an overwhelmingly Catholic membership and which seemed to identify Repeal with the advancement of the Catholic religion. These fears were reinforced by O'Connell's response to the Government's attempts to remove Catholic grievances during 1844–5. The Charitable Bequests Act of 1844 was opposed by the majority of Repealers, both ecclesiastical and lay, while the trebling of the Maynooth grant in 1845 – a measure which exposed Peel to biting attacks from ultra-Protestant organisations and politicians – was greeted with scarcely any show of gratitude. Last, but not least, O'Connell and Archbishop MacHale treated Peel's proposal, presented to Parliament in 1845, to reform and broaden, in the Catholic interest, the structure of Irish university education, with the profoundest hostility. The fatal flaw in this scheme, from O'Connell's point of view, was the absence of adequate safeguards to protect Catholic students from influences subversive of all religious belief. The 'godless colleges' should therefore be opposed because they would inevitably breed religious indifference. Supported in this stand by most of Ireland's Catholic bishops, he thereby not merely confirmed the suspicions of Protestant Ulster; he also provoked the second major revolt against his leadership by the *Nation* group.

From the foundation of the paper Gavan Duffy and Thomas Davis, who was himself of Protestant stock, had sought to define Irish nationalism in terms which surmounted both religious antagonisms and the social and economic barriers which separated landlord from tenant. To their mind, any form of 'nationality' which was socially or religiously divisive had to be opposed because it was a contradiction in terms. A nationalism which fragmented a people was a corruption of a noble ideal. It was thus simply because Peel's Academical Institutions (Ireland) Bill, whatever its defects, did promise to reduce sectarian passions by giving a common university training to the children of Ireland's middle classes, that the *Nation* gave the measure its qualified approval.

Given the *Nation*'s views, there was a degree of inevitability about the clash which occurred in May 1845 between Davis and O'Connell, the principal spokesmen for these two diametrically opposed schools of thought. Although the memory of this dispute was partly obliterated by

O'Connell's conciliatory gestures towards his younger opponent and by his genuine sorrow at Davis's tragically early death in September 1845, there were few guarantees that this conflict, emanating from radically different assessments of Ireland's needs, would not be repeated in the near future. By July 1846 the worst fears of Ireland's Repealers had been realised when the 'Young Ireland'–*Nation* element formally severed its connection with the Repeal Association.

The formalisation of the split between O'Connell and 'Young Ireland' stemmed indirectly from the onset of the Irish Famine and the impact of that fearsome disaster on national politics. The magnitude of the failure of the potato crop in the autumn of 1845 exercised a cataclysmic effect both on Ireland itself and the House of Commons. Faced with what was styled an 'imperial calamity', Peel had to decide how best he could insulate Ireland from the threat of mass starvation. On the positive side he came out in favour of a restricted programme of public works to tide Ireland over her immediate difficulties and the importation into the country of limited supplies of Indian corn. These measures, however, paled into insignificance compared with two other problems which confronted him – namely, whether or not he should repeal the Corn Laws, and whether or not he should try to tackle the vexed question of land reform. In the end the land issue was quietly dropped after the Government had made a token and completely abortive attempt to pass a measure dealing with compensation for improvement. But to be offset against this 'failure' was the fact that the existing system of agricultural protection had been completely dismantled by June 1846. The importance of this latter act was to be twofold. In the first place, it provoked a heated debate about the social and economic consequences of repeal for landlord and tenant farmer. Secondly, it constituted a turning-point in the history of mid-nineteenth-century politics; for it divided the Tory party as bitterly as tariff reform was to do during Balfour's 1902–5 administration. Peel and that section of the Tory party which followed his lead – the future Peelite group – accepted the overwhelming need for free importation of grainstuffs to alleviate the increasing amount of social suffering in Ireland, while the majority of the party remained firmly in favour of protection. Operating in this volatile environment, Peel had only been able to carry repeal of the provision laws because of the external support which had been given to him in the division lobbies by the Whigs.

The magnitude of this upheaval at Westminster affected thinking in Repeal circles about the utility to Ireland of a renewed alliance with the

Whigs. O'Connell for his part was immediately enthusiastic about re-establishing that close co-operation which had existed between Irish Repealers and the Melbourne ministry. As early as January 1846 he had begun to outline the terms on which he would be prepared to enter into an informal understanding with any future government which Russell might form. Among other things, he argued, the Whigs should conduct a more drastic overhaul of the structure of Irish municipal government than had occurred under the 1840 Irish Corporations Act. They should also extend the scope of the franchise in Ireland beyond the terms of the 1832 Irish Reform Act – a measure which O'Connell had once described as 'the new-fangled phrase now used in polite society to designate the Tory ascendency'.[24] Provided these concessions were made, the two sides could agree to differ on Repeal. The 'Young Irelanders', however, thought that Ireland would best be served by the total separation of Irish Repeal M.P.s from all British-based political parties: for such an alliance as O'Connell envisaged could only have a corroding effect on Repeal at a time of crisis in the internal affairs of the Irish nation. Whig patronage, they asserted, had once before blunted the enthusiasm of individual M.P.s for Repeal in the late 1830s. The movement could not afford to risk a revival of this practice in the mid-1840s.

Throughout the winter months of 1845 and the first half of 1846 the debate about the future direction of the Repeal Association continued. But it was no longer a debate between Gavan Duffy and newer members of the *Nation* group, such as John Mitchel and Thomas Meagher, on the one hand, and the Association's established hierarchy on the other. There were signs that Smith O'Brien, O'Connell's chief lieutenant, was drifting towards the more rigid concept of Irish nationalism which the 'Young Irelanders' preached. This showed in several small but cumulatively significant ways. First, Smith O'Brien was openly sceptical not only about Whig intentions towards Ireland but also about the willingness of Parliament itself to do anything positive towards easing the plight of the famine-stricken peasantry. Second, when in April 1846 he was placed in custody for refusing to serve on a committee of the House of Commons – he argued that he was serving his constituents better by remaining in Ireland – he was disgusted by the lack of support he had received from the committee of the Repeal Association. Whereas the 1782 Club, composed almost entirely of 'Young Irelanders', had given him its enthusiastic backing during this time of personal tribulation, scarcely a word of approbation for his act of defiance had come from the senior officials of the Repeal leadership. When, therefore, the long-anticipated confrontation between 'Young' and 'Old' Ireland finally took place in July 1846, O'Connell had no guarantee that Smith O'Brien would automatically take his side against his youthful opponents.

The confrontation was ostensibly concerned with the abstract question of whether or not moral force was in all countries and in every circumstance the only legitimate means of campaigning for a political goal. The universality of this principle, upheld by O'Connell and his son John, ruled out all talk of armed insurrection against any political system, no matter how corrupt or oppressive or incapable of reform from within it was. As O'Connell had put it almost two years earlier, 'The greatest and most desirable of political changes may be achieved by moral means alone . . . no human revolution is worth the effusion of one single drop of blood.'[25] The 'Young Irelanders', Thomas Meagher in particular, were to attack this doctrine with great vigour. Although they were prepared to accept that the Repeal agitation should be conducted on 'moral force' lines, they refused to accept this principle as a universal panacea for the redress of all political grievances. When O'Connell made it clear that unconditional subscription to this thesis was a necessary undertaking for all those who desired to remain members of the Repeal Association, the 'Young Irelanders' and Smith O'Brien walked out of the debate. By acting thus they formally severed their connection with the organisation they had served so well. O'Connell could now press forward with his Whig alliance – Russell had returned to power in June 1846 after Peel's administration had been brought down on its Irish Coercion Bill – but without the backing of most of Ireland's most articulate young nationalists.

The immediate reaction to rank-and-file Repealers to this secession was stunned disbelief. For the previous four years they had been taught to believe that the *Nation* was fulfilling a valuable role in the national struggle; now they were asked to ban it from their Repeal reading-rooms. Similarly they had been accustomed to treat Smith O'Brien as second only to O'Connell among the Repeal leaders; now he had formally severed all connection with the Association. Although Catholic bishops such as Cantwell and Higgins did much in the succeeding months to restore the faith of most Catholic Repealers in O'Connell by painting the seceders as 'schoolboy philosophers and sanguinary Repealers' and implying that the *Nation* was a 'Voltairean newspaper' tending 'to the overthrow of Catholic faith and morals',[26] it was none the less impossible to prevent, in the short term, a wide-spread questioning of the wisdom of forcing the 'Young Irelanders' out of the movement. In the North of England, for instance, Repealers from Manchester, Leeds, Stalybridge and Liverpool felt constrained to 'regret and disapprove of the policy and proceedings that have had the effect of driving our much-valued and much-beloved countryman, Mr Smith O'Brien, and so many other able, honest, and uncompromising compatriots from the Association'.[27] In Ireland the protest movement expressed itself through the Dublin Remonstrance of November 1846 – a document which denounced both the forging of the Whig alliance and the 'moral force' resolutions which had been instrumental in disrupting the unity of the Repeal front.

Faced by these tangible signs of unrest within the Repeal ranks and compelled to acknowledge that the much-vaunted understanding with the Whigs had produced few concrete results for Ireland, now experiencing the second successive failure of the potato crop, O'Connell tried to placate his critics by conducting negotiations with 'Young Ireland' on the peace resolutions themselves. Meeting the seceders in Dublin in December 1846, he went so far as to concede that he was willing to confine the doctrine of 'moral force' to an exclusively Irish context. This offer, however, was insufficient to entice 'Young Ireland' back into the fold. What they by now also wished to discuss were the closely related questions of the Whig alliance and Government patronage, and the introduction into the Association's affairs of some degree of public control over the management of the 'Repeal Rent'. The sequel to these far-reaching demands was the breakdown of the talks and the formation in January 1847 of the Irish Confederation.

VI

The Irish Confederation came into being at a time when Irish society was in a state of flux. For one thing, the rigours of the Famine were already causing deaths from undernourishment and producing moves towards the consolidation of holdings. For another thing, in the realm of Government policy Russell was about to acknowledge, albeit reluctantly, that the food requirements of the Irish people could not be met by market forces alone and that it was economically impossible for Ireland to set in motion public works on the scale required to provide employment for the landless labourer. In the political field there were also signs of change. In January 1847 the so-called 'Irish Party' emerged, composed of Tories, Whigs and Repealers, and pledged to press at Westminster for schemes of land reclamation and drainage work, and for some recognition of the principle of compensation for improvement. Last, but not least, came the death in May 1847 of Daniel O'Connell – an event which was genuinely deplored by Smith O'Brien and his colleagues but which also deprived the Repeal Association of their one leader of national stature. In every respect his successor, his son John, was a man of infinitely fewer accomplishments.

On the whole, however, the Irish Confederation failed to exploit this situation to its own advantage. Partly this was because of the hostility its activities encountered from the Catholic clergy. But partly also it was a product of the essential conservatism of its Council. For the Council's policy aims were virtually identical with those which the dead O'Connell had followed in the early days of the Repeal movement. Like O'Connell, Smith O'Brien was dedicated to obtaining Repeal by relying on 'moral force' methods. Like O'Connell, too, the Confederate Council devoted little real thought to socio-economic issues. Repeal was a political goal; all detailed examination of how to improve the lot of the peasantry would have to wait until an Irish Parliament met again on College Green. If, then, the Repeal Association drifted aimlessly for most of 1847 under John O'Connell's guidance, the Irish Confederation did little to inspire any hope of salvation in a wretched peasantry struggling against the fearsome consequence of the potato blight.

It is against this sombre backcloth that James Finton Lalor's appearance on the Irish political scene has to be set. Lalor from the outset was convinced that the key question facing Irish society was not Repeal but the problem of land tenure. The Irish peasant's greatest need in 1847 was not an Irish Parliament but the acceptance by all Irish landlords of the principles of Ulster tenant right. To achieve this goal Lalor came out in favour of a nation-wide campaign to secure the Irish tenant against the evils of arbitrary eviction, rack-renting and noncompensation for the improvements he had made to his holding. Initially, however, this social programme created scarcely a ripple of interest in the Confederate ranks. Although Lalor himself was active on behalf of tenant right Leagues in Tipperary and Kilkenny during the course of the year, he only made his first important recruits on the Confederate Council in November 1847. They were John Mitchel and Devin Reilly.

By early 1848 Mitchel, convinced of the validity of Lalor's analysis, had tried to persuade his colleagues to break out of the political straitjacket which they had imposed on the activities of the Confederation.

Everything was to be gained by committing themselves to land reform. Moreover, to give such a policy a sense of urgency they should also exhort all tenant farmers to refuse to pay the poor rate until tenant right had become the law of the land. To Smith O'Brien and Gavan Duffy, however, Mitchel's ideas were fraught with danger, the more so as he was also beginning to speak of armed resistance to the Crown. As they interpreted it, the course of action Mitchel was now advocating suffered from two major defects. In the first place, a poor-rate strike would hit hardest the most destitute sections of society. It was, therefore, either an impracticable proposition, or if 'practical', then inhumane in its consequences. In the second place, to accept the policy Mitchel had outlined would sound the 'death knell' on the comprehensive type of nationalism to which the *Nation* had always been dedicated. Landlord would then be arrayed against tenant, instead of both classes co-operating together for Ireland's political regeneration. What therefore Mitchel and Lalor had brought to the forefront of the Confederation stage was a debate about ends. To the land reformers the socio-economic issue of the land was of prime importance; beside it questions of constitutional proprieties paled into insignificance. On the other hand, to the overwhelming majority of the Confederate Council Repeal remained what it had always been – a largely political objective.

In the short run Gavan Duffy and Smith O'Brien had little difficulty in securing a decisive majority in favour of their more cautious programme of constitutional reform, although at high cost. For this verdict, delivered by the Confederation in early February 1848 after a protracted debate, resulted in Mitchel, Devin Reilly and John Martin resigning from the Confederate Council and the appearance on 12 February 1848, under Mitchel's editorship, of the *United Irishman*. This newspaper, during its brief life, was to be noted both for its militant republicanism and its social radicalism. There was thus a real possibility that the Confederation might further hinder the progress of Irish nationalism by fragmenting into two rival schools of thought. That this did not ultimately occur owed less to the skilled diplomacy of its leaders than to the reaction of the Irish people to the revolution of February 1848 in France.

The overthrow of Louis Philippe's 'July Monarchy' acted as a catalyst on Irish nationalists in general and on the Confederate leaders in particular. Gavan Duffy and Smith O'Brien had now real cause to examine critically the basic premises of their organisation and how best to overcome the obstacles which still stood in the way of their success.

One immediate result of this rapid reappraisal was to drive them nearer to the position of Mitchel than had seemed possible a fortnight earlier. While, for instance, they were still not persuaded to take up the question of the land, they no longer frowned upon thinly veiled 'military' threats to the Government. By March 1848 Gavan Duffy had gone so far in this direction as not to rule out the use of force to obtain Repeal if the Whig ministry spurned all offers of a negotiated settlement, and Smith O'Brien had stressed the virtues of setting up, and enrolling in, a National Guard. Such suggestions as these, backed up by Mitchel's vitriolic articles in the *United Irishman*, were accompanied by two other developments. First, the Confederate clubs had begun to organise drill practices among groups of pike-armed members, and to act as the nucleus of a 'National Guard'. Secondly, the Confederation had concluded an informal alliance with Feargus O'Connor and the English Chartists.

This last step above all marked a major break with the past. For the Confederates, like O'Connell before them, had hitherto avoided all contact with 'the insane or dishonest Radicals of England, who, instead of appealing to common sense, declare their reliance on arms; and instead of resorting to reason and justice, talk of swords, rifles, and physical force'.[28] As late as August 1847 Mitchel had endorsed this stand by writing in biting terms against such fraternisation: 'Between us and them there is a gulf fixed, and we desire, not to bridge it over, but to make it wider and deeper.'[29] Such sentiments had initially been reciprocated by many English Chartists. According to Julian Harney, for example, 'Smith O'Brien and his friend were no advocates of democratic principles, all they wanted was an Irish middle-class supremacy dignified by a national flag.'[30] The pressure of events, however – especially the Confederation's conviction that they would need Chartist support to mount a diversionary military operation in the North of England in the event of an armed uprising in Ireland – had done much to soften old antagonisms. In January 1848 the first signs of the coming *rapprochement* was the appearance of James Leach, a prominent Manchester Chartist, at the Confederation's birthday celebrations. Thereafter the scope of the contacts between the two movements gradually widened until, despite Smith O'Brien's private misgivings, a deputation from the Confederation cemented their understanding with O'Connor at a Manchester rally, arranged, appropriately enough, for St Patrick's Day (17 March 1848).

The sudden upsurge of Repeal activity was not without its effect on Lord Clarendon, head of the Irish Executive and Lord-Lieutenant. Fearing that the situation would deteriorate rapidly unless prompt action were taken against the Confederates, Clarendon resolved to prosecute Meagher, Mitchel and Smith O'Brien for sedition. This decision, taken towards the end of March 1848, was not, however, sufficient in his eyes to restore stability to a troubled land. In addition, therefore, he sought to persuade Russell's Cabinet to suspend the operation of habeas corpus in Ireland as long as the present tensions should last. Not unexpectedly Russell, analysing the Irish scene from the more detached position of London, at first refused to institute such a sweeping suspension of the rule of law. Instead he compromised, asking his Lord-Lieutenant to be content with the Treason Felony Act which had been passed in April. It was ultimately to be this statute, with its penalty of transportation for all those who tried to stimulate treasonable acts 'by open and advised speaking', which did more than anything else to undermine faith among Confederates in 'moral force' methods.

Significantly neither Smith O'Brien nor Meagher, when they were brought to trial on the sedition charge, had been prosecuted under the broad terms of the Treason Felony Act. Both had been acquitted. John Mitchel, who just prior to his own court appearance had broken with the Confederation because it would not adopt his radical republican notions, was not to be so fortunate. His articles on military tactics in the *United Irishman* and his defence of armed resistance to the authority of the Crown conformed so closely to the definition of treason felony that the decision was made to charge him with committing this newly created offence. In the upshot he was sentenced at the end of May to transportation to Tasmania for a period of fourteen years.

The verdict had two immediate consequences. In the first place, the severity of Mitchel's sentence led to renewed talks between the Repeal Association and the Irish Confederation about the desirability and practicability of reunification. By early June a provisional agreement was reached to dissolve both of the existing organisations and to replace them by an Irish League. Confederate clubs, however, were to continue in being to act, if the need arose, as quasi-military bodies. Second, even the most conservative Confederate spokesmen began to think of the possibility of an armed uprising as the best means of breaking Ireland's association with the rest of the United Kingdom. Yet those who thought thus were basing their hopes of success on a totally unrealistic appraisal of the social environment in which they would be operating. For one thing the Irish peasantry, bowed down by the weight of the three successive potato crop failures and already experiencing the horrors associated with widespread evictions, was in no condition to answer any call to throw off the 'British yoke'. More important, the Government, as strong as the Irish peasantry was weak, was as well able to meet any potential uprising as the 'Young Irelanders' were powerless to launch one. Nothing proved this more conclusively than the closing chapter of the Repeal agitation. For when in late July Russell, once more yielding to Clarendon's entreaties, at last suspended habeas corpus, the hastily planned uprising became a fiasco. By the end of the same month Smith O'Brien's experiment with the doctrine of physical force had come to an ignominious end in Tipperary. Ahead for him and his fellow-conspirators lay the treason trials and exile from their native land. Behind them they left a dispirited people, disillusioned with Repeal for a generation. The Irish peasant had lived to see both O'Connell's 'moral force' methods and the idea of armed insurrection totally discredited. At the end of seven years' agitation for Repeal – 1841–8 – the Union seemed as immutable as ever. Faced by this catalogue of disaster and disappointed hopes, the Irish peasantry in the early 1850s turned away from constitutional issues and took up Lalor's cry of tenant right. Repeal was thus decently interred until it was resurrected by Isaac Butt and Parnell in the 1870s and 1880s under the new title of Home Rule.

BIBLIOGRAPHICAL NOTE

The economic and social background of Ireland in the first half of the nineteenth century is still only broadly covered by G. O'Brien, *The Economic History of Ireland from the Union to the Famine* (Longmans, 1921) and T. W. Freeman, *Pre-Famine Ireland* (Manchester U.P., 1957). The rapid growth of Ireland's population during the hundred years preceding the Famine and the ineffectiveness of government legislation to halt the process of subdivision have been well documented by K. H. Connell, *The Population of Ireland 1750–1845* (O.U.P., 1950). Some of Connell's findings, however, have been recently disputed both by M. Drake, 'Marriage and Population Growth in Ireland 1750–1845', *EcHR* 2nd ser., xvi (1963), and by L. M. Cullen, in two articles: 'Problems in the Interpretation and Revision of Eighteenth Century Irish Economic History', *TRHS* 5th ser., xvii (1967) and 'Irish History Without the Potato', *Past and Present*, 40 (1968). Irish agriculture on the eve of the Famine has been examined in depth by E. R. R. Green in his contribution to R. D. Edwards and T. D. Williams (eds), *The Great Famine* (Nowlan & Browne, Dublin, 1962, ed.). The effect of the Famine itself on government policy is discussed in detail by C.

Woodham-Smith, *The Great Hunger: Ireland 1845–9* (Hamish Hamilton, 1962). The important theme of the impact of nineteenth-century economic theorists on successive administrations' approach to the 'Irish question' is well documented in R. D. Collison Black, *Economic Thought and the Irish Question 1817–70* (C.U.P., 1960). A microcosmic study of the growth of the textile industry in part of Ulster has been made by E. R. R. Green, *The Lagan Valley 1800–50: a Local History of the Industrial Revolution* (Faber, 1949). C. Gill, *The Rise of the Irish Linen Industry* (O.U.P., 1925) is still the seminal study of the development of one of Ireland's major nineteenth-century industries.

The best introduction to the political background of Repeal is to be found in the two volumes which R. B. McDowell has devoted to politics and public opinion – *Irish Public Opinion 1750–1800* (Faber, 1944) and *Public Opinion and Government Policy in Ireland, 1801–46* (Faber, 1952). For the history of the Catholic Association and the campaign for Catholic Emancipation, see J. Reynolds, *The Catholic Emancipation Crisis in Ireland, 1823–29* (Yale U.P., New Haven, 1954), The same question is examined from a different angle in G. I. T. Machin, *The Catholic Question in English Politics 1820 to 1830* (O.U.P., 1964). The early phase of the Repeal question – that is, from 1830 to 1834 – still awaits its historian. It is, however, touched upon by J. Broderick, 'The Holy See and the Irish Movement for the Repeal of the Act of Union with England, 1829–47', *Analecta Gregoriana*, lv (Rome, 1951), and A. Macintyre, *The Liberator, Daniel O'Connell and the Irish Party 1830–47* (Hamish Hamilton, 1965). Both these works are indispensable studies of different facets of the period under review. A. Macintyre explores with great skill the practical consequences for Ireland of the Lichfield House Compact, while J. Broderick looks at both the part the Irish Catholic clergy played in the Repeal agitation and the pressures which were placed on the Holy See by the British Government to condemn clerical intervention in politics. The Repeal agitation and the changing attitudes of Peel to Ireland are exhaustively analysed in K. B. Nowlan, *The Politics of Repeal* (Routledge, 1965) and in the same author's contribution to Edwards and Williams (eds), *The Great Famine*.

Specialist studies of various aspects of the Repeal agitation have been made by an assorted company of historians. The aims and objectives of the Irish Federalists are analysed by B. A. Kennedy, 'Sharman Crawford's Federal Scheme for Ireland', in H. A. Cronne, T. W. Moody and D. B. Quinn (eds), *Essays in British and Irish History in Honour of James Eadie Todd* (Muller, 1949). Several essays and monographs have been devoted to the subject of 'Young Ireland'. R. D. Edwards, 'The Contribution of Young Ireland to the Development of the Irish national idea' in S. Pender (ed.), *Féilscríbhinn Torna* (Cork U.P., 1947), tries to analyse what the 'Young Irelanders' contributed to the concept of a distinctive Irish nationalism. D. Gwynn has examined the clashes between 'Young' and 'Old' Ireland over Peel's proposal to reform Irish higher education in *O'Connell, Davis and the Colleges Bill* (Cork U.P., 1948). The same author has also traced the course of the 'Young Ireland' movement from its inception to its inglorious end in his *Young Ireland and 1848* (Cork U.P., 1949). The causes of the split in July 1846 between 'Young' and 'Old' Ireland are outlined in Randall Clarke, 'The Relations between O'Connell and the Young Irelanders', *Irish Historical Studies*, iii (1942–3). The Irish Confederation-English Chartists' *rapprochement* in March 1848 is touched upon briefly in D. Read and E. Glasgow, *Feargus O'Connor* (Arnold, 1961). The central position of O'Connell in Irish political life has been discussed in D. Gwynn, *Daniel O'Connell, the Irish Liberator* (Hutchinson, 1930), M. Tierney (ed.), *Daniel O'Connell, Nine Centenary Essays* (Browne & Nolan, Dublin, 1949), J. H.

Whyte, 'Daniel O'Connell and the Repeal Party', *Irish Historical Studies*, xi (1959).

Irish participants in the events of the 1830s and 1840s have left a vast collection of material for the historian's use. Apart from unpublished letters and contemporary newspaper reports, these records fall into two broad groups. First, there is that part of O'Connell's voluminous writings which was published in W. J. Fitzpatrick (ed.), *Correspondence of Daniel O'Connell, the Liberator*, (2 vols Murray, 1888). Although these are far from exhaustive, they give a good insight into the mind of O'Connell, the practical politician. Second, 'Young Irelanders' such as C. Gavan Duffy and John Mitchel have attempted to write a history of the troubled times through which they and the Repeal agitation passed in the 1840s. Sir C. Gavan Duffy tried to trace the course of the Repeal movement from 1840 to 1849 in two distinct works – *Young Ireland: A Fragment of Irish History, 1840–45*, 2 vols (Allen & Unwin, 1896) and *Four Years of Irish History, 1845–49* (Cassell, 1883). Both of these studies are immensely readable, but are heavily weighted in favour of the 'Young Irelanders'. J. Mitchell, *The Last Conquest of Ireland (Perhaps)*, (Cameron & Ferguson, Glasgow, n.d.), is again an attempt to write the history of Ireland in the 1840s from the author's own distinctive standpoint.

NOTES

1. *PP* (1831–2), xix, qq. 11909, 11912.
2. J. F. Broderick, 'The Holy See and the Irish Movement for the Repeal of the Union with England, 1829–47', *Analecta Gregoriana*, lv (1951), 35–6.
3. A. Macintyre, *The Liberator* (1965), p. 144.
4. O'Connell to P. V. Fitzpatrick, 14 Apr 1835 (W. J. Fitzpatrick [ed.], *Correspondence of Daniel O'Connell* (1888), ii, 12).
5. Ibid., p. 7.
6. *Liverpool Mercury*, 29 Jan 1836.
7. *Leeds Times*, 16 Sept 1837.
8. O'Connell to W. Rathbone of Liverpool (*Liverpool Mercury*, 22 Jan 1836).
9. O'Connell to Fitzpatrick, 6 Feb 1839 (Fitzpatrick, op. cit., ii, 168).
10. O'Connell to MacHale, 25 July 1840 (ibid., ii, 246).
11. *Liverpool Mercury*, 1 Jan 1841.
12. *Leeds Times*, 23 Sept 1843.
13. Broderick, loc. cit., p. 125, quoting Cantwell.
14. *Leeds Times*, 30 Sept 1841.
15. Ibid., 4 Nov 1843.
16. K. B. Nowlan, *The Politics of Repeal* (1965), p. 48.
17. Sir C. Gavan Duffy, *Young Ireland* (1896), i, 122.
18. Broderick, loc. cit., p. 149.
19. N. L. I. Smith O'Brien Papers, 434 (1214): 'Address to Smith O'Brien on behalf of the Blackburn, Lancs., Repealers . . . dated 23 July 1844'.
20. Ibid., 434 (1216): O'Brien to Blackburn Repealers, 25 July 1844.
21. B. A. Kennedy, 'Sharman Crawford's Federal Scheme for Ireland', in H. A. Cronne, T. W. Moody and D. B. Quinn (eds), *Essays in British and Irish History in Honour of James Eadie Todd* (1949), pp. 250–1.
22. N. L. I. Smith O'Brien Papers, 434 (1277): Crawford to O'Brien, 18 Nov 1844.
23. Cronne *et al.*, op. cit., p. 252.
24. Macintyre, op. cit., p. 35.

25. D. Gwynn, *Daniel O'Connell, The Irish Liberator* (1903), p. 266.
26. D. Gwynn, *Young Ireland and 1848* (Cork, 1949), p. 81.
27. *Nation*, 5, 12 Sept, 3, 17 Oct, *Leeds Times*, 24 Oct 1846.
26. O'Connell to N. Maher, 23 Oct 1838 (Fitzpatrick, op. cit., ii, 156).
29. *Nation*, 15 Aug 1847, quoted in Sir C. Gavan Duffy, *Four Years of Irish History, 1845–49* (1883), p. 450.
30. *Northern Star*, 8 Aug 1846.

8. The Public Health Movement

C. H. HUME

THE improvement of the health of a community has always posed many problems to the pioneers of public health. There must be available knowledge of sanitary engineering, town planning and building as well as medical skill; general and local acts must be passed which local authorities and medical workers must attempt to apply, often at the same time having to overcome resentment or apathy among those involved.

The need for some organisation of public health was stressed early in the nineteenth century by John Roberton, who wrote that 'by far the greater proportion are cut off by diseases induced by want of care, and propagated by want of attention both to themselves and their inferiors in society'.[1]

Agitation for reform of sanitary conditions in the nineteenth century came not from the people most at risk, and only to a minor degree from local authorities, but mainly from medical and other individuals who were concerned about health problems in all classes of society.

Even in its early phases the Industrial Revolution brought about significant changes in the distribution and condition of the population. Industrialisation resulted in the expansion of old and the creation of new communities and led to the migration of large numbers of people from rural areas. Irish immigrants, to whom even the squalor of the industrial areas may have been an improvement upon conditions at home, increased the size of certain urban communities, particularly Liverpool, Manchester and Glasgow. In Scotland there was a marked shift of population from the Highlands to areas south of the Forth. The rise of industry and its demand for labour does not altogether explain the movement of population, but only the predilection for certain areas. Nor does it explain why people were willing to move in the first place. Among the reasons was the pressure of a steadily increasing population on limited land, a situation periodically aggravated by crop failure.

The result was the overcrowding of certain areas, particularly in towns where conditions were already bad, with inadequate new housing and inefficient refuse removal, drainage and water supplies. Some local authorities, along with the various local Commissioners of Paving,

Sewerage and Improvement, did attempt to ameliorate conditions by obtaining Local Improvement Acts, although such attempts were sometimes frustrated by lack of finance and the opposition of private interests.[2] By 1820, however, local government was generally unable to cope with the increasing problems of growing towns.[3] These factors, along with periods of industrial depression and destitution, tended to produce unhealthy and undernourished groups, a prey to disease both endemic and epidemic.

I

Until the 1830s there were only sporadic attempts by local and central government, and by a few early reformers, to improve sanitary conditions and to deal with outbreaks of disease. Between epidemics no preventive measures were thought necessary, the outbreaks being considered 'acts of God'. Many years were to pass before it was possible to overcome the fatalistic acceptance of disease exemplified in the preface to the Cholera Prevention Bill of 1832, with its assertion 'whereas it has pleased Almighty God to visit the United Kingdom with the plague called cholera . . .', and the public health movement largely devoted itself to reports deploring conditions and overcrowding.

As well as investigation of bad housing, sanitation, water supply and disease itself as factors influencing public health, the study of health and population statistics has often interested workers in this field, particularly at that time when there was marked population movement. For about eight decades before 1830 population increased all over the country, most rapidly in those towns where it was affected by migration.

The population, which had been increasing in the late eighteenth century, increased even faster between 1800 and 1830, in England and Wales by 5,004,000 (55 per cent) and in Scotland by 756,000 (47 per cent). In London and Edinburgh the population between 1801 and 1830 increased by 63 per cent and 24 per cent respectively and in Glasgow, Leeds, Birmingham, Liverpool and Manchester the populations more than doubled during this period.[4]

An overall growth in population obviously depends on two basic factors, birth and death rates and the balance between them. Many economic historians have held that the main factor between 1750 and 1830 was the falling death rate and a birth rate maintained at a high level, except between 1816 and 1830 when the birth rate was falling.[5] Factors affecting the birth rate were the marriage age, fertility, the demand for child labour and the fall in neonatal mortality due to advances in medical knowledge.[6] Factors producing the fall in death rate included medical advances and eighteenth-century agricultural improvements.[7]

Crude death rates for towns are in themselves of no more value than simple population figures in estimating the nation's health; only when they are considered in conjunction with estimates of population density and shift, immigration and migration, and causes of death do they become more meaningful as health statistics.

The rise in the death rate just before 1830 detected by Griffith[8] was probably the result of overcrowding, malnutrition and industrial disease in the newly expanded towns. The child mortality rate (more than half of which was due to infectious disease) reversed the fall achieved in preceding decades by children's hospitals and dispensaries and by smallpox vaccination. Malthus asserted in his *Essay on Population* in 1798 that 'It would appear by the present proportion of marriages, that the more rapid increase of population supposed to have taken place since the year 1781 has arisen more from the diminution of deaths than the increase of the births.' Birth rates were maintained between 1781 and 1830 in spite of cyclical unemployment and wage cuts.

Much more important are the figures of the incidence of disease, mortality due to specific diseases, comparative death rates, and disease incidence in towns and rural areas, particularly during epidemics.

The Registration of Births and Deaths Act of 1837 made it possible to obtain more accurate figures of births and deaths in England and Wales, and the provision was extended to Scotland in 1854. These records were to specify causes of death, a provision which was to prove valuable in health statistics. Before 1830 the main diseases rife in the community were typhus fever, smallpox and dysentery. From the beginning of the nineteenth century free vaccination of children reduced the incidence of smallpox although epidemics occurred in 1817 and 1825, when there were epidemics of typhus among adults. Even at that time it was realised that typhus and dysentery occurred more often and spread more rapidly in conditions of poor personal hygiene and poor sanitation.

II

In most large or growing towns housing presented a problem, largely because of a growing labouring population which had moved to the sources of employment. Such workers accepted poor living conditions and many crowded together in 'single rooms' or cellars. New accommodation for the increasing numbers of working people in industrial towns was in many cases badly built. The modern view that town planners should consider the public health was certainly not widely held. Even new houses tended to be cramped; in the North of England 'back-to-back' houses were common, in Scotland well-built tenements with inadequate sanitary facilities were constructed, and in the Midlands ill-ventilated courts were surrounded by buildings. The construction was frequently unsound, lacked proper drainage and had open sewers outside. Overcrowding remained a problem well into the nineteenth century as new building did not keep pace with the population growth and shift.

Refuse removal, drainage and water supplies, in most places barely adequate, became grossly overburdened by the growing urban population. The fact that these conditions were associated with ill health was recognised, and the conditions were deplored by many writers who observed them in the large cities of Britain, and in the years prior to 1830 several men were concerned with public health problems. Although their work was an important and necessary part of the development of health consciousness, their names are not as well known as those of some later reformers.

Among the early reformers were Thomas Perceval and John Ferriar of Manchester, who influenced the formation of the Manchester Board of Health in 1795; some recent writing has emphasised the importance of their work.[9] Another writer tends, however, to minimise the importance of these men in the light of the work of later and more effective reformers.[10] In Scotland Robert Graham, Robert Cowan and James Cleland published reports on public health in the early nineteenth century.[11] The contribution of William Jenner's work on smallpox vaccination was also important in the first decades of the century.[12]

With the growth of manufacturing industries and mining, industrial disease and injury became more common as a result of factors such as poor ventilation, long hours and inadequate sanitation, and also as a result of the danger inherent in the processes themselves. An extensive survey of occupational disease and its resulting mortality and morbidity was carried out by Charles Turner Thackrah of Leeds in 1831–2. He examined the differences in mortality rates in urban and rural communities and noted the high incidence of respiratory disease among those working in dust-laden or polluted atmospheres, the skin diseases found among grocers, bricklayers and bakers due to sugar, lime and flour respectively, and the effects of lead and silver absorbed through the skin of potters and silverers. He gave an exhaustive account of many types of occupations and their hazards, showing the need for supervision and reform of industrial processes.[13] Robert Baker, a Leeds factory inspector, carried on his work in the eighteen-forties and fifties.[14]

It is clear that by 1830 the existing standards of housing, sanitation, water supplies, conditions of work and knowledge of basic hygienic principles, especially among the working classes, were a danger to the whole community and required major improvements. These conditions were not new. They had been described and deplored by many people, and tentative measures had occasionally been taken against them in the face of public apathy and general unconcern. But it was not until after 1830 that these clamant facts were brought forcibly to the notice of the public and the Government by 'agitators' and stated in published reports to be a danger to the country. The growth of population and industry meanwhile continued to impose new stresses on an already tottering sanitary structure.

III

During the years 1830–8 there were two strong stimuli to action: first, the outbreak of Asiatic cholera in Britain for the first time and second the rise of Edwin Chadwick as a government administrator and later as a sanitary reformer.

The cholera epidemic broke out in 1831 in Sunderland. During 1832 it became widespread, affecting most parts of Britain but being concentrated in the poor quarters of the towns.

'The virus, for all its opportunities, showed a marked preference for, an almost exclusive selection of the lowest and least cleanly localities, and a considerable preference for persons of drunken or negligent habits', wrote Creighton in 1894.[15] Some authorities, however, consider that, unlike typhus, cholera was liable to attack the middle classes as much as the labouring population, as their improved water supplies could disseminate the disease rapidly if the infection became waterborne. Professor Briggs[16] has shown that the disease was found in better-class localities which had a good water supply, while poor localities with no water supplies might well escape it.

Early in 1831, realising the risk of cholera spreading to Britain from the Continent, the Government had sent two Medical Commissioners to St Petersburg to study the disease. Their report, combined with the growing alarm among Government officials, resulted in the institution of a Board of Health which announced general facts about the prevalence of disease in unclean conditions and among those in poor health. The main preventive provisions were strict quarantine, isolation of cases, the establishment of temporary fever hospitals and fumigation of infected furniture, clothing and rooms.[17]

Local boards of health were to be set up in the large towns and were to appoint inspectors who would submit daily reports on the health of their own districts. The board was to give assistance and advice to the poor if deficiencies in food, clothing, ventilation, cleanliness and drainage facilities were reported. Reports from the local boards were to be sent to the Central Board.

As doubts were expressed as to the legal powers of the boards, temporary 'Cholera Acts' were passed in 1832[18] to allow them to enforce various measures. Although this legislation strengthened the boards' position, it could not coerce the people into individual effort in spite of the fear of the disease. The City of London and Birmingham were the only places in which local authorities made major efforts to carry out the recommendations of the national Board.

One important view of the epidemic was propounded by a Dr McCann of Newcastle, who had had experience of cholera in India. He insisted that early treatment in the 'premonitory' phase was of the greatest importance, and that special dispensaries should be set up for treatment of the first symptoms. In 1832 McCann was said to have arrested a severe outbreak near Wolverhampton by this treatment of incipient cases.[19]

As usual, after the epidemic had died down some officials held that it had been 'much less fatal than the preconceived notions had anticipated' and that 'the alarm was infinitely greater than the danger'.[20] It was considered, however, that the public had become more aware of the dangers to every section of the community during an epidemic, and it had been shown that it was possible to prevent the spread of cholera by early treatment of suspected cases.

The emergence of Edwin Chadwick as a public figure in the 1830s was the result of his work for the Royal Commissions on factory labour and Poor Laws. His investigations of schemes for the care of the aged, young and insane poor in almshouses and hospitals, industrial schools and organised asylums between 1832 and 1834 gave him an insight into the conditions of the poor. After the passing of the Poor Law Amendment Act in 1834, he was appointed Secretary to the Commissioners after being rejected as a commissioner.[21]

Chadwick's concern at the lack of public health administration was aroused as a result of his work for the Poor Law Commission, and also followed his interest in the 'sanitary idea' which stemmed from his research for essays on health statistics and preventive police in the late 1820s. These essays had led to Chadwick's appointment as secretary to the ageing Bentham, whom he assisted in the completion of the *Constitutional Code*. Bentham's influence on Chadwick, though strong, was not enough to cause him to accept the offer of an annual income from Bentham to become an exponent of his views alone.[22] It was, however, from 1838 on that Chadwick turned his whole attention to public health questions, having been again rejected as Poor Law Commissioner to replace Thomas Frankland Lewis.

In 1837 an Act was passed for the registration of births and deaths in England and Wales. Chadwick was the instigator of the provision that causes of death as well as the crude death rates should be recorded, a modification which he considered would highlight the areas where preventable diseases could be attacked and public health improved. The assistant Registrar-General, appointed at Chadwick's suggestion, was William Farr, who held the post for forty-two years and became one of the important names in public health owing to his brilliance as a statistician and to the large number of reports which he produced.

During Chadwick's years as the Poor Law Secretary he battled many times with the Commissioners over the administration of the new Act. He was by all accounts a very difficult man to deal with, headstrong, humourless, extroverted and egotistical. But he was also tireless in his schemes for 'social engineering', and he was incensed at the sight of 'unnecessary' disease, waste or suffering. This facet of his character no doubt gave him the ability fearlessly to pursue his ideas for sanitary reform, although his successes were certainly not won by persuasion but rather by coercion of his opponents.

During the Poor Law investigation of 1832–4 Chadwick had considered the health of the pauper population. Improvements of their conditions (for example in housing) might in the long run prove to be less expensive, he thought, than continually supplying poor relief to those suffering illness as a result of bad conditions. By 1838 it was apparent to the Commissioners also that disease both endemic and epidemic was placing a great burden on the poor rates and that it would be good economy to alleviate poor conditions. A letter on this subject, drafted by Chadwick, was sent in 1838 from the Commissioners to the Home Secretary, Lord John Russell, and resulted in an inquiry into the prevalence of disease and the conditions of the working classes in the metropolis. This inquiry was carried out by three medical men who were to become leading figures in the cause of health reform, Neil Arnott, James Phillips Kay and Thomas Southwood Smith.[23]

Arnott, a London physician, had previously been a ship's surgeon and had become noted for his interest in the improvement of seamen's health. By the time of the inquiry he was well known also for his interest in furthering health improvement and education.[24]

Kay, later Sir J. P. Kay-Shuttleworth, practised for some years as a physician in Manchester and in 1832 had published an account of *The Moral and Physical Conditions of the Working Classes* of that city. Later he became an assistant Poor Law Commissioner, which led to his association with Arnott and Southwood Smith.[25]

Southwood Smith had practised as a minister of religion before and for some time after turning to medical studies. In the early 1820s he was appointed physician to the London Fever Hospital, a post which fitted him well to investigate disease and the conditions encouraging it in the metropolis. He worked also among the poor as physician to the Eastern Dispensary and the Jews' Hospital in Whitechapel. He had acted with Chadwick on the 1833 Factory Commission. In 1825 his first article on sanitary matters was published, 'Contagion and Sanitary Laws', studying the relationship between epidemics and bad sanitary conditions, and in 1835 he published his *Philosophy of Health*, which became influential in drawing popular attention to simple practical ideas of preventive health and hygiene. From 1839 to 1854 he was a zealous worker in the cause of sanitary reform in association with Chadwick. Like Chadwick and Arnott he had been a follower of Bentham.[26]

The three investigators submitted two reports. Kay and Arnott wrote 'On the prevalence of certain physical causes of fever in the Metropolis which might be prevented by proper sanitary measures'. Southwood Smith gave his views 'On some of the physical causes of sickness and mortality to which the poor are particularly exposed and which are capable of removal by sanitary regulations, exemplified in the present condition of the Bethnal Green and Whitechapel districts, as ascertained in a personal inspection'.[27] These accounts, based partly on personal inspection and partly on medical reports from Poor Law medical officers, brought several salient facts to the notice of Parliament. In areas inhabited by many thousands, healthy conditions were unattainable under existing circumstances. The rather insanitary personal habits of the population were probably of less significance in producing disease (and in fact inevitable in the circumstances) than overcrowding, poor ventilation, lack of organised refuse disposal and insufficient water supply, all of which were the concern of local governing bodies. In 1839 Southwood Smith asserted in a supplementary statement that[28]

Such is the filthy, close and crowded state of the houses and the poisonous condition of the localities in which the greater part of the houses are situated from the total want of drainage and the masses of putrefying matters of all sorts which are allowed to remain and accumulate indefinitely, that during the last year in several of the parishes, both relieving officers and medical men lost their lives in consequence of the brief stays in these places which they were obliged to make in the performance of their duties.

In a further appendix Southwood Smith reported 'On the prevalence of Fever in twenty Metropolitan Unions and Parishes during the year ended the 20th March 1838'.[29]

These reports were the first official results of inquiries directed by Governmental agencies into the possibilities of preventive medicine and the improvement of the conditions of the poorer classes. No further action was taken until in 1839 the bishop of London, Dr Blomfield, probably at the instigation of Chadwick, suggested in the Lords that a similar survey should be made of the prevalence of disease among the labouring classes in other parts of England and Wales. A resolution was passed to this effect, and the large-scale investigation which commenced was further extended in 1840 to include Scotland. This inquiry was not finally completed until 1842 owing to the extensive nature of the undertaking, lack of finances, minimal Government interest, the change of Government in 1841, and the general suspicion aroused by Chadwick and his inquiries.

IV

During this period another 'sanitary' agitator, the Radical politician Robert Aglionby Slaney, secured the Select Committee on the Health of Towns in 1840 to investigate the health of inhabitants of large towns with a view to improving their sanitary arrangements. Chadwick disapproved of this body which re-interviewed many of his witnesses, and he saw no merit in its rather general recommendations. But in fact the report,[30] issued after three months, did stimulate some interest among members of the failing Whig Government. It recommended a general buildings Act, a general sewerage Act and a Board of Health in each large town with a sanitary inspector to enforce regulations; and attention was drawn to defects in burial grounds, water supplies, lodging-house conditions and the provision of public baths.

Lord Normanby, the Home Secretary, introduced three bills dealing with borough improvements, urban building regulations and drainage improvement. Chadwick was annoyed, not only by these proposals, but still more by Normanby's 'ban' on the continuation of his own inquiry. These three bills were defeated, but their proposals were periodically discussed for three years. From 1841 Normanby became, in Opposition, an enthusiastic supporter of sanitary reform.

Chadwick was requested by Sir James Graham, the new Home Secretary, to complete his report for the 1842 session. He produced two volumes of local reports from all over the country and a third volume consisting of his own treatise, the 'Report on the Sanitary Condition of the Labouring Population of Great Britain'.[31] In February 1842 the report was completed but the Poor Law Commissioners, George Lewis in particular, refused to have it published in its original form, because of its severe criticism of the London water companies, the metropolitan Commissions of Sewers, the medical profession and local administration. It was eventually published in July 1842 under Chadwick's name alone, having been redrafted on the suggestion of John Stuart Mill and with additional material collected in the interim. As the report was a House of Lords paper it was scarce in its official published form. To enable as wide a distribution as possible Chadwick arranged a separate publication of a large edition to be sold and given away.

The reports covered towns of all sizes, villages both industrial and agricultural, lodging-houses, miners' housing, all types of cottage dwellings, and drainage and sewerage. The financial burden of ill health in the community was described with suggestions for legislation; and attention was drawn to the proved efficacy of those preventive measures which had been previously adopted. Information for the reports was collected by means of the Poor Law organisation; the assistant Commissioners sent out to various towns and districts details of the information required by Chadwick. The reports were sent back by Poor Law medical officers and by many other people concerned with social medicine, physicians, dispensary surgeons, clergymen, prison officers and factory owners. Chadwick himself, with Arnott, visited several towns and wrote some of the local reports.

In the preface to his report, Chadwick stated that he was not concerned with the treatment of disease but with collecting evidence of the means available to improve the observed poor conditions of the housing, habits and general environment of the labouring classes. He pointed out that the cases described were not isolated incidents but were examples of very frequent occurrences.

The report has remained justly famous as the first full account of poor living conditions and their effects, and of possible remedial measures, and as a result Chadwick's name is one of the most important in the field of health reform. Benjamin Ward Richardson described him as 'the pioneer of that modern sanitary science which has worked in the course of half a century such true marvels for the prevention of disease'.[32] Although Richardson, as a contemporary biographer, may have been over-enthusiastic, Chadwick's contributions to public health stimulated interest in a way no other worker had done before, and made 1838 a turning-point in the sanitary movement.

Chadwick's recommendations were that the removal of solid refuse and sewerage from houses and outside privies could be effectively carried out by the suspension of the matter in water, which would then be removed by glazed circular-bored drains. Better water supplies would be necessary both for this drainage method and for supply to private houses. Geological factors should be considered as a basis for economical and efficient drainage. He suggested that there should be appointed officers with a knowledge of science and civil engineering who would be responsible for devising new local public works, to ensure people's confidence in the improvements and to protect rate-payers and the labouring classes from inefficiency and waste of money. Medical officers should be appointed to prevent disease caused by bad conditions (for example poor ventilation) in places of work or assembly.

There was no immediate move to implement Chadwick's recommendations, and he spent the year following their publication in preparing a report at Graham's request on burial practices. This question had been omitted from his report in 1842 as a Select Committee on Interments had produced a report in that year.[33] Chadwick's supplementary report,[34] published in 1843, confirmed the Select Committee's advice on the discontinuance of intramural burial and also described many social factors concerned with the expense of burials to the poor, the lack of mortuaries and the danger to the health of a family if removal of a body were delayed.

While Chadwick was studying burial practices, his 'sanitary report' was producing mixed reaction ranging from derision to whole-hearted support. Graham proposed in 1843 a Royal Commission on the Health of Towns and rejected Normanby's three health bills, which by this time had passed the Lords and had reached a second reading in the Commons. The purpose of the Health of Towns Commission was not to question the general principles of Chadwick's report but to investigate more fully the legislative and financial side of the proposed improvements, and Chadwick himself drew up a programme for the Commission. It was to suggest effective legislation and to establish

> the best means of promoting and securing the Public Health under the operation of the Laws and Regulations now in force, and the usages at present prevailing with regard to the drainage of lands, the erection, drainage and ventilation of buildings, and the supply of water in such towns and districts, whether for the purposes of health, or for the better protection of property from fire.

The Commissioners, under the Duke of Buccleuch, included Lord Lincoln, Sir Henry de la Beche (a geologist), Professor Richard Owen, Arnott, Lyon Playfair (a chemist), Smith of Deanston (a cotton-mill manager and authority on land drainage), Slaney and Captain Denison and Robert Stephenson (engineers). Chadwick took virtual command and organised the investigation and reports. Questionnaires were sent to the fifty towns which had the highest annual death rates and the Commissioners personally studied for themselves the conditions in the most populous areas. Of fifty towns investigated, forty-two had very bad drainage and thirty had a poor water supply. Only one town had reasonable drainage and six good water supplies. Reports were sent to Chadwick by supporters of his campaign, including W. H. Duncan of Liverpool, Haycock of York and the engineer Thomas Hawksley of Nottingham.

The first report of the Health of Towns Commission was published in 1844. It provided an outline of the Commissioners' views, particularly on the state of town drainage and water supply. Few new facts emerged, but the evidence emphasised what Chadwick considered to be the immediate need for improvements in sanitary engineering. The second report[35] in 1845 consisted of proposals for future legislation, with a long memorandum by Chadwick explaining the recommendations on sewerage, drainage and water supply. He considered that local authorities had shown themselves incapable of managing those matters efficiently.

These reports ended the Governmental investigation into health

THE PUBLIC HEALTH MOVEMENT

THE PUBLIC HEALTH MOVEMENT 195

matters which had begun with the 'Fever Reports' of 1838. During the Health of Towns inquiry in 1844, Slaney and Normanby became impatient with the delay in definitive action and Normanby produced a petition from 3000 Edinburgh inhabitants demanding sanitary legislation. Chadwick was convinced that all evidence should be amassed and the most efficient measures determined before any legislation was introduced.

In spite of all the published reports there was no great increase in general public support, and Chadwick decided to inaugurate a campaign to spread propaganda. The Health of Towns Association, formed in 1844, had a central committee in London and local associations in the provincial towns. Chadwick, although not a member of the Association, was its virtual leader and directed its action, provided much of the propagandist information and wrote many of its reports. Among its members were Ashley, Normanby, Slaney and Southwood Smith. The members gave public lectures, organised pamphlet distribution and petitions and produced publications such as the *Weekly Sheet of Facts and Figures*.

In 1845, after the final report of the Health of Towns Commission had been presented, the introduction of sanitary legislation was announced in Parliament. Lord Lincoln, First Commissioner of Woods and Forests, introduced measures, based on the report, which Chadwick and the Health of Towns Association criticised as having many weaknesses. The Bill was introduced at the end of the 1845 session but immediately dropped until the 1846 session. Introduced in 1846, the Bill was again withdrawn owing to Peel's resignation and the change in government. In 1847 Lord Morpeth introduced a Health Bill which was also dropped because of more pressing Government matters, in spite of the change of attitude everywhere as a result of the Health of Towns Association and its propagandists. Morpeth reintroduced his proposals in 1848[36] and they were passed in the same year as the Bill for Promoting the Public Health.[37]

V

The Act of 1848 established a central 'General Board of Health' which lasted for five years. The Board was empowered to initiate sanitary reforms in any town on receiving a petition from one-tenth of its ratepayers or where the death rate from all causes reached 23 per thousand per annum. Municipal authorities were to be responsible for local public health, and where there was no elected council, a local board of health would be established.

Several other measures were passed while the Public Health Bill was under consideration. Acts of 1846 dealing with the removal of nuisances and the prevention of epidemic disease were eventually embodied in the measure of 1848. The Liverpool Sanitary Act was passed in 1846, giving the town council powers to carry out sewerage, drainage and water supply improvements, and appointing W. H. Duncan as the first Medical Officer of Health in Britain. In 1847 the Waterworks Clauses Act and Town Improvement Clauses Act were passed to encourage local reforms. These were overshadowed by the 1848 measure, but remained important in Scotland, where the Public Health Act did not apply. It had been recognised in 1847 that the 1848 measure would not apply to London and a Royal Commission was appointed under Chadwick, the Metropolitan Sanitary Commission, which made its reports in 1847-8. In consequence a measure providing for the appointment of the Metropolitan Commissioners of Sewers was passed in 1848 as the Metropolitan Sewers Act.

Any immediate results of the 1848 Act were overshadowed by the outbreak of cholera in Britain for the second time and the consequent involvement of the Board. In addition, the Board was controversially involved with the problem of the water supply and drainage of the metropolis, which had been excluded from the Act, and the Board's own investigations were resented by the Metropolitan Commissioners.

In spite of these problems the Board applied the new health regulations successfully for six years; by the beginning of 1850, 192 towns had requested legislation and the Act had been applied in 32; by 1853 there were 284 petitions and the Act had been applied in a total of 182 cases. The work of the Board, however useful, made it unpopular with certain local authorities and individuals, and in 1854 the Board was disbanded and a new Board to be appointed every two years set up in its place. One of the first tasks of this Board, as in the case of the Board of 1848, was to deal with a cholera outbreak, this time in 1854-5.

One important result of the cholera epidemics in 1848 and 1854 was three independent reports on the spread of disease by John Snow, William Budd and John Simon.[38] Snow, of London, studied the predisposing factors and spread of disease in the two epidemics and published his results in 1849 and 1854. The famous case described was that of the Broad Street pump which supplied water to a certain district where cholera was rife, apart from a small area which used a different water supply. After removal of the pump handle the number of cases quickly declined. Budd, of Bristol, published articles and a book on cholera and typhoid spread, in which he reached the same conclusions as Snow, and remarked on the prevention of spread within a family by proper disposal of infected excreta. Simon's report 'On the London Cholera Epidemics of 1848–49 and 1853–54 as affected by the consumption of impure water' described the evidence that in areas with impure water the incidence of cholera was higher than in areas with a clean water supply.

VI

There were other workers in the cause of health reform during the period of agitation with which Chadwick is most associated. Robert Baker, of Leeds, was active in the field of industrial health, studying conditions of work and their effects on health rather than the industrial diseases themselves. Prior to his appointment as a factory superintendent in 1834, he had studied also the cholera outbreak in Sunderland and noted the prevalence of cases near open sewers. Duncan, of Liverpool, was influential in obtaining Local Improvement Acts in the 1840s, culminating in the Liverpool Sanitary Act of 1846, which gave the town council power to institute many improvements. This work was continued even more effectively by Duncan as Medical Officer of Health from 1846.[39] The contribution of John Simon to public health was more as administrator than as agitator; as Medical Officer of Health to the City of London from 1848 to 1855, he laid down a pattern of public health administration which was followed successfully by many later medical officers.[40] The Radical surgeon Thomas Wakley, who became the first editor of the Lancet in 1823, supported health legislation in his journal. He also praised the publication of facts about the high incidence of pulmonary tuberculosis, and the relationship of disease to bad social and working conditions.[41]

Agitation for public health reforms as such was not marked among the general population but among individual pioneers such as Chadwick, and the legislation passed by 1850 to improve conditions detrimental to health was the result of the work of these people. Possibly ignorance of the specific causes and spread of disease, as well as fear of it, caused those of the general population who recognised the need for drastic improvements of living conditions to combine with the Chartists, and those who recognised the causal agents of disease in industrial processes and deplored the poor conditions of work joined the factory reform movement, both of which can be called with truth 'popular movements'.

BIBLIOGRAPHICAL NOTE

The background of public health achievements and developments in the nineteenth century is dealt with adequately in W. M. Frazer, *History of English Public Health* (Ballière, Tindall & Cox, 1950) and George Rosen, *A History of Public Health* (MD Publications, New York, 1958). A more detailed account of public health administration in England in the nineteenth century can be found in John Simon, *English Sanitary Institutions* (Cassell, 1890) although this book is less easily obtainable. Thomas Ferguson, *The Dawn of Scottish Social Welfare* (Nelson, 1948) fully describes social and health conditions and attempted improvements in Scotland. Many descriptions of urban conditions and town planning during the industrial revolution are given in William Ashworth, *The Genesis of Modern British Town Planning* (Routledge, 1954). Charles Creighton, *A History of Epidemics in Britain II* (reprint, Cass, 1968) contains a detailed account of diseases prevalent in Britain during the eighteenth and nineteenth centuries, with figures of incidence in different areas concerning both endemic and epidemic disease.

The life of Edwin Chadwick, his career as a public health pioneer and his relationship with colleagues and friends are described in R. A. Lewis, *Edwin Chadwick and the Public Health Movement* (Longmans, 1952) and S. E. Finer, *The Life and Times of Sir Edwin Chadwick* (Methuen, 1952). Lewis gives more detail of the administrative side of public health and the Commissions and reports with which Chadwick was associated, while Finer describes more fully Chadwick's personality and his influence on those working with him. A recent edition of Chadwick's *Report on the Sanitary Condition of the Labouring Population of Great Britain* (1842) has been published with a foreword by the editor, M. W. Flinn, (Edinburgh U.P., 1965), who gives a useful account of the political, economic and social background to the report and of the administration involved in the collecting of material for it, and a summary of Chadwick's chief aims and recommendations.

The lives of important public health pioneers of the period are described in W. M. Frazer, *Duncan of Liverpool* (Hamish Hamilton Medical Books, 1947); Frank Smith, *The Life and Times of Sir James Kay-Shuttleworth* (Murray, 1923); Royston Lambert, *Sir John Simon* (McGibbon & Kee, 1963) and A. Meiklejohn, *The Life, Work and Times of Charles Turner Thackrah* (Livingstone, Edinburgh, 1957). Major Greenwood's book *Some British Pioneers of Social Medicine* (Cumberlege, Oxford, 1948) contains short accounts of early pioneers such as Perceval and Ferriar as well as Chadwick, Simon and Farr.

Basic accounts of the population problems of the eighteenth and nineteenth centuries are found in G. Talbot Griffith, *Population Problems of the Age of Malthus* (Cambridge U.P., 1926) and M. C. Buer, *Health, Wealth and Population in the Early Days of the Industrial Revolution* (Routledge, 1926). *Population in History*, ed. D. V. Glass and D. E. C. Eversley (Arnold, 1965) contains a number of articles by H. J. Habakkuk, T. H. Marshall, D. V. Glass, D. E. C. Eversley and Thomas McKeown and R. G. Brown which deal with various controversial aspects of the population problem.

NOTES

1. John Roberton, *A Treatise on Medical Police and on diet, regimen, etc.* (Edinburgh, 1808), p. xv.

2. Sir J. H. Clapham, *An Economic History of Modern Britain* (Cambridge, 1964), p. 538; Asa Briggs, *The Age of Improvement* (1959) p. 46.

3. G. Kitson Clark, *The Making of Victorian England* (1962), p. 18.

4. B. R. Mitchell and Phyllis Deane, *Abstract of British Historical Statistics* (Cambridge, 1963), pp. 5, 6.

5. T. H. Marshall, 'The Population Problem during the Industrial Revolution', *Economic History*, i. (1926–9); D. V. Glass, 'Population and Population Movements in England and Wales, 1700 to 1850' from D. V. Glass and D. E. C. Eversley (eds), *Population in History* (1965), p. 239; G. Talbot Griffith, *Population Problems of the Age of Malthus* (1926), p. 28.

6. D. E. C. Eversley, 'Population, Economy and Society', Glass and Eversley, op. cit., p. 39; Thomas McKeown and R. G. Brown, 'Medical Evidence related to Population Changes in the Eighteenth Century', Glass and Eversley, op. cit., p. 299; T. H. Marshall, loc. cit., pp. 431, 434–5; H. J. Habakkuk, 'English Population in the 18th Century', *EcHR* 2nd ser., vi (1953–4).

7. Thomas McKeown and R. G. Brown, loc. cit., pp. 304–7; H. J. Habakkuk, loc. cit.

8. Talbot Griffith, op. cit. p. 39.

9. B. Keith Lucas, 'Some Influences affecting the Development of Sanitary Legislation in England', *EcHR* 2nd ser., vi (1953–4).

10. E. P. Hennock, 'Urban Sanitary Reform a Generation before Chadwick?', *EcHR* 2nd ser., x (1957).

11. A. K. Chalmers (ed.), *Public Health in Glasgow* (Glasgow, 1905), pp. 5, 7.

12. Charles Creighton, *A History of Epidemics in Britain* (Cambridge, 1894), ii, 564–6.

13. A. Meiklejohn, *The Life, Work and Times of Charles Turner Thackrah* (Edinburgh, 1957), pp. 3–8, 51–7, 120–5.

14. W. R. Lee, 'Robert Baker: the First Doctor in the Factory Department', *Br. J. of Industrial Medicine*, xxi (1964); F. Beckwith 'Robert Baker', *The University of Leeds Review*, vii (1960).

15. Creighton, op. cit., pp. 799–800.

16. A. Briggs, 'Cholera and Society', *Past and Present*, 19 (1961).

17. J. Simon, *English Sanitary Institutions* (1890), pp. 170–1.

18. 2 Will. IV, cc. ix–xi.

19. Simon, op. cit. pp. 174–5.

20. *Annual Register*, lxxiv (1832), pp. 305–6.

21. R. A. Lewis, *Edwin Chadwick and the Public Health Movement 1832–1854* (1952), p. 19.

22. Maurice Marston, *Sir Edwin Chadwick (1800–1890)* (1925), pp. 20–2.

23. Simon, op. cit., p. 181.

24. Ibid., p. 185.

25. Frank Smith, *The Life and Work of Sir James Kay-Shuttleworth* (1923), pp. 14, 35. Kay's book has been reissued (Frank Cass, 1968).

26. Simon, op. cit., p. 187.

27. Fourth Annual Report of Poor Law Commissioners, *PP* (1837–8), xxviii, app. A.

28. Simon, op. cit., p. 183.

29. Ibid., p. 184.

30. Report of the Select Committee on the Health of Towns, *PP* (1840), xi.
31. *PP* (1842), xxvi.
32. Benjamin Ward Richardson, *The Health of Nations* (1887), ii, p. 1.
33. Report of the Select Committee on Intramural Interments, *PP* (1842), x.
34. Supplementary Report on Intramural Interment, *PP* (1843), xii.
35. 1st and 2nd Reports of the Health of Towns Commission, *PP* (1845), xviii.
36. *PP* (1848), v.
37. 11 and 12 Vict., c. 63.
38. John Snow, *On the mode of Communication of Cholera* (1855); William Budd, *Typhoid Fever, its Nature, Mode of Spreading and Prevention* (1873); *PP* (1856), lii.
39. W. F. Frazer, *Duncan of Liverpool* (1947), pp. 35, 45.
40. Royston Lambert, *Sir John Simon* (1963), pp. 114, 603.
41. Charles Brook, *Battling Surgeon* (1945), pp. 33, 167.

NOTES ON CONTRIBUTORS

W. H. CHALONER, M.A., Ph.D. (Manc.), is Reader in Modern Economic History in the University of Manchester. Publications include *The Social and Economic Development of Crewe, 1780–1923* (1950), *People and Industries* (1963), two histories of insurance companies, new editions of several nineteenth-century books and (with A. E. Musson) *Industry and Technology* (1963). With W. O. Henderson he has also published new translations of W. G. Hoffmann's *British Industry, 1700–1950* (1955) and of Friedrich Engels's *Condition of the Working Class in England in 1844* (1958).

DEREK FRASER, M.A., Ph.D. (Leeds), is Senior Lecturer in History in the University of Bradford. Publications include *The Evolution of the British Welfare State* (1973) and his edited volume on *The New Poor Law in the Nineteenth Century* in the 'Problems in Focus' series (1976).

W. H. FRASER, M.A. (Aberd.), D.Phil. (Sussex), is Lecturer in History in the University of Strathclyde and editor of the Scottish Labour History Society's magazine.

Mrs C. H. HUME, M.B., Ch.B. (Glas.), was Assistant Lecturer in Anatomy in the University of Glasgow.

M. E. ROSE, B.A., D.Phil. (Oxon.), is Senior Lecturer in Modern Economic History in the University of Manchester. Publications include *The Relief of Poverty, 1834–1914* (1972).

J. H. TREBLE, B.A., Ph.D. (Leeds), formerly a Research Assistant in the University of Birmingham, is Lecturer in Economic History in the University of Strathclyde.

J. T. WARD, M.A., Ph.D. (Cantab.), is Professor of Modern History in the University of Strathclyde, having formerly been a Bye Fellow of Magdalene College, Cambridge and Lecturer in Modern History in Queen's College, Dundee. Publications include *The Factory Movement, 1830–1855* (1962), *Sir James Graham* (1967) and a new edition of John Fielden's *Curse of the Factory System* (1969).

ALEX WILSON, M.A. (Glas.), D.Phil. (Oxon.), is Director of Studies in Management and Industrial Relations in the Department of Extra-Mural Studies of the University of Manchester. Publications include 'Chartism in Glasgow' in Asa Briggs (ed.), *Chartist Studies* (1959), and *The Chartist Movement in Scotland* (1970).

Index

Shaw, Sir Charles, 143
Sheffield, 2, 33, 41–2, 80, 81, 84, 88–90, 96, 101, 105, 109, 111–12, 119, 142
Sibthorp, Charles de Laet Waldo, 14, 61
Simon, Sir John, 196–7
Slaney, Robert Aglionby, 191, 194–5
Slavery, 19, 37, 56
Smiles, Samuel, 1
Smith, Adam, 6, 10, 64, 74, 154
—, James, 194
—, James Elishma, 106–7
—, Sydney, 3–4, 18
—, Thomas Southwood, 190–1, 195
Snow, John, 196
Society for Promoting Christian Knowledge, 19
Society for Promoting National Regeneration, 68, 104
Society for the Propagation of the Gospel, 19
Society for Suppression of Vice, 19
Somerville, Alexander, 141
Southey, Robert, 60, 63
Sparke, Edward Boyer, 18
Spooner, Richard, 33
Stalybridge, 100, 145, 174
Stanhope, Philip, 4th Earl, 82
Stanley, Viscount (14th Earl of Derby), 17, 156–7
Stephens, Joseph Rayner, 9, 24, 68, 69, 70, 72–3, 87, 89, 142
Stephenson, Robert, 194
Stocks, William, 86
Stretton, George, 41
Strickland, Sir George, 7th Bt, 73
Sturge, Joseph, 123, 164
Sugden, Sir Edward (1st Lord St Leonards), 124
Sutton, Charles and Richard, 40
'Swing Riots', 8, 39, 78
Sykes, Sir Tatton, 4th Bt, 4

Taylor, Sir Herbert, 53
—, John, 122
—, John Edward, 41
—, William Cooke, 57
Thackrah, Charles Turner, 70, 186–7
Thompson, James, 40
—, Matthew, 65, 84
—, Thomas, 40
—, Thomas Perronet, 137
—, William, 16, 102

Thomson, Charles Edward Poulett (1st Lord Sydenham), 68, 73
Todmorden, 62, 84, 88
'Tolpuddle Martyrs', 8, 81, 105, 108, 110
Tone, Wolfe, 152, 155
Tooke, Thomas, 136
Trollope, Anthony, 3
—, Mrs Frances, 70
Turner, James, 65–6
Twiss, Horace, 25

Unitarians, 22, 145

Victoria, Queen, 1, 64
Villiers, Charles Pelham, 141
Vincent, Henry, 90, 123, 124, 130

Wakefield, 46
Wakefield, Edward Gibbon, 16
Wakley, Thomas, 197
Wales, 48, 49, 82, 118, 119, 130, 184
Walker, William, 62, 70
Walmsley, Sir Joshua, 160
Walter, John, 79, 87, 90
Warrington, 58
Warwickshire, 33
Watkin, Sir Edward William, 1st Bt, 143–4
Watson, Joshua, 19
Weatherhead, David, 69
Welch, Edward, 104, 107
Wellesley, Arthur (1st Duke of Wellington), 14–17, 24, 34, 42, 43, 44–6, 81, 137, 153, 155–6
Wesley, John, 57, 59
Wharncliffe, James, 1st Lord, 45
Wilberforce, William, 19
Wildman, Abraham, 69
Wilkes, John, 11, 31, 40
William IV, King, 1, 40, 44, 45, 53
Wilson, George, 141
Wing, Charles, 70
Wiseman, Nicholas Patrick Stephen, 23
Wood, John, 62, 65–6, 70
Woollen and worsted trade unions, 97–8, 101, 104, 113
Worcester, 39, 105
Wordsworth, William, 60
Wyvill, Christopher, 31

York, 70, 194
'Young England', 15, 22, 61, 63
'Young Ireland', 169, 171, 172–4, 179